ROAD TO REDEMPTION

ROAD TO REDEMPTION

DAMEON K. WROE

PUBLISHED BY
Another **EP**® Publishing Company

Copyright ©2024 by Dameon K. Wroe
Another **EP**® Publishing Company

All rights reserved. All materials and/or supporting text written in this book are the original work *and* creation of the author, and are protected by applicable copyright laws on file with the Library of Congress Copyright Office. Any photocopying, reproductions, publications, alterations or duplications of this book and the information contained within it, without the author's *or* the publisher's expressed written consent, is a violation of applicable laws. It is equally a violation of applicable laws to copy, post, re-post, print or otherwise transfer any text from this book onto any social media platforms, for *any* reason whatsoever, without the author's *or* the publisher's expressed written consent. No part of this book shall be altered or interpreted by any entertainment company or entity for the purposes of attempting to re-create this storyline to be used in any feature film(s), commercial advertisement(s), theatre stage play(s), or any other theatrical production(s) for the sake of generating revenue, without written permission from the publisher and from the author.

To book this author for public speaking engagements, workshops, podcast interviews, author appearances, talk show interviews or book signing events, address all inquiries in writing to:

Another **EP**® Publishing Company
Post Office Box 300
Walnut, CA 91788-0300
or by email at: anothereppublishingcompany@gmail.com

Printed in the United States
9 8 7 6 5 4 3 2 1

ISBN#: 978-0-9740685-4-1

> If you purchased this book without a cover, you should know that this book is stolen property. It was reported as "**unsold**" or "**destroyed**" to the publisher and neither the author nor the publisher has received any payments for this "stripped book."

★ ★ ★ ★ ★

TABLE OF CONTENTS

Introduction		*i*
1	The Foundation	1
2	Training & Experience	45
3	An Undisputed Work Ethic	87
4	Malicious Prosecution—1995	121
5	My Second Shooting Incident	149
6	Railroaded	169
7	But God	255
8	What Google Never Told You!	309
References		325

★ ★ ★ ★ ★

INTRODUCTION

I CAN'T BREATHE! As I force myself to push forward to write my truths, I can feel my heart rate increasing rapidly. I couldn't stop my heart from beating outside of my chest if I wanted to. This is my moment of truth… to share with the world what *really* happened that night; it is finally time! My fingertips are not typing as fast as they once did, because the images of what got me to this place are distracting me from being in the present… images that I wish for no one to have to remember.

My hunger to clear my name and move on with my life challenges my anxiety to remain calm but, when the sounds and scenic triggers of that night replay in my mind, over and over again… I can't breathe! The volume of the voices in my head is diligently attempting to derail me from the mission at hand but, as far as I'm concerned, failure is not an option. The level of psychological and emotional discomfort and trauma that I will have to endure to share this testimony is unimaginable but, for the sake of revealing facts that have never been told to the public until now, there's absolutely no turning back. This book is more than 20 years overdue, but now… it's harvest time.

The real-time sounds of surface street traffic set the tone for this uncomfortable and unfortunate walk back down memory lane, as the sights and sounds of emergency vehicles passing outside my window trigger flashbacks that vividly describe how a tragic, work-related encounter changed my life forever.

Before I go any further with the details of these events, I want to make some things crystal clear. It is not my objective to solicit your pity. It is not my objective to solicit your sympathy. In no way, shape or form do I desire to tell a one-sided story to paint *myself* as a victim, in an effort to persuade you to feel sorry for me, or to ignore the fact that a life was lost. Up until now, a one-sided story is the ONLY story that has been told so far. Now… it's time for the *real* version, the truthful version of that same story to finally be told! In the end, I am confident that my innocence will be revealed, and that I will be redeemed.

In telling the facts of my story, the truest version ever told, I am going to do what I had always done throughout my intermittent, 12-year history of being a private security officer. I'm simply going to tell the truth so that, for the first time ever, society can finally get the 110% *truthful version* of my story directly from me, rather than the tainted version that the internet, the decedent's family and newspapers all over San Bernadino County have used to slander my name for *their* financial and political gain, and to use relentlessly negative media coverage of my case as a means to groom the public into thinking that I was a cold-blooded murderer, long before I even got to trial. These are the types of tricks

INTRODUCTION

that *they* play on a regular basis so that *they* can obtain the only thing that they care most about at the end of the day… high conviction rates and a more favorable chance at getting re-elected to maintain their positions! As you will later discover, the fabricated case that *they* built against me did not turn out the way that *they* had all hoped for… because God wouldn't allow it! God was on my side from the beginning to the bitter end.

The good news is, some of the events that occurred that night no longer come to my mind as readily as they once did in the past. The sad news is, most of the events that unfolded that night are engraved in my memory forever, and I remember them as if it were just 24 hours ago. In the event that you were one of the many people who passed judgement on me and wrote me off *before* ever taking the time to get to know me for yourself, I'm about to overwhelm you with so much factual proof that I was railroaded, and unjustly prosecuted, that you will have no other choice but to re-evaluate your perception of me.

At every possible crossroad where I can give you factual evidence that I was the high-value target of *"white privilege"* and *"malicious prosecution"* in America, I'm going to lay it all out for you so that you can research it for yourself and see that I'm telling you the truth. Unlike any book that I have ever written before in my life, I'm going to take you as deep into my mind and my thought process as I can possibly take you. I'm going to describe things to you so vividly that you're going to feel like you were there to witness everything that happened with your own two eyes.

The things that I'm about to describe to you really happened to me in real life! There's no script… there's no agents and casting directors… there's no stunt-doubles, there's no studio audience and, most certainly, there was never a dress rehearsal on the days that my life flashed right in front of me on more than one occasion. The only thing that I had to fall back on in the midst of danger and second-by-second chaos and violence against me was my training, my experience, my *expert* ability to sense when danger was present… **and my will to survive!**

By the end of this book, you are going to see for yourself that my malicious murder charges were never about *right* vs. *wrong*… my charges were always about *black* vs. *white*; it was about a Black man who shot a young White man who, in the eyes of my oppressors, did nothing wrong that night (which will also be proven to be a lie). You are about to experience every possible emotion that I felt on the tragic night that I had to defend my life back on the night of January 1, 2004.

If you are honestly a truth-seeker, then my accounts of the deadly confrontations that I'm about to share with you will resonate with you almost immediately. If you are *not* a truth-seeker, then the facts as I will lay them out in the chapters ahead will never be enough to influence you to use your common sense to recognize the truth for yourself, once you have had time to evaluate the information offered by both sides. If you are the type of person that hates authority, and feel as though people who violate the law should be praised rather than punished, then you might as well stop

INTRODUCTION

reading this book right now because, chances are, no matter how much of the truth I tell you, you are still going to judge me unfairly—the same way that many others before you have already done.

My goal is not to try to convince you that I'm being honest, my goal in writing this book is simply to reveal the truth about how the man who attacked me more than 20 years ago forced me to make a split-second decision to decide if I wanted to live or die. In the forthcoming chapters, you will get a chance to see my true character and also my work ethic, by learning that my actions were carried out with fairness, professionalism, integrity and that they were performed within the rules and guidelines of the law. I challenge you to hold off on your thoughts about this book until you have read it in its entirety. This book is like a movie... if you take your eyes off of it for too long you're definitely going to miss a key detail that points towards my innocence and my desire to be redeemed!

I'm going to be the first one to admit that this book is going to be hard to read at times, because the truth really does hurt—especially when something that you truly *want* to believe as being factual is not factual at all. In the lives of those who wish to voluntarily live a lie each day, by justifying their hate and corruption, this book will be the bright spotlight that exposes who they really are. With regards to the two court cases that I am going to disclose in this book, you will most definitely see a consistency of systemic racism and racial profiling by members of a broken, racist judicial system that has historically targeted black men for hundreds upon hundreds of years. Sadly, I was no exception to their racist rules, protocols, and tactics.

The *average* person who gets involved in the private security industry typically does the bare minimum to get by on the job each day. They work just hard enough so that they don't get fired, and they are usually getting paid just enough money so that they don't quit. The *average* security officer is one who will oftentimes show up for work late, but occasionally jump at an opportunity to get to go home early. When given an important task while on the job, the *average* security officer can almost always be expected to not meet nor exceed the company's expectations. I could have easily walked in the footsteps of these same *average* security officers, but there was just one problem… I was anything other than *average*.

Everything that I have ever accomplished in my lifetime I have accomplished by simply believing in myself, trusting the effectiveness of how I use my gifts and talents, pursuing a higher education, getting trained by proven experts in my fields of interest, by working hard and by praying to Almighty God that He constantly cover me with a hedge of protection wherever my two feet may go. Nothing more, nothing less, and nothing else.

"Most kind, most merciful, and most gracious Father God: before I ask You for anything, I first want to thank You for everything! I thank You for waking me up out of my bed to see another day that was not promised unto me, so that I can finally complete this book. I thank You for sending Your one and only Son to die a cruel death on Calvary's cross so

INTRODUCTION

that a feeble man like me could one day have an opportunity at eternal life in Glory with You. I thank You for surrounding me with good people who love me, who believe in me and who accept me for who You have manifested for me to be. It is at this hour that I humbly approach Your throne of mercy and grace with a heavy heart, asking that You walk with me on this uneven journey to find closure and healing.

As I re-live some trying and difficult times in my past to tell this story, I ask that You keep me sheltered and protected in the palms of Your unchanging hands. I ask that You allow me to speak my truths from the heart, without reservation and without the fear of how others will receive it. Give me the strength and the courage to be as transparent as I can possibly be, so that the world can see *You* in *me*. I ask that You open up every door that man has slammed shut in my face, and that You close every door that has been opened up against me, in attempts to hinder opportunities that You have already customized just for me. It's in the mighty name of Your Son, Jesus Christ, that I pray and ask for these blessings. Amen!"

1
★ ★ ★ ★ ★

THE FOUNDATION

THE MARATHON STARTED quite a long time ago in Sacramento, California… somewhere between the age of seven or eight, to be exact. Back in those days, children were to be *seen* but not *heard*. When grown-ups were talking, or entangled in a fierce game of dominoes or spades, you'd dare not interrupt them by asking an unimportant question, or by inviting yourself to be a part of their conversation! For nearly all children back in my day, the consequences for involving yourself in grown folks' business was rather steep, to say the least. If you were a young Black kid back in the 70's, you would have had better luck teaching a shark how to chew gum than butting into adult conversations— thinking you *wouldn't* get popped upside the head. Only White kids got spankings back then; Black kids either got popped upside the head or flat-out whooped. That was back in the day when kids were actually afraid of their parents.

For a young kid like me, life in my younger days was extremely strict and regimented, yet sprinkled with intermittent moments in time to explore the things that quickly sparked my interests. Like most young kids in my neighborhood, my greatest forms of entertainment consisted of playing outside on the block with my friends, going Bass fishing with my dad, and making new friends up at the Robertson Community Center on Norwood Avenue, where all the cute girls in the surrounding neighborhoods would typically hang out.

The community center offered quite a few summer programs and youth activities for us that kept us out of trouble and gave us something constructive to do with our idle time. You see, my sister was a member of the drill team that was subsequently formed at the community center, based on all the girls who desired to sign up. This gave me the perfect advantage to always be around all of the girls that other boys in the neighborhood were in competition for. The more girls that my sister became friends with, the more my chances of being noticed by them increased.

Although I had signed up to be on the basketball team, I would oftentimes shout out, "Sub!!" so that an alternate player could come in the game to take my place, while I took time to catch my breath. Growing up through my childhood years, I struggled with asthma for quite a long time. Even though I wanted to take a break to catch my breath, so I could get back in the game and help my team win, the short breaks also gave me an opportunity to drool over the cute girls on the drill team as they practiced their routines on the sidelines. Once I had finally found a cutie to take notice of me, it was time to get back in the game and show her how I was able to hustle up and down the court, scoring points for my team. When balling up at the community center got

THE FOUNDATION

old and boring, it was time for us kids to walk back home to the block to find something more interesting to get into.

During the times I was not outside playing with my friends, we were always at church or either at a church activity. My mother and my grandmother always made it a point to enroll my sister and I into what was known as Vacation Bible School. Remember Vacation Bible School? It was usually an annual summer program that was hosted by many local churches, including my grandmother's church where we also attended. Vacation Bible School was where us kids learned things like how to recite the books of the Bible, by singing them in song format so we would remember them more efficiently.

Once we memorized the songs, we could ultimately recite all of the books in the Bible by memory as well, because our teachers made it fun. Another thing I recall being taught very early on in my upbringing was learning about the Ten Commandments. Looking back on my childhood, these lessons were some of the most memorable and impressionable training moments of my life, because it was in these early stages of development where the differences between right and wrong were engraved into my young mind forever. Little did I know as a little boy, that the spiritual training grounds I was exposed to at such an early age would mold me into the man that I have become today. Keep this fact at the forefront of your mind at all times as I quarterback these stories for you because, from this moment forward, it will answer many questions that you will have in between the spaces of what I say and what you may struggle to believe.

Attending church and learning about God at a very early age felt like both a blessing and a hardship. Since mostly every adult in my immediate family (on my mother's side) was raised in the church, my sister and I got that same upbringing. Even though we were really young, we were brought up with a very strong Christian foundation. It was church on Sunday mornings, church on Sunday evenings, and mid-week Bible Class on Wednesday nights. Sometimes going to church all the time made me sad because, when it was time to get ready to get dressed to go to church, that took away my time to play with my other friends in the neighborhood. As time went on, going to church felt less and less like sitting in detention and a little bit more like fun, because I was making new friends there who I enjoyed seeing every weekend.

Church taught me a lot about the differences between right and wrong but, the way our Sunday School teachers would always explain it to us in class, *wrong* was oftentimes synonymous with the word *sin*. With this is in mind, there were quite a few things that I remember about my childhood. Although my childhood started off with having both of my parents in the home with me, my mother eventually divorced my father because she just finally got sick and tired of being sick and tired.

The more and more I went to church and learned about sin, the more and more I slowly began to understand my home life a little bit better. As best as my memory can recall, my father started out being a rather fun person to be around. In the beginning, I remember him always laughing a lot... almost like a prankster. I recall him playing random games with my sister and I when we were all home together with nothing specific to be doing. Sometimes when he knew I was in my room, he would call out my name as if he was calling me to come help him do something. When I finally made it to the part of the house where I thought I heard him calling me from, he wasn't there. When I walked out of the room and went looking for him somewhere else, I could hear him calling out for me again from the same area. When I walked back over to that part of the house that I thought he was calling me from again, he was still nowhere to be found.

It was at this time that I realized that he was hiding from me and testing me to see if I could find him. Whenever I would finally find him, he would jump out of his hiding place and let out a big, scary roar... and I'd take off running down the hall, back to my room to hide from him. It didn't take long for the fun-loving environment around the house to change and, unfortunately for everyone except my father, the change was not a happy one.

Since I was just a young kid with no life experiences, I didn't know why my father was always yelling and screaming at my mother... I just knew it was *sin*. I didn't understand why my father felt the need to make smoking weed and getting high more of a priority than spending quality time with his family... I just saw it as *sin*. I saw a very dark side of my father that I never thought I'd ever see in a million years, and I didn't like it! For every time that I ever saw my mother crying, as a result of something that my father either said or did, it caused me to develop a sincere hate for him.

What made me even more angry inside was the fact that I sometimes witnessed things that my mother went through with my father, and it gave me an overwhelming feeling of helplessness because I was not old enough, strong enough nor brave enough to do anything to stop it from happening. Since I was too afraid to stand up to my father back then, I kept my emotions bottled up inside and I hid my feelings from everyone because, as a child, I felt that no one wanted to hear how I felt about the grown-up things that were happening all around me. Since mental health awareness was not on society's radar back in the 70's, I felt like my father didn't care about how his actions were molding me into a person that would ultimately go on to hate him for decades to come, and/or have a propensity to possibly repeat his very same behaviors once I became an adult.

My father's temper and sporadic drug use had gotten so out of control that my mother just couldn't take it anymore! Sometimes when I would hear my father pulling into the garage on his motorcycle, I would run down the hallway to my room, shut my bedroom door and pretend like I was asleep… just so I didn't have to speak with him or engage him in any way. Other times when he came home, I'd literally go into my room, shut my door and find a place to hide, because I was always afraid of him coming home in one of his unpredictable moods and then taking his aggression out on me, my sister or my mother, as if *we* were the reason why *he* had such a terrible day.

As my young childhood years continued to progress on, my father became a pretty scary person to be around, and I did not always enjoy how his presence made me feel at times. When he and my mother would have rather loud disagreements, my internal instincts made me feel like busting in his room or openly confronting him to stop his rampage, but that self-preservation side of my young mind told me, "Don't do it… you'll be in danger of getting hurt!" These ended up being the times in my life where I wished my father would either leave the house or hurry up and fall asleep so the shouting would stop. When my father was either sleeping or gone, those were the times we experienced the most peace in the house.

One of my fondest memories, while there at our single story house on Douglas Street, was the day that my mother finally moved my sister and I out of there. There was no time to really digest what had suddenly happened. I remember looking out of the kitchen window and wondering to myself, "Why is my grandfather here? Why is his pickup truck facing the street instead of the garage door?" Things had just got real!

It didn't take long for me to put two and two together and figure out that my grandfather was there as a result of God answering my prayers… my grandfather was there to help my mother move us away from my father. Like most life-changing things, it took some getting used to but, to be honest, it didn't take long! After leaving Douglas Street, we lived with my grandparents for a short time. Compared to where we had just come from, it was a place that finally felt like home! The yelling and the shouting were gone. The constant fear of wondering when the *big bad wolf* [my father] would appear was gone. The fears of having to step in to suddenly protect my mother and my sister were also gone and, just like that, a solid foundation was being built for me to have a fresh start at a new life! Next stop… 264 Olmstead Drive in Sacramento, California.

Things at my grandparent's house weren't all that different from the way things had always been. I still had the ability to play with all of my regular friends and see them as often as I had always done. Since I was only a kid, and had no real concept of *expectations*, I thought living at my grandparent's house was going to be a fun little walk in the park. I would soon learn that I was as wrong as wearing two left shoes. It was still church on Sunday mornings, church on Sunday evenings and mid-week Bible Class on Wednesday nights. When I wasn't outside playing with my friends in the neighborhood, my mother had me indoors either doing homework, practicing my handwriting or learning my numbers. Even if I didn't come home with homework from school, my mother always made sure that she had some extra work that I could be doing at home. In order for me to be able to go outside and play with my friends, I had to make sure that all of my homework, extra homework, and household chores were finished first.

Adjusting to life at my grandparent's house was effortless. There was always some type of fun or adventure to be found there. One of the first lessons I remember learning while at my grandparent's house was taught to me by my grandfather, when he taught me how to play pool. My grandparent's house was the only house on our block where there was a pool table. If you wanted to play a game of pool, you either had to know someone in the neighborhood who had a pool table or you had to pay money to go play pool down at a local pool hall. My grandfather started teaching me how to play pool at the approximate age of seven and, from that point on, his expectations of me winning became greater and greater, based on what he knew he had taught me.

Once I had begun to feel more confident in all of the things that my grandfather had taught me about pool, I would always invite some of the neighborhood kids over to my grandparent's house to play pool with me in the garage. Of course there were times when I would lose some games here and there but, for the most part, none of the kids wanted to keep on playing pool with me because they saw for themselves that I was too hard to beat! It made my grandparents proud to see that I had gotten so good on the pool table that I was winning almost every game while playing with my friends. However, when my head and my ego had gotten too big, my grandfather always had a way of humbling me when he'd come out of the house into the garage and tell me, "Rack'em!!"

After I was finished racking the balls for a new game of pool, my grandfather reminded me of who was the real boss on the table… him! When my grandfather would break, he'd hit the balls so hard that they literally flew in all different directions, with at least 3 to 4 balls falling into the pockets. For me, it was all downhill from there. After a while, I never desired to play my grandfather in pool anymore, because I was already expecting him to win. However, the more and more I played him and lost to him, it was just a matter of time before my losses started to turn into wins! All it took was for those first few wins against my grandfather to give me a renewed sense of always maintaining a winning attitude, not just in the game of pool, but winning in the game of life as well.

Although shadowing my grandfather in the protocols of the game of pool taught me valuable lessons, there was no place I'd rather be than right by my grandmother's side on any given day. My grandmother and I were like two peas in a pod... we were inseparable... we were like bacon and eggs... peanut butter and jelly. Wherever you would find my grandmother, I was usually an arm's reach away from her. Taking it upon myself to be my grandmother's shadow everywhere she went, allowed me to learn my grandmother's likes and dislikes, as well as adopt some of her very peculiar pet peeves about life in general.

Since she was at home so frequently, my grandmother had a very keen eye for noticing anything suspicious in the neighborhood; she was a one-woman Neighborhood Watch Program. Whether it was an odd-looking vehicle driving through the neighborhood, or simply a person walking down the street with a certain stride, my grandmother didn't miss a beat if something in the neighborhood wasn't right. No matter what it was or who it was, my grandmother saw everything! Whenever I saw my grandmother standing at the front door, looking through the black, iron screen door, I knew there was some activity going on outside on the block that drew her attention, and I was usually standing right behind her. If she wasn't monitoring activity behind the stealthy security of the iron door, she was conducting surveillance through a small opening of the kitchen curtains.

In all of my years of developing an inseparable relationship with my grandparents, I never knew them to have ever called the police to report any suspicious activity in the neighborhood because, where we lived, many residents were always afraid of retaliation if the police ever disclosed who called them. The fact that my grandmother always saw people in the neighborhood doing bad things and never called the police really bothered me as a kid. I had always been taught that when you do something wrong, you will be held accountable and made to answer for your actions. I strongly believe that this knowledge that was instilled in me at such an early age triggered something inside of me that would define the next few decades of my life.

"What do you want to be when you grow up?" This was one of the most common questions that children have always been asked by adults. Whenever this question was asked, the typical response would be either fireman, policeman, doctor, nurse or lawyer. As for me, I recall being that young kid who initially thought it would be so cool to become a firefighter so that I could ride around on that huge, red truck, putting out fires and going through red lights without stopping. There was just something about the power that fire engines had when those lights and sirens were activated. As soon as motorists would see those emergency lights or hear that siren, they knew that they had an obligation to pull over and get out of the way! Thanks to other kids on the block that I would often play with to cure our boredom, it wasn't long before we all started to play Cops and Robbers. After deciding who would be the cops and who would be the robbers, the stage was set, and it was lights, camera, ACTION!

In the beginning, it was really fun playing the role of the robber, because the robber's job was to never get caught or captured. Seeing as though I was one of the fastest kids on the block, rarely could anyone playing the role of the cop ever catch me. You see, in this game of cat and mouse, if you wanted to catch me, you had to be faster and smarter than me… that was my mentality for playing the game. Outsmarting the kids playing the role of the cop made the game more challenging and more fun for a kid like me. When there were no kids to play with on some days, I found myself in the house with my grandmother, either helping her prepare food in the kitchen, or sitting in the living room with her while she binge-watched some of her favorite television shows.

Some of our favorite shows that we would enjoy watching together were *T.J. Hooker, Starsky and Hutch, Hawaii Five-O, Magnum P.I., Matlock, Hunter,* and *Murder She Wrote.* When those shows became redundant and boring, we became engulfed in reruns of other popular shows back then such as *S.W.A.T., Adam-12* and *Columbo.* All of these shows were an amazing showcase of excitement, and non-stop action. Watching these shows was almost like playing Cops and Robbers with my friends in the neighborhood, and I had a front-row seat in my grandmother's living room on

THE FOUNDATION

a regular basis. When my grandmother had to eventually get up and pull herself away from watching TV, it wasn't long before my grandfather retired to the living room to sit and watch TV from his favorite Lazy Boy chair. My grandfather loved some of the same shows as my grandmother, but his favorite shows to watch were shows such as *Bonanza* and *The Rifleman*.

In many of these action TV series that I grew up watching, I seemed to always lean towards rooting for all of the *good guys* to catch and punish all of the *bad guys*. You see, since I had been taught right from wrong at such a young age, I discovered that I really didn't like any of the bad guys, because the bad guys most often reminded me of my father. Although my father was sometimes a fun person to be around as a kid, I also experienced his other side… the dark side. When my father was in one of his bad moods, it was really a bad, terrible mood. The best way that I can describe it is that he was a bully. He was mentally, emotionally, verbally and sometimes physically abusive. At the times I started to see these traits in my father, I was too small and too weak to do anything about his unreasonable behavior towards others in our family because I was just a kid. Kids back in my day did not DARE question or challenge any adult, even if it were someone other than our actual parents. Children in that time were to be *seen*, and not *heard*.

With these mental pictures in mind, I got tired of seeing bad people do bad things to good people. I got sick and tired of seeing people being mistreated or bullied by other people. I felt such a high measure of sorrow and sadness for those who were being bullied and did not have the courage or the strength to fight back so, as I got older, I made it my mission in life to be the voice of those in society who were always being unfairly treated and picked on, and I decided to fight for them so that their fears of being picked on or bullied had been taken away. Little did I know that watching all of these popular TV shows with my grandmother over the years would be the foundation for my desire to fulfill what would ultimately become my childhood dream… becoming a police officer.

Once my mother and father's divorce was finally over with, my mother moved my sister and I to Los Angeles County in 1980 when I was just nine years old. Fortunately, she was able to take advantage of an opportunity to have her job transferred from her then Sacramento office to an office in Southern California, where one of her primary goals was to give us a fresh, new start in a fresh, new environment.

As any other child would have been in a brand new environment, I couldn't help but be overly inquisitive about my new city, my new school, my new friends, and all the other things that were happening around me. Normally, when my sister and I were in the car with my mother, riding around town with her while running errands or going to scheduled activities, we were oftentimes not allowed to ride in the front seat. Assuming it was for safety reasons, since we were so young, I took it upon myself to become my mother's back seat observer. Just as I had witnessed my grandmother do on many occasions before we moved to Southern California, I found myself taking particular notice of bad or illegal things happening wherever I went.

THE FOUNDATION

If I saw someone run a red light, I would think to myself, "If I were a police officer right now, I'd pull that car over and give them a ticket for running that red light." If I saw someone roll through an intersection without making a complete stop behind the limit line, I would think to myself, "If I were a police officer right now, I'd pull that car over and give them a ticket for not making a complete stop, and running that stop sign." If I saw any cars passing my mother at a high rate of speed, I'd think to myself, "If I were a police officer right now, I'd pull those cars over and give all of them a ticket for speeding." If I saw someone in the grocery store stealing things, and walking out of the store without paying for them, I'd say to myself, "If I were a police officer right now, I'd stop that person and tell them that they're under arrest for stealing, because taking something that doesn't belong to you is a crime, and it's not right." The more I found myself saying, "If I were a police officer right now," the more passionate I became about finding out what steps I would eventually have to take in order to actually become a police officer one of these days. With this fact in mind, the stage to begin that transition was officially set!

Once I learned that I would be attending Nogales High School for my first year of 9th grade, I knew that this educational experience would ultimately become the training grounds for the next phase in my life, upon me finishing out my term there and eventually graduating after four years. At first, I wasn't very happy about the required classes that I had to take, but at least I got to pick a few of my own elective classes that were being offered to me. The Home Economics class that the high school was offering seemed pretty fun, especially after it was told to me that the students get to actually eat the food that they would be learning how to cook in that class. Then, there was one other course that I had stumbled upon that not only caught my eye, it made my heart smile. The other course that subsequently got my attention was none other than Criminal Justice.

I didn't know what to expect when I first started showing up to my Criminal Justice class, but I will say that I fell in love with the class much faster than I anticipated I would.

The class instructor's name at that time was Juan Rodriguez. During the year that I first entered his class, Mr. Rodriguez was a sergeant with the Los Angeles County Sheriff's Department—Industry Station. I really came to admire him for the way he carried himself. He was always neat and clean, and he was very impressive by how eloquently he spoke when he was teaching. By the time that I had already spent a few short weeks in his classroom, the admiration I had for him continued to grow, and really start to peak my interest even further. One thing that I remember about him that stood out the most was the fact that his pants always appeared to be heavily starched, and he always had the perfect crease running down the center of each pant leg. The bottom hem of his pants appeared to always sit right on top of his shoes, as if maybe he had served in the military.

Mr. Rodriguez was such an intriguing person by the way he carried himself. Oftentimes, when I got bored of studying classroom learning materials, I would study Mr. Rodriguez. He was a very, no-nonsense instructor who was

THE FOUNDATION

very well spoken and very passionate about the manner in which he taught his class. Not only did he tell us some of his exciting patrol stories, he was constantly bringing in very interesting training videos. Even though the training videos he'd have us watch were primarily re-enactments of actual crimes that took place, they showed me the realistic side of law enforcement that none of my grandmother's favorite TV shows could have ever prepared me for.

Of all the videos we watched, the ones that stood out the most to me were the videos that showed many different scenarios and tactical variations of patrol procedures. Although the training videos were quite informative and interesting, they were also a vivid reminder of how dangerous it can be working as a law enforcement officer. Even after 36 years have passed since seeing these training videos that I last saw in high school, there are two very impressionable lessons I learned from watching them.

The very first lesson that I have always been able to readily recall is that patrol should NEVER be routine. When a police officer gets into the habit of doing routine patrols in the areas that they are assigned to patrol, it gives criminals in that area an opportunity to learn or otherwise predict that officer's patrol routine. Once criminals start to feel overly confident that they have learned an officer's patrol routine, it gives them courage to conduct criminal activity during times that they feel that the police will not be coming around until a specific period of time has elapsed.

The second lesson that I learned was from watching a video of an officer who was making a simple traffic stop for a common traffic violation. As the officer approached the driver's side of the vehicle to make contact with the driver, the driver intentionally waited for the officer to get as close to the driver's side window as possible before he suddenly reached his arm out of the window and opened fire on the officer, striking him multiple times and fatally wounding him. Seeing this happen to the officer, who was just doing his job, made me pretty angry and eager to start taking the necessary steps to one day becoming a police officer. From this moment forward, one consistent theme you will hear throughout this book, is how these lessons played a very vital role in everything I did in the field of private security over an intermittent span of about 12 years.

During my time in Mr. Rodriguez's class, I was on a learning streak that made me stand out to him as a student who was definitely committed to taking the next steps needed to become three steps closer to one day putting on a Los Angeles County Sheriff's Department uniform.

As the days and months wore on in my Criminal Justice class, I felt like I just couldn't be stopped. Even if I was not doing very well in my other classes, I was doing exceedingly well in my Criminal Justice studies. Whenever Mr. Rodriguez would ask the class a question, to test our memory of the material that he had been teaching us, my hand was always the first two or three hands to quickly go up in the air. If Mr. Rodriguez called on other students first, I always had the answers if they didn't. Mr. Rodriguez had a very special way of showing me that his faith and his trust in my ability and knowledge was growing.

THE FOUNDATION

During the first few times that we had a substitute teacher, I was eventually called up to the teacher's desk. My first instinct was that I was in trouble for something but, the more I thought it through, I quickly rejected that theory because I was never in trouble in Mr. Rodriguez's class. On more than one occasion, the substitute teacher called me over to his desk to ask me questions about classroom protocols. I can remember one particular substitute teacher called me up to the desk at the front of the classroom. As he was reading some written instructions that Mr. Rodriguez had left behind, he asked me if I could help him return test papers to the students in class from a previous test

Mr. Rodriguez had given us. It was easier for him to ask for my help in accomplishing this task, because he knew that I already knew who all the students were in the class. I later learned from Mr. Rodriguez that all of the substitute teachers had given him positive feedback about how helpful I was to them while he was away, and that, in some cases, I helped the teachers set up and/or operate classroom equipment so that we could watch more training films and videos.

When Mr. Rodriguez saw how serious I was about getting into the field of law enforcement, he didn't waste any time suggesting to me that I should get involved with the Los Angeles County Sheriff's Department Deputy Explorer Program. From that very moment, I approached my mother with the idea to see if I could get her blessing with getting me to and from the academy if I were to submit my name to become a candidate for the program. After getting my mother's blessing, the rest was history.

The Deputy Explorer Program was only held on Saturdays, beginning promptly at 0600 hours out on the *grinder*, north of the solid, white line, facing south. The *grinder* was just a fancy term for *parking lot*. Whenever we were told to assemble out on the *grinder*, it meant that, as soon as humanly possible, all explorer recruits were expected to be out in the empty section of the large parking lot that was designated for much of our training operations. Our training included marching, physical training (P.T.), and learning how to open ranks in our respective platoon formations for uniform inspection. With the exception of our classroom, the *grinder* was the primary area on the academy grounds where we would either begin or end whatever tasks we were given for the day by our drill instructors. From the perspective of a 17-year-old kid, our drill instructors frequently scared the living crap out of me! Less than halfway through the program, it felt as though someone had tricked me into signing up to be in a military boot camp!

The majority of our drill instructors were sworn LA County Sheriff's Department personnel, and some were senior explorers who had already graduated from their explorer academy, and were actively going through the process to become sworn law enforcement officers. These drill instructors were so intimidating, my biggest fear while at the academy was doing something wrong and having them notice it and call me out on it. I never wanted to be the one in my academy class who got scolded by either Deputy DeVusser, Deputy Barker or Deputy Emerton! I'll never forget the time that Deputy Emerton stood in the front of our

THE FOUNDATION

classroom and said, "Class, upon my command, you will fall out into your respective locker rooms, where you will have six minutes to change into your full P.T. gear and meet out on the *grinder*, north of the solid white line, facing south. Class, fall out!!"

Even though our drill instructors were extremely intimidating, their stern demeanor helped me to better understand and appreciate the value of always being professional, even while maintaining an unshakable command presence in the performance of my duties and responsibilities. Deputy Emerton was a very well-known, no-nonsense type of deputy... and everyone knew it. Just when you thought he was going to cater to you, and give you some one-on-one instruction time about something, he would randomly blurt out things to the class like, "The LA County Sheriff's Department is a quasi-military organization. If you don't know what *quasi* means, it means *semi*. If you don't know what *semi* means... look it up!!" With Deputy Emerton, it was always cut and dry.

Just as I had felt by being in my Criminal Justice class with Mr. Rodriguez, it didn't take me long to fall in love with everything I was learning in the explorer academy at the S.T.A.R.S. Center in Whittier, California. The academy consisted of relentless training on things such as learning California penal codes, radio codes, health and safety codes, business and professions codes, as well as California vehicle codes. Additional things that I learned in the academy consisted of powers of arrest, elements of a crime, patrol tactics and/or patrol procedures, how to properly call a pursuit, weaponless defense, searching and handcuffing techniques, as well as narcotics identification and how to safely shoot firearms. Prior to graduating from the academy, we were also made to learn how to identify a wide variety of gang signs.

Learning the gang signs was quite useful because, whenever we were out on a ride-along with the deputies, we were able to identify specific gang turfs by the hand signs we saw people throwing up while we were out patrolling in the community. The drill instructors who dedicated their time and energy to teach us kids about the complexities of what law enforcement is all about, really made a life-long impression on me in particular and, as you will see in the chapters ahead, the lessons that they taught me in the academy proved to be extremely instrumental in helping me to survive and overcome some very brutal and dangerous encounters later in life as a private security officer.

Just as many of the things that Deputy Emerton had taught us in the academy, Deputy Barker was another drill instructor who made quite a lasting impression on me. Whenever we would be in the gymnasium, partnered up to practice our weaponless defense techniques, Deputy Barker always used that time to remind us that the academy is where we need not be afraid to fail at learning something because, in the academy, we could always reset, go back, start over, and fix what we may have done wrong. He would often say, "In the academy, you can always keep practicing until you get it right, but if you get it wrong too many times out on the street, you can get yourself hurt or killed… or even get your partner or an innocent bystander

THE FOUNDATION

hurt or killed if you don't know what you're doing." Those types of statements being made to a kid like me, were like deeply-rooted seeds that had been engraved in my memory forever. As an inexperienced, 17-year-old kid, little did I know that those very words and principles would ultimately save my life on more than one occasion.

More than halfway through the explorer program, I found it very ironic that my drill instructors in the academy echoed an all too familiar admonishment, concerning the potentially life-threatening situations that we may find ourselves in after graduating from the academy. The takeaways I always got from these law enforcement experts could never be more clear, "No matter how dangerous an encounter with a suspect may be, you must *always* fight to have the will to survive… no matter what! Your training and your will to survive will *always* get you through," they'd often say to encourage us.

I was definitely on the fast track to becoming more and more noticed by my drill instructors, in a positive way. Whenever our drill instructors would give us writing assignments in class, they used to always preach to us that our papers needed to be neatly written. For any explorer recruit that turned in a paper that was sloppy and poorly written, the drill instructors would make that person re-write the entire paper until it was legibly written. It didn't take long for a few of the drill instructors to notice that all of the written assignments that I turned in were always neatly written. Anyone who was to ever look at my hand-written work could always tell that I took great pride in my writing ability.

At some point, the drill instructors started to offer us volunteer opportunities to either be a class sergeant or a platoon sergeant. It was an absolute honor to be chosen to be a class sergeant or a platoon sergeant. When you stepped up to be in one of these positions, it meant that a recruit got the opportunity to show all of the drill instructors that the recruit had a commendable level of leadership, and that he/she was not afraid of taking on the responsibility that came along with that position. Considering these facts, I knew that I wanted to be in one of these positions, but my strategy for getting there was very clever and intentional.

My grandmother had always told me, as a child, that it was best to learn from *other people's* mistakes, so that's exactly what I did while in the academy. Once I saw other recruits fulfilling the term of their role as either a class sergeant or platoon sergeant, I paid very close attention to everything the drill instructors yelled at them for either *doing* or *failing to do*. Once I felt confident that I fully understood what the drill instructors expected from us while in that role, it wasn't long before I finally became a class sergeant.

I'll never forget the time when one of my drill instructors announced to the class that I was going to be the next class sergeant. Although I was glad to finally be in that distinguished position, I was also very nervous… okay, I was flat-out scared. Rather than continuing to allow that fear to keep on intimidating me not to do my job successfully, I chose to embrace the fear, to help me overcome the very emotions that were trying to hold me back. I remember my first task as a class sergeant like it was yesterday.

THE FOUNDATION

"Class… upon my command, you will fall out into your respective locker rooms, where you will have six minutes to change out of your civilian clothes and into your full P.T. gear, and report to the *grinder*, north of the solid white line, facing south. Class… fall out!!"

Once I finished that powerful directive to the class, and saw everyone exiting the classroom to hurry up and get out to their respective locker rooms at my command, that was the boost in confidence that I felt I needed to get through the rest of the academy. Even after my time as class sergeant had ended, I would later go on to be platoon sergeant before ultimately graduating from the academy in June of 1989.

Seemingly, things that were hard for the other cadet recruits came much easier for me, thanks to everything that I had already been learning in my high school Criminal Justice class. Whenever I saw other recruits in class, or even in our training activities outside of the classroom, I would help them out with getting better at understanding things like laws, elements of crimes, patrol procedures, searching and handcuffing techniques, and patrol procedures. I can never forget the female cadet recruit in my platoon who really struggled with learning her California penal codes. Our class was so large that we were broken up into four different platoons. I was the platoon sergeant for the fourth platoon.

I can vividly recall the day all four of our platoons were out on the *grinder*, and we all opened ranks for inspections by our drill instructors. During inspection, the drill instructors walked up and down each row of recruits, looking us over with a fine-tooth comb, looking for anything on our uniform that was out of place. If our uniforms had any *ropes* [long, untrimmed threads] hanging from them, we were immediately called out for it, in an embarrassing fashion. If our uniform *gig line* [alignment of shirt, belt buckle, and pant/fly seam] was out of place, we got the tongue-lashing of a lifetime. If our drill instructors quizzed us on our penal codes, and we didn't explain them correctly, the embarrassment they imposed on us for not knowing our codes would surely make us remember them for the next random inspection.

Whenever the drill instructors would come to a particular girl in my platoon to ask her about her penal codes, she was always confused about the differences between 211 PC and 459 PC. "Recruit… what's a 211?" the drill instructor would routinely shout at her. "Burglary, sir," she'd reply. "Burglary?" the DI asked angrily. "Yes sir," the recruit would sound off. "Well if a 211 is a burglary, recruit, then what's a 459?" With her voice noticeably shaken and unsure, the recruit answered, "Robbery, sir." Already knowing the answers to these questions, I just knew within my heart that this recruit was about to get the worst shouting of her life by giving the wrong answers to every question that was asked of her.

As the drill instructor's became increasingly angry at this recruit, for obviously not knowing her penal codes, the stern voice of Deputy DeVusser told the recruit, "Recruit… if you can't tell me the difference between a 211 and a 459 by next week, I'm going to give you a writing assignment so long that you're going to think that the Holy Bible is a bedtime story!! Do you understand me?" "Sir, yes sir," the recruit shouted without hesitation. To make a long story short, we never saw that recruit ever again... she quit.

We started off with approximately 200 cadet recruits in my explorer class but, by the time graduation day came, less than 150 recruits actually graduated. On the day of graduation, we were no longer referred to as recruits, we officially became known by Explorer Cadet. Beyond any shadow of any doubt, it was the most rewarding feeling to have been included in the number of all of my fellow classmates that graduated. During this time of my young life, I felt as though I was three steps closer to reaching my childhood dream of becoming a law enforcement officer. Little did I know that an unforeseen setback was waiting right around the corner for me, not even three months after graduating from the academy.

During the entire time that I was going back and forth to the academy to become an LA County Sheriff's Department Deputy Explorer Cadet, my mother and my then step-father were in the midst of a pretty rocky divorce. My step-father was not a very pleasant person to be around. He was quite a fun person to be around when he and my mother had initially started dating. However, once more time had gone by, and we were spending more and more time around him, his true colors started to really come out... and I didn't like him one bit after that.

At some point, his temper and his frequent fits of out-of-control rage in our home got him kicked out of the house by a family court judge. Once my step-father was no longer in the home with us, I could see that maintaining the monthly needs of the house was really starting to wear on my mother. She oftentimes tried her absolute best to handle things on her own without my sister and I knowing the truth about the real stress she was enduring but, me being so attentive to detail, I knew she was hurting financially during that time. For weeks and weeks, I sat on my bed upstairs in my room and tried my best to come up with some possible ways I could make some extra money to help my mother out financially, and to help out with a few bills here and there. Even though mama did her best to hide her stress and hardships from us, it broke my heart into pieces one night when I started to walk downstairs and heard her in her bedroom with the door shut, noticeably crying. It was at that time that I knew I had to do something, and fast!

During this time, I had a job at a local Taco Bell that was about a mile away from my house. Most of the time I was working, I was assigned to work either the drive-thru window or the front registers as a cashier. Working in this capacity gave me insight as to how much money the restaurant was bringing in during my shifts. Every time I handled cash during my shift, I would oftentimes think to myself, "If I could just get my hands on this kind of cash, I could help my mother pay some bills around the house and she wouldn't even know where I got it from; she would probably just think I was giving her my entire paycheck." Once I had persuaded myself to believe how possible this plan could actually be, the blueprint to make it a reality was slowly beginning to be drafted in my mind. It was just a matter of a few weeks when I realized that I had to recruit someone to help me pull this off, and I was more than willing to share half of the money. All I needed was someone who I trusted that would go the distance with me, and who wouldn't tell a soul about what we were about to do, because failure was not an option at that point.

Somewhat reluctantly, I sarcastically mentioned my plans to steal money from the restaurant I was working at to my friend Steven, who was also in my academy class. Little did I anticipate, my plan to stage a robbery at my job had surprisingly peaked his interest, and he wanted to know more about how we would pull it off. He confided in me by telling me that he was also under a lot of financial stress to make more money, because he and his wife had a baby on the way and money was extremely tight. He saw my idea as a way to also make some quick money to help his family stay afloat. After both of us had just recently graduated from the explorer academy a few months earlier, it was unthinkable that we were even entertaining the idea of carrying out such a dangerous crime without any regard for what our consequences would be if we were to get caught.

As Steven and I got further and further into going over the details of our plan, I continued to make it crystal clear to him that he would definitely have to come into the restaurant with a gun but, to ensure that no one got hurt in the process, the gun was NOT to be loaded under any circumstances, which he agreed to. Being the foolish kids we were, we decided to go through with the crime to make some quick money, but our plan failed miserably!

The very next day, while I was home alone, there was a determined knock at my front door. Not expecting anyone to be coming over to the house, I very quietly tip-toed down the stairs to see who was at the front door. Before I even got near the door, the doorbell began to ring, so I knew there was a sense of urgency to enter by whoever was on the other side of the door. As I looked out of the peephole, I recognized it to be my drill instructor, Detective Barker. At that time, Detective Barker was assigned to the Walnut Sheriff's Station and, when he got the case assigned to him, he took it personal when he learned that I was somehow connected to the robbery.

Upon staring through the peephole for several seconds, I initially found it to be very strange that Det. Barker was standing on my porch, but his partner was standing at the far end of our walkway, hiding behind the rock décor on the corner of our garage, and holding what appeared to be a stainless steel revolver in his left hand. I eventually opened up the door and let Det. Barker and his partner inside the house for what I knew would end up being a *come to Jesus* topic of discussion.

Detective Barker was one of my favorite drill instructors in the explorer academy. I admired him because of his command presence he always displayed while he was training us. He was always a very matter-of-fact type of person who didn't play around. If you ever caught him laughing, or even smiling, it was a treat, and could have easily been mistaken for the assumption that there was something about you that he actually liked. He was one of many deputies who participated in the historic Baker to Vegas run. One time, while out on the academy P.T. field, he informed me that he was impressed with me because he saw that I was

THE FOUNDATION

frequently able to keep up with him on the days that the drill instructors would have us run anywhere between one to two miles around the academy track.

Whenever we would run in platoon formation, that wasn't the time for me to prove to the drill instructors that I was capable of keeping up with *them*, running in platoon formation was a time for all of us recruits to show the drill instructors that we understood the cadence of marching, or running in a quasi-military style formation, and demonstrating that we could operate in sync as one entire unit.

The very first question that Detective Barker asked me was, "Dameon... how long have we known each other?" I humbly replied, "About six months or so, sir." He then began to ask me some very detailed questions about what happed at my job on the night of the robbery. Every answer that I gave him was a colorful recollection of what I chose to tell him about the incident. The very next statement out of his mouth was the very statement that changed my young life forever. "Dameon... Steven is in custody, and he told us everything!" Almost immediately, my chin sank into my chest, and I found it hard to even look Det. Barker in his eyes after that. The tears of disappointment began to fall down my face, but it was too late for crying!

Once I confessed to my involvement in the robbery, I immediately began explaining to Det. Barker why I went through with what I already knew was the wrong thing to do. I simply told him, "My mom needed me, sir! Ever since my step-father unexpectedly moved out of the house, it seems like my mother has had a hard time keeping up with the bills by herself, and things have just been a little hard for her... and I was just trying to get some quick money to help her out. I couldn't just sit back and watch my mother struggle and not try to help her."

Looking back, it was nothing less than a blessing that God chose Det. Barker to be the one to come to my house to arrest me. Whenever a felony arrest warrant is issued for a suspect to be picked up, it is not in any way a very welcoming process. Almost all of the time, the protocol is for a *team* of deputies to show up to take a suspect into custody, especially when they have knowledge that a firearm was used in the commission of a crime. It is also customary for deputies to completely surround a suspect's house before knocking on the door and announcing their presence. You can expect them to surround the entire house or property with guns drawn, helicopters circling the residence, K-9 unit on scene, and sometimes utilizing the Special Enforcement Bureau (SEB), also known as S.W.A.T., to take extremely violent suspects into custody.

Thanks be to God that I did not bring that type of embarrassment to our neighbors by causing that level of commotion on our street. I had already embarrassed my family enough by even being caught up in such a horrible situation. Based on the fact that Det. Barker was one of my drill instructors in the academy, he knew me... he knew I was a mild-mannered kid. He also knew that I came from a good home and, most importantly, based on how well we got along at the academy, he knew that I wouldn't run or make his job any harder to do than it already was.

THE FOUNDATION

Detective Barker never spoke to me like a suspect, he spoke to me with empathy and the realization that I was just a scared little 17-year-old kid who accepted the fact that I had made a terrible mistake. Somewhere embedded in the tone of his voice, it almost felt as though he was talking to me as a mentor. As the conversation between Det. Barker and I continued, he told me things about the robbery that even I didn't know. Despite the fact that Steven and I repeatedly discussed the fact that the gun he would use for the robbery would not even have bullets in it, Det. Barker informed me that, once they arrested Steven and recovered the gun he used in the robbery, the gun in fact had six *live* rounds in the clip. He went on to disclose to me that what led them to Steven, after the robbery, was the fact that, during the commission of the robbery, Steven's mask fell off at some point while he had the manager in the office, demanding entry into the restaurant's safe.

It was at that time that, when Steven's mask fell off, the manager got a quick glance at Steven's face, and recognized him as someone that he went to high school with. When this information became available to deputies who responded to the scene, Jason, the restaurant manager, told deputies that he could definitely identify Steven if he ever saw his face again. From the crime scene, one of the deputies drove the restaurant manager to his home nearby, where he retrieved his high school yearbook to see if he could find Steven's photo. It was told to me that the manager and the deputy went through every single page of the yearbook and, low and behold, there was Steven's photo on the page. At that time, the manager made a 100% positive ID that Steven was the masked assailant who pointed a gun at him and demanded all of the cash in the safe before fleeing the location.

Not only was my stomach in knots after hearing this information, I felt extremely betrayed by the fact that Steven's handgun was loaded with six rounds of live ammunition, when we specifically discussed that there would be no bullets in the gun at all. As if that wasn't enough, the gun he chose to use in the robbery was a .45 caliber, semi-automatic handgun. If the manager would have struggled with Steven in any way, trying to prevent the restaurant from being robbed, and the gun would have accidentally been fired, a round of that caliber would have had a permanent and devastating outcome! It was truly the grace and favor of God that no one got hurt during this foolish incident.

Before taking me into custody, Detective Barker escorted me to my upstairs bedroom, where he and his partner confiscated every garment of my Deputy Explorer uniform that had a Los Angeles County Sheriff's Department patch on it. I was extremely hurt and disappointed with myself that I allowed my poor judgement to ruin everything that I had worked so hard to achieve by investing all of that time into graduating from the academy. For many years after that incident, I was also upset with myself that I betrayed the honor and the trust of the Los Angeles County Sheriff's Department, my drill instructors, and my fellow explorer cadets from my academy class who looked upon me with integrity, and held me in high esteem. I screwed up bigtime, but I knew that, somehow, my life had to go on.

THE FOUNDATION

The shame and disappointment that I held against myself for many years made it all the more shameful to explain to my mother the real reason why I did it. My mother did not even learn about the above details until this very book was already under construction so, for an entire 35 years, my mother had no idea what provoked me to participate in such a crime. In the event that you should feel yourself starting to develop any type of negative or judgmental assumptions about me for what I did as a child, first, be sure to reflect back on the things that *you* did as a child that you were also not proud of. The obvious difference between me and most people in the world, is that I had the courage and the thick skin needed to allow myself to be honest and vulnerable enough to share with the world what most people in society would choose to keep hidden from everyone, for the fear and embarrassment of anyone ever finding out what they did. Not many people would ever risk that, but I did.

Since the year that I published my first book back in May of 2000, my objective goal with my writing talents has always been to show people who have made mistakes in life how to turn negatives into positives and move on with their lives. It's not always comfortable to talk about but, if the failures of *my* past can possibly help steer some other young kid away from going to prison, or possibly getting killed by making the same poor choice that I made, then I will talk about my own personal failures to anyone who will listen. They may not always appear when we want them to, but I truly believe that there are so many blessings that can be laid at our feet if we just have faith that *our* life lessons that we speak about are making a positive difference in the lives of those who feel like they have no one that cares enough about them to help guide them through the bumpy roads in life.

After going through the court process, I was eventually found guilty of conspiracy to commit armed robbery. My punishment for my role in this stupid idea of a crime was one week in Los Padrinos Juvenile Hall, along with probation and 260 hours of community service at Frank G. Bonelli Park. After serving my time in juvenile hall, I was determined to live my life by being a much more productive member of society. It was extremely hard to look my mother in the eyes when I came home from juvenile hall, because, after all that my mother had taught me about God, and about the importance of making responsible choices in life as a Christian, I knew without question that I had let her down tremendously... and it took me many years to forgive myself for the shame and embarrassment that I brought upon her and upon our family. I knew that it was too late to take back what I had done, but I also knew that the only *true* way I could ever apologize to my mother, and demonstrate to her how disappointed I was with myself, was to make a commitment to never do it again and, proudly, I kept that commitment!

Unlike *my* term of one week in Los Padrinos Juvenile Hall, Steven wasn't so lucky. After his court hearings were over and done with, he received three years in state prison for armed robbery. Since the both of us were affiliated with the Los Angeles County Sheriff's Department Explorer Program, the court was relatively lenient in our sentences, because we could have easily been given much more time than what we received.

THE FOUNDATION

For those who struggle with sharing the back-story of some of the most vulnerable incidents of *their* past, I will be the first to proclaim that it is everything *other than easy*! It takes a great deal of mental, emotional, and psychological strength to be *this* transparent about talking openly about things in my past that I am not proud of, **knowing** that there are people in this world who are eagerly awaiting to pass judgement on me the very moment they receive the information. In more cases than not, even *misinformation* will do just fine, as far as they are concerned.

Understanding long ago that God gave me a talent to write, and to tell profound stories at a very early age, I have been collecting influential pieces of documentation over the course of many years that serve as evidence that is representative of the *real* person I am at heart, despite what society may think of me. As proof of this fact, I hereby submit to you, and quote, the authentic words of Mr. Jason E. Reiff, the Taco Bell restaurant manager that was robbed at gunpoint many years ago by my former friend, Steven. The terms and conditions of my juvenile probation were largely determined by the recommendations that the court received from the probation department.

It is a common practice of the probation department to submit a written recommendation to the court as to what the terms and conditions of a defendant's probation should be. I was fortunate enough to have had many people submit character letters to the probation department on my behalf, describing what type of person they knew me to be. While gathering my research to include in this book, I came across a heart-felt letter that was dated October 11, 1989. This character letter was written by Mr. Jason E. Reif and, in his own words, this is what he had to say about the incident.

> "To Whom It May Concern,
>
> Concerning the incident that took place here at Taco Bell on the approximate date of August 31, 1989 involving Dameon Wroe, it was obviously a poor mistake on Dameon's part. Since the first day Dameon began working here at Taco Bell, I had an opportunity to watch Dameon in various areas. He was a fast learner and without a doubt a hard worker. Dameon was also respected for his ability to work with people while on the job and no doubt even when he was not working.
>
> I can honestly testify that Dameon is deeply and truly remorseful for the incident in which he was involved in. Roughly a week following his arrest, Dameon saw fit in his heart to write a letter to all Taco Bell employees apologizing for the incident that took place at the restaurant. Dameon did not fully state the exact reason why he did what he did, but everyone understands how Dameon is as a person and we have no harsh feelings toward him for what he has done.

THE FOUNDATION

> Dameon has always struck me as a person who is constantly setting high goals for himself and never quitting until they have been fulfilled. Despite what has happened to Dameon, now and in the past, he has not given up on himself, and neither have I!"

It disturbs me to my core to see that, even in the 21st Century, we live in a world where people who know absolutely nothing about you have the most negative things to say about you at times. It saddens me that, even today, we still dwell in a society where people who know nothing about your integrity will believe a fabricated, one-sided lie about you in a heartbeat without *ever* taking the time to get to know you for themselves. Hopefully, the letter above, written by Jason E. Reiff, will at least cause *my* readers to have a change of heart, if they find within themselves that they are also guilty of pre-judging me without taking time to notice the good within me for themselves! Despite all of the negative information that my oppressors have said about me all over the internet to slander my name, I am one of the most giving and down-to-earth people you will ever meet in your lifetime... and there is plenty of documented evidence that will be made available to the public to support this truth as time goes on.

As a person who grew up in the church, ever since I was a teenager, I knew that what I did back then was terribly wrong, but I did it anyway. Even though I felt justified in *why* I did what I did at that time, I eventually took ownership of the fact that I wasn't helping my mother at all. In fact, I was hurting her much more than I ever dreamed I would have done. The main thing is that, through that distasteful experience in my young life that I brought upon myself, I learned the value of talking to people in my circle about all subsequent challenges that I went through as a young person, and it forced me to search for more productive solutions to my problems, rather than breaking the law to get what I felt like I needed for me and my family. In my eyes, that's a *flex*!

It convicted me even more that this poor manger, who had a gun pulled on him during a robbery, based on *my* stupid idea, could have been fatally injured in the commission of my ignorant plan and, even after he learned that I had something to do with it, he found it in his heart to openly forgive me. Forgiveness in today's society seems to be too scarce to come by, but I sincerely hope that, one day, as a society, we can come together for the greater good of humanity to fix that problem. I hope and I pray that, one of these days, people will stop maliciously judging me simply because *my* sins are different than *their* sins!

For any young Black boys or young Black men out there in the world who may read this book one day, I would like to offer these empowering nuggets of information. If you find that you are currently in a similar situation that I just finished describing from my childhood, in the previous paragraphs, I strongly urge you to find a friend or family member that you trust enough to go to, and tell them about the struggles that you feel like you're dealing with. Don't

THE FOUNDATION

allow your pride to keep you from reaching out to people in your circle who might be in a position to help you deal with the many thoughts hiding in the dark corners of your mind.

Don't allow yourself to get to a point where you are faced with making desperate decisions. Most people who make desperate decisions during desperate times typically make the wrong decisions. If you have never been incarcerated, you're definitely not missing out on anything! Being incarcerated is *literally* hell on earth, and worse than *everything* that you may already be experiencing as a free person. As you will see in the chapters ahead, the people that you assume will be there for you, if and when you get incarcerated, will not be there for you at all. Never let any hardship or struggle cause you to have the false perception that you won't get caught if you commit a crime to get the things that you feel like you need or want in life. **No crime is worth your freedom, Black man!** There is no amount of money that you can steal or take by unlawful means that is worth the hell and psychological torture you will experience by being in prison!

If you have never been to prison before, believe me when I tell you... YOU ARE ALREADY WINNING IN LIFE!! Historically speaking, our oppressors in this country have systematically laid traps for us, as Black men, that will eventually put us in a position where we will never see our families again, if we allow ourselves to get caught up in a justice system that *they* control the way that *they* see fit!

For those of us Black men who have sons that we are raising, we have a duty and a responsibility to demonstrate to our sons that there *is* a better way to handle conflict, rather than picking up a gun and killing each other. This is the exact type of behavior that our oppressors are counting on us to continue. We need to teach our sons that there are more respectable ways of making money than obtaining it by way of illegal acts. If you find that you are a young Black man who does not have any positive role models or mentors to guide you to be successful in life, go online to Barnes & Noble or Amazon and order my book *Modern Day Mentor*. I wrote that book specifically for young Black boys and Black men around the world who need positive advice on mentoring and how to become better decision-makers.

Rather than spending the rest of your life dwelling on who was never there for you while you were growing up, dwell on the fact that you can be the one in your family to break those curses and change the narrative of your family history by breaking the cycle of generational dysfunction. If this is something that has never been done within your family, make a decision that *you* are going to be the first person to make it happen… with God's help, of course. Don't wait until you find yourself entering a prison facility to find God… find God now, while you still have a chance to make more productive decisions!

At this point in your reading, you're probably thinking to yourself, "Why would he share in his book such a terrible thing he did as a kid?" Somewhere in this world, right now, is a fully grown adult who is still holding themselves hostage for something wrong that they did as a child. Somewhere in the world, right this minute, is a fully grown adult

THE FOUNDATION

who has still not forgiven themselves for something stupid or dishonorable that they did as a child. My goal in sharing my story from my youth is to free people from themselves, and be an example to them that, since God forgives, it is finally okay for them to completely forgive themselves and move forward in their lives… that's why. If sharing my past failures as a kid will help someone in today's society get from where they are to where they are trying to go, it was all worth sharing!

2
★ ★ ★ ★ ★

TRAINING & WORK EXPERIENCE

IN A FORMAL BUSINESS LETTER dated May 13, 1992, Capitol Records attorney Eva Saks confirms that Capitol Records, Inc. ("Capitol") had accepted "H2O" as the first recording artist under an official, written agreement between Capitol and Black Tie Music, Inc., effective February 3, 1992. Back in the early 1990's, I became the fourth member of an R&B singing group called *"H2O,"* which stood for Hard 2 Overcome. On the night that we were scheduled to perform at The Roxy in West Hollywood, my then manager, Shirley Block, came upstairs to our dressing room, seemingly bursting in with an obvious excitement. She went on to tell us that we had to "throw down" during our performance that night because Herb Trawick was out in the audience to see us perform, and that he brought The Whispers with him to check us out. At that time, Herb Trawick was the personal manager for recording artist Brian McKnight, who was signed to Mercury Records at that time.

As we were less than 30 minutes away from hitting the stage, our nerves were seemingly becoming more and more shot. Our anxiety was all over the place that night because the house was packed, and we were scheduled to go on stage right after the live performance of rapper Ice T. and his crew. Now, keep in mind, at that time, the entire world knew who Ice T. was and, because we were not signed yet, almost nobody knew who we were. Despite the fact that we were not a household name, we went on stage and killed it!

When Ice T. and his crew left the stage after their performance, they left all of their mic stands and band equipment all over the stage, which decreased the amount of space we had to do our dance routine. After getting fully dressed in our full wardrobe for our show, we had to come out on the stage in front of everyone, move all of Ice T's equipment further back on the stage, exit the stage again to wait for the MC to announce us, and then come back out on stage again and act as if no one had just seen us come out and remove all of the equipment from the previous performance. Once our music started to play, and we began our dance routine, the rest was history.

We exited the stage and went straight back upstairs to our dressing room… hot, hungry, and out of breath! Shortly after settling in our dressing room, my manager walks in and tells us that we did so well with our performance that The Whispers were requesting us to go outside and have a brief meeting with them, in the alleyway that sits in between The Roxy and a local bar and grill next door. When we walked outside and walked up to Herb Trawick and The Whispers, they were all smiles, and appeared eager and honored to meet us. Though only Scotty and Walter were the only Whispers present with Herb at that time, they expressed to us how impressed they were with our performance.

TRAINING & WORK EXPERIENCE

Scotty and Walter praised our determination to have a successful show, citing that, even though we had to come on stage and set up our own mics and move equipment out of our way, we did a fantastic job. Scotty and Walter went on to explain to us that they were in the process of solidifying a formal deal with Capitol Records that would allow The Whispers to sign acts directly to their entertainment company [Black Tie Entertainment] and utilize Capitol Records as a major record distribution arm.

At the end of our alleyway meeting, adjacent to The Roxy, The Whispers presented a question to us that would change the history of our lives forever, "How would you guys like to be the very first act to get signed to Black Tie Entertainment?" After we accepted their offer, we were eagerly looking forward to signing our official record deal and start working on recording our first album. However, in reality, until that magical moment were to happen, I still had to hold on to my full-time day job to keep the bills paid.

After putting my second semester of college on hold at Mt. San Antonio College to try to land a record deal, I made a commitment to myself that, if the music business didn't work out for me, I would go back to school to pursue my degree in Criminal Justice and try to get a job as a law enforcement officer.

Like many aspiring entertainers, I already had a full-time job when I entered the entertainment industry. I was working in the security department at Universal Studios Hollywood when my former group members and I had already signed our deal with Black Tie Entertainment. Though

I was assigned to work at Universal Studios, the actual company that employed me at that time was American Protective Services (APS), who was contracted to provide security services for the MCA/Universal properties. At the time I began working at the Universal Studios property, CityWalk was still under construction, but scheduled to open for business approximately a few months after my start date. When I initially reported to the security department, I was primarily a uniformed officer. Every morning, outside of the *tours* security office, our captain would hold shift briefings each morning before we started our shift, so that every officer would know in advance which part of the theme park they were going to be assigned to work at for the day.

Initially, the job was kind of boring because, being one of the new guys, I was always getting assigned to the various parking structures. Over time, I began to start inquiring how long it would take me to be able to work in other areas of the entertainment center, rather than being stuck in the parking structures all day long. Because of the daily activity inside of the theme park that I would always monitor coming over the radio, it didn't take long for me to determine that all of the action that was happening from day to day was happening *inside* of the theme park, not in the parking structures. Most of the radio chatter that I was monitoring during my shift was primarily coming from our plain-clothes security officers inside the park.

I learned a lot from those plain-clothes security officers during my first several months of working there. Whenever those officers came over the radio to report something, I

TRAINING & WORK EXPERIENCE

could easily tell that they had been working there a long time before me, because they knew where everything was. When the officers got on the radio and told our dispatcher that they were following shoplifting suspects who had just left a particular gift shop, I couldn't tell if the officers were located in the upstairs portion of the theme park (*tours*) or the downstairs portion of the theme park, also known as lower lot or *Studio Center*, because the theme park was so huge!

The more familiar I started to become with knowing where all of the common places of the theme park were located, it became easier to do my job, and my confidence in *how* I was doing my job began to increase as well. The more action I got myself involved with during my shift, the more experience I gained. During our morning shift briefings, our captain assigned each officer his/her unit number for the day. Whenever you heard an officer give their unit number over the radio, you knew exactly what part of the property that officer was assigned to work. As best as I can remember, the most active units in our department were…

Tours Security Watch Commander:	40
Tours Security Lieutenant:	41
Tours Security Dispatcher:	42
Plain-Clothes Security Officer:	46
Plain-Clothes Security Officer:	46A (46 Adam)
Plain-Clothes Security Officer:	47

Plain-Clothes Security Officer:	47A (47 Adam)
Uniformed Security Officer:	49
Uniformed Mobile Patrol Officer:	61
CityWalk Security Dispatcher:	81
Sheriff's Department Deputies:	95
	95/Gross
	95/Belda
	95/Collins
	95/Dane

Since I understood the potential dangers that came along with being employed as a security officer, monitoring my radio was always of the utmost importance to me because, if I ever heard that one of my fellow officers came over the radio needing any type of help or assistance, I had already made up my mind that I would automatically abandon my post to go and help that officer until he/she was no longer in danger, and that the person causing the problem was in handcuffs.

Based on training that I had already received in my Criminal Justice class in high school, as well as what I learned in the sheriff's explorer academy, I knew that our radios were the lifeline that stood between us and any person attempting to harm us, or other innocent guests who were there to visit our theme park.

Still functioning as a new-hire, I quickly learned that there was one particular security officer who was always

TRAINING & WORK EXPERIENCE

catching people sneaking into the theme park without paying for a ticket to enter. His radio traffic also suggested to me that he was also very well known for making a lot of petty theft arrests, by catching people stealing miscellaneous items from gift shops. If he saw someone stealing from a gift shop, he would get on the radio immediately upon exiting the store behind the suspect and call it in. Here is a short example of what our radio traffic would sound like once we knew someone was about to be detained or arrested...

Plain-Clothes Security Officer:
46 to 42

Tours Security Dispatcher:
42

Plain-Clothes Security Officer:
Be advised, I'm just leaving the General Store, and I'll be 10-15 with one.

Tours Security Dispatcher:
Copy, 10-15 with one from General Store. Do you need a 95 unit to 87 you?

Plain-Clothes Security Officer:
Stand by, I'll let you know shortly.

Tours Security Dispatcher:
10-4

Uniformed Security Officer (Me):

49 to 42

Tours Security Dispatcher:

42

Uniformed Security Officer (Me):

Advise 46 that I'm right across from the General Store if he needs me.

Tours Security Dispatcher:

Copy... 46, did you copy 49's traffic? He can 87 with you if you need him to.

Plain-Clothes Security Officer:

Yeah, 10-4, have him come on over.

Tours Security Dispatcher:

Copy... 49, go ahead and 87 with 46.

Uniformed Security Officer (Me):

10-4, en route.

Sheriff's Department Deputy:

This is 95/Collins, I'm 10-8 from the substation, I'll be heading over also.

Tours Security Dispatcher:

10-4, 95.

TRAINING & WORK EXPERIENCE

Since I was still a newbie with the company, I was initially intimidated and afraid to get on the radio and communicate directly with the plain-clothes officer who was about to make an arrest, so for the longest time I would only get on the radio and communicate directly with the dispatcher, so that she could direct me on what to do and when to do it, just in case my assistance wasn't needed. There was something very peculiar about this plain-clothes security officer that I admired about him every time I heard his voice come over the radio. I could always tell that he had a distinct, command presence about himself, and that he was one of the best officers that the company had at that time. He was solid and knew his job like the back of his hand. In the scenario above, here is what was being said in the radio transmissions from start to finish.

Realizing that the suspect he was observing had stolen multiple items from the gift shop, and walked right by the store's cash registers several times without making any overt attempt to pay for the merchandise, the plain-clothes security officer was notifying the security dispatcher that he was exiting the General Store gift shop, and that he was about to arrest the suspect for shoplifting. The security dispatcher indicated that she understood the plain-clothes officer's radio traffic, and proceeded to ask him if he needed a deputy sheriff unit at his location. The plain-clothes officer advised the dispatcher to stand by for further information concerning the arrest he was about to make. This was done because the officer had no way of telling if the suspect was going to be cooperative or combative to avoid being arrested, which does happen in many cases.

The dispatcher then acknowledged that she was standing by for updated information. While waiting to hear back from the plain-clothes security officer, I got on the radio to advise the dispatcher to tell the plain-clothes officer that I was very close to his location, in case he felt like he needed backup. The security dispatcher relayed my message to the plain-clothes officer over the radio as I had requested. At that time, the plain-clothes officer advised the dispatcher that he did in fact want me to meet (87) him at the arrest location. The dispatcher complied with the plain-clothes officer's request, and I went over to meet with him.

Since all deputy sheriff's assigned to the MCA/Universal property monitored our radio traffic, as well as their own county issued radios, Deputy Collins got on our radio frequency to let our dispatcher know that he was just coming on duty, and that he was heading over to our tours security office at his own discretion, for further investigation of the person we arrested. Now that you have a better understanding of the details explained in this scenario, let's talk about why it was often times beneficial for the sheriff's deputies to work so closely with us on the Universal Studios entertainment center property.

When a suspect is about to be taken into custody by a plain-clothes security officer, they sometimes have difficulty believing that the person attempting to arrest or detain them is a legitimate employee of the security department. This can sometimes provoke the arrestee to become hostile and bold enough to either fight us to get away, or take other evasive measures to elude us. Having a uniformed security officer

TRAINING & WORK EXPERIENCE

on scene to assist the plain-clothes officer in making his arrest serves as confirmation to the suspect that they are in fact under arrest, and that fighting to get out of it will likely be a fight that they will ultimately lose, thus encouraging the suspect to remain compliant. After this arrest process was fully carried out, I started to notice that I was beginning to build a more favorable rapport with the plain-clothes officers and my supervisors, many of whom were much older than me and had been working at the theme park much longer than me.

Once I had proven myself to the plain-clothes security team, and my supervisors, my days of being assigned to the parking structures were over. Since the more experienced security officers were starting to take notice of my skillset, and my detail-oriented ability to do the job, they began to suggest to the upper management team that I would be a greater asset to the security team if I were given an opportunity to work with them on plain-clothes assignments. After these plain-clothes officers were able to successfully convince upper management to give me a chance to work in this capacity, I officially became a member of the undercover security team. It was already evident to me that these guys were really good at what they did and, with that understanding in mind, I knew that I had to be just as good or better than them in order to maintain my undercover status. I didn't just meet their expectations, I exceeded them on a regular basis.

Based on the fact that I was already a very observant person by nature, I noticed a pattern among other plain-clothes security officers that had a particular theme, relating to how they did their job. Most of them would make a lot of misdemeanor arrests, usually for petty thefts, as defined under California Penal Code Section 488.

When deputies would come to our security office to assist us with petty theft arrests, they would transport the *arrestee to their sheriff's substation on CityWalk for booking, but we were making the actual arrest as a private* person, most commonly referred to as a *citizen's arrest* or *private person's arrest.* In order for a police officer to make an arrest for a misdemeanor crime, the police officer must have physically witnessed that misdemeanor crime take place. If the misdemeanor occurs outside of a police officer's presence, then the officer must inform the person who witnessed the crime that they will need to make a private person's arrest, typically by filling out and signing a Private Person's Arrest Form that will be used as documentation in the arrested person's booking process. A police officer cannot make an arrest for a misdemeanor crime that he/she did not witness.

On the other hand, in order for a police officer to make an arrest for a felony crime, the felony need not have been committed in the presence of the officer. As long as a felony has been committed, a police officer can make a felony arrest, as long as he/she has probable cause to believe that the person being detained or held did in fact commit the felony. During the time that I worked as a security officer at Universal Studios Hollywood (1992-1994), any stolen property with a value of $400.00 or less was classified as misde-

TRAINING & WORK EXPERIENCE

meanor petty theft (488 PC), punishable by time in county jail upon conviction. Any stolen property with a value greater than $400.00 was classified as felony grand theft (487 PC), punishable by time in state prison upon conviction.

Currently, the new legal threshold for those same crimes has changed dramatically. Currently, any stolen property with a value of $950.00 or less is classified as misdemeanor petty theft (488 PC), punishable by time in county jail upon conviction. Any stolen property with a value greater than $950.00 is classified as felony grand theft (487 PC), punishable by time in state prison upon conviction.

All of this knowledge, for me, was simply a review of everything that I had already learned, either in my high school Criminal Justice class or in the sheriff's academy, where I had trained to become an explorer cadet. When the existing plain-clothes security officers began training me on what to look for while we were out, methodically patrolling the entertainment center, they taught me to make sure that I allowed a shoplifting suspect to fully exit the gift shop first before I stopped them and identified myself as security.

If I were to stop someone outside of a gift shop, and falsely accuse them of shoplifting, the company could have been held liable for my false accusations if the person did not in fact have any stolen merchandise on them after exiting the store. In some cases, I personally witnessed random people put stolen items in their pocket or in their purse, but then have a change of heart and put the items back before leaving the store. In those cases, even though I initially saw the person stealing, I would ultimately end up letting them go without being approached for investigation. However, I routinely followed that person around the park to other gift shops to see if they would attempt to steal—sometimes they did, and sometimes they didn't.

In order for me to stand out, and show my superiors that my work ethic was just as admirable as the other security officers, my strategy was to focus primarily on felony arrests. With my understanding that each crime has certain elements that must be met before an individual can be arrested for committing that crime, I focused on burglary arrests, identifying entertainment center guests that were intentionally going around to multiple gift shops, clearly intending to commit petty thefts. Once the Universal Studios theme park opened for business each day, I would start my shift by dressing up like a tourist who was just roaming around the park to see all of the attractions, just like all of the other guests who had purchased a ticket. I would carry around a plastic gift shop bag, and fill it with random items from my security office to make it look like I actually purchased something from one of the stores in the park. I also carried around programs and maps of the scheduled theme park shows, to give my tourist look a little bit more believability.

There were even many times when I followed a shoplifter out of a gift shop and right into the stadium seating area of an actual show to continue my observation. After the show was over, my partner and I would continue to follow the shoplifter to see if he/she would commit another theft at a new gift shop. If it became evident to us that the

TRAINING & WORK EXPERIENCE

shoplifter was not making any overt efforts to enter another gift shop, we would just stop him/her, identify ourselves as park security, and take the person into custody for the previous theft that we did in fact witness.

Each time I knew I was about to enter a specific gift shop to look for shoplifters, I would go to a discreet location and notify our tours security dispatcher, via my two-way radio, that I was about to enter that store and that, while inside of that store, I would be turning off my radio until I was out of the store. Once inside the gift shop, I would eventually locate a person inside the store that I had observed stealing items.

Once I observed that person put a stolen item in their pocket or in their purse, my training alerted me to start maintaining continuity of that stolen item. Continuity of evidence is a legal term that simply means, as a security officer targeting shoplifters, once I see a person put a stolen item in their front, right pocket, that same stolen item must still be in their front, right pocket once they exit the store and I detain them. If the shoplifter were to move the stolen item from their front, right pocket to an inside, jacket pocket, then I would have automatically known to recover the stolen item from the subject's inside, jacket pocket because I visibly followed that stolen item without ever taking my eyes off of it.

Once I would finally detain a shoplifter, after observing them steal merchandise from two or more gift shops, I would ultimately place them under arrest for burglary (459 PC). One of the elements of burglary is when a person enters a four-sided dwelling or structure with the *intent* to commit theft. Arresting a person for burglary, after only shoplifting at one store, would not be a fair charge, because it's extremely difficult to prove *intent to commit theft* after observing that a person only shoplifted from one store. For this reason, I routinely made it my own personal protocol to follow a shoplifter around the entire Universal Studios Hollywood theme park until I was satisfied that I was able to establish *intent* for a felony burglary arrest.

It didn't take long for me to rapidly gain the attention and the respect of my supervisors, their bosses, as well as my fellow plain-clothes security officers. Equally, after working directly with the various sheriff's deputies that were assigned to the Universal Studios property, they were impressed to learn that I was a former explorer with the Los Angeles County Sheriff's Department several years prior.

I am persuaded to believe that most people who have counter-productive contact with private security officers, tend to think that security officers can't do anything to them. Even in my personal experiences of having worked in the security industry, most people looked at security officers as rent-a-cops, toy soldiers, wannabe cops, or some other derogatory term that best described their level of disrespect and disdain for the security profession. Many of the people I arrested while working at Universal Studios Hollywood also felt that same way about me. They felt that I had no authority to detain them and ask them questions. They felt that I had no authority to arrest them, because I was not a police officer. Many of them voiced directly to me that I didn't know what I was doing, and tried to con-

TRAINING & WORK EXPERIENCE

vince me that my actions would eventually result in them suing me for false arrest... which never happened. There were quite a few people that I arrested in the past that felt like I could not even handcuff them, until I handcuffed them and escorted them to the sheriff's substation on CityWalk to be turned over to the sheriffs to get booked for the very crime(s) that I in fact arrested them for. They messed around and found out!

When the deputies would show up to our security office to inquire about an arrest we made, they had the capability to investigate things about the arrestee that were beyond our capability. For example, once we had all of the suspect's personal information that we needed to include in our arrest report, we would then forward that information to the deputy on scene, so that he/she could run that person's name over their county issued radio to find out if they had any wants or warrants... the same protocols that a deputy would follow if they were pulling someone over on a traffic stop. In many cases, most of the people I personally arrested did not have any pending wants or warrants, but a small handful of subjects that I arrested during my employment there, did in fact have felony warrants that they were ultimately taken to jail for.

Still to this day, I'm persuaded to believe that most people who visit CityWalk today, don't even realize that there is a jail facility on the CityWalk premises, which sits on the second floor, right above the old Camacho's Cantina restaurant, courtesy of the Los Angeles County Sheriff's Department—West Hollywood Station. This is one hotel that you don't ever want to check into! Once my reputation as one of the top-performing security officers continued to get noticed by my superiors, and fellow officers, I noticed that I was being included in more and more public safety operations on the MCA/Universal property. Little did I know at that time, that the experience I would gain while working for this organization would be pivotal in helping me to keep the public and myself protected from harm and criminal activity, as long as I was on duty and being entrusted with doing my job with such integrity, precision, and high expectations.

I always loved it when the security department would get memos that a concert was coming up at the old Universal Amphitheatre, headlining top rock or heavy metal bands. The types of people that these kinds of concerts would bring in was guaranteed to keep us on our toes before, during, and after the event. We used to hide in tactical observation points on the premises and target common locations where concert-goers would hide weapons or drug paraphernalia, usually metallic or small, glass weed pipes. When they came back to these locations to retrieve their hidden weapons after the concert was over, they never found the weapons they hid because we had already found them and confiscated them.

Most of the weapons we would find and confiscate were knives and brass knuckles. On one or two occasions, myself and my partners would find switchblade knives and those leather, heavy-metal style gloves studded with metal spikes. Concert-goers would hide these items before standing in line for their scheduled concert because they knew they would be scanned with metal detectors once they got to the front

TRAINING & WORK EXPERIENCE

of the line at the main entrance to enter the concert. On the other hand, if we observed anyone in possession of brass knuckles, we would arrest them on sight, since brass knuckles are a dangerous weapon and have the ability to inflict great bodily injury, up to and including death. After the arrest process was complete, we would oftentimes return to the main entrance of the park in different clothing so we wouldn't be noticed, and start our surveillance patrols all over again.

Our specialized plain-clothes security operations on the MCA/Universal Studios property was so organized and discreet that our uniformed security officers would not even know that we were on the premises. Not only did they never see us in the performance of our duties, they also could not hear or monitor our radio traffic because we had radios that were set to a specialized frequency. I had never been a part of such an organized security company like APS, but these were some of the best times I ever had during my 12-year, intermittent work history in the private security profession. I can honestly say that I have never met another person in the private security industry who has had a more experienced, diverse, and decorated work history than me—I'm just being honest.

Before my time had come to an end, working security at Universal Studios Hollywood, I was fortunate and blessed to have earned a chance to be a part of several more impressive opportunities that gave me a chance to further enhance my training and professional growth. I was *selected* to be a member of the Special Problems Unit, more commonly called the SPU Team, and I was also selected to be a member of the CityWalk Suppression Unit (CSU), most commonly referred to as the CSU Team. Being a member of either one of these teams was a very special honor and accomplishment but, truth be told, I had the most fun in actively honing my skills while being used as a plain-clothes asset on the SPU Team.

What made me feel most honored about being a member of the SPU Team was that not just anyone could *apply* to be on the SPU Team. The only security officer candidates who could be considered for the SPU Team were candidates who were *specifically chosen* by members of the MCA/Universal Corporate Security Division. Most of the people who made up the corporate security team, during my time there, were retired law enforcement officers. They came from high-ranking positions that they held while employed by their respective police/sheriff agencies. Looking back on those days of my young life, I'm still blown away today that those men and women saw something upstanding within me that I may not have fully noticed about my own abilities back then.

Should any of them come across this book, I use this publication as my personal opportunity to say to them, "Thank you so very much for believing in me enough to put your name on the line for a youngster like me, by entrusting *me* to perform the many tasks that I was able to perform at CityWalk as a young man. Your belief in me, coupled with my experience and knowledge of the law, made it possible for me to prove to the world around me that not all security

TRAINING & WORK EXPERIENCE

officers are to be considered *average*!" Still with me? If so, tighten up your seatbelt as we continue this roller coaster ride of training and experience that afforded me the chance to take part in some historic opportunities while employed in the private security arena.

Once all of the SPU Team members had been identified, two intense, mandatory training sessions were scheduled with the corporate security staff and members of our security team, who would be the security officers tasked with successfully carrying out the missions that we were about to be sent out on. I recall the first training session being conducted by the corporate security executives and our supervisors within the security department. The objective of the initial training session was to inform all of us about the biggest crimes that were occurring on the MCA/Universal property at that time. We were informed that a spike in tourist complaints were coming in, as a result of people having their vehicles broken into while visiting the Universal CityWalk entertainment center. We were also informed of people being robbed by pickpockets, possibly working in small groups in various areas, taking money or other personal items right out of peoples' pockets or opened handbags/purses.

A *pickpocket* is someone who will blend in with very large, crowded areas and reach around other people to steal items off of the person of another, then make an immediate getaway to avoid detection. Our second SPU Team training was the training that had me feeling like my accomplishments as a security officer were about to rapidly soar to the next level. The MCA/Universal Corporate Security Division had the insight to hire former Special Investigation Section (SIS) detectives of the Los Angeles Police Department to come in and train us on surveillance and investigation tactics.

I specifically recall one of our instructors teaching us that, in other countries, there are actually schools and workshops where even children are taught how to properly steal from people's pockets without being detected. The SIS instructors taught us that members of these criminal organizations would wire purses, bags, and even pant pockets with red indicator lights so that, if a child reached into a purse and accidentally touched the sides of the handbag, alerting the unsuspecting victim, the red indicator light would light up, letting the student know that they failed to successfully take money or other valuables from the purse without being detected.

A major reason why these illegal acts were taught to children is because, if a child got caught, they would face very little punishment for their acts... or no punishment at all. Punishments for adult criminals are always higher than punishments for minors. Not only did this fact blow me away, it made me angry to know that there are adults in this world who would even want to teach children how to steal and break the law! Not long after taking this training class, facilitated by the former SIS detectives, I eventually got my chance to demonstrate my displeasure with adults who teach kids how to steal. I will never forget one of my most meaningful arrests during my time in the security department at Universal Studios.

As I was scouting for shoplifters in the gift shop directly next to Guest Relations, I observed some small children who

TRAINING & WORK EXPERIENCE

were roaming around in the store with no adult or guardian with them. As I continued to pay attention to the kids, they clearly had no idea I was watching them. Whoever the children were with, I knew that an adult had to be somewhere nearby them. As I continued to watch them, I noticed a female in her mid to late 20's sitting in the shade, on a window ledge right outside of the gift shop. Sitting right next to the young lady was a much older woman, seemingly in her late 50's to early 60's.

I then noticed the two, small children, no more than about seven or eight years old, methodically coming in and out of the store to steal small souvenirs. The elderly woman would hand the kids a large, plastic souvenir mug and direct them to go into the store and fill the mug with keychains, ink pens, and refrigerator magnets. Anything that was small enough to fit into the mug was fair game for the two women. Once the mug was full with stolen items, the kids would put the top on the mug to conceal the stolen items, and then exit the store and hand the mug off to the elderly woman.

The elderly woman would then hand the mug off to the younger woman sitting next to her, and the younger woman would then empty out the stolen contents into a diaper bag that was hidden underneath her baby stroller. Once emptied, the younger woman would hand the mug back to the elderly woman, and the elderly woman would give the mug back to the children so that they could re-enter the gift shop and continue stealing more of the same items. This went on about a total of three times. Once my partner arrived at

Guest Relations to back me up, we briefly spoke about what the women were observed doing and, within just a few minutes, my partner and I approached both women, identified ourselves as park security, and arrested them both for burglary, while using their children in the commission of a crime. I have no sympathy, nor any respect for any adult who intentionally teaches children how to steal, or otherwise break the law! Zero tolerance!!

On designated days, and during specific timeframes, myself and other SPU members would walk up and down CityWalk for an entire shift, specifically targeting anyone who drew unnecessary attention to themselves, and appeared to fit the profile of the pickpocket teams we were looking to identify. When we were not seemingly onto any of the pickpocket teams we were hoping to arrest, we broke up into teams and went into the parking structures for a few hours, looking for anyone who appeared to be discreetly trying to break into vehicles. Some nights we patrolled the parking structures on foot and from stationary observation points.

There were other times, usually when special events were taking place that the security department would rent undercover passenger cars for us to drive around in, looking for potential car thieves and trying to catch them in the act of stealing a car or burglarizing parked vehicles. In each operation, we had a direct connection with each individual sheriff's deputy on duty. On weekends, when the night-life on CityWalk was at its highest peak, we also had the assistance of the mounted (horseback) units of the Los Angeles

TRAINING & WORK EXPERIENCE

County Sheriff's Department. If you've never seen deputies on horseback in action before, they have a command presence that strongly urges potentially unsavory characters to behave themselves, or get dealt with in ways they would never forget. Those horses utilized by the sheriff's department are **no joke!**

While my time and experiences at Universal Studios and Universal CityWalk were filled with many memories of fun, exhilaration and excitement, there were also some memories that stayed with me over the course of a few decades that reminded me of how fortunate I am to still be alive today.

After working an eight hour shift one day, I went home to shower and change clothes, only to hurry back to CityWalk in time for my then girlfriend's lunch break, so that I could spend time with her. Though I was off duty, I still parked my car in what used to be known as the Z-Lot, a parking lot designated for only employees. As I began to execute a left turn into an empty parking spot, I observed two Black males about five parking spaces beyond where I ultimately parked. They were walking side-by-side towards my car, and seemingly having a discussion about something.

Just as I had put my car in park and opened up my door to exit my vehicle, I looked in my rear view mirror and noticed the two males stop, almost directly behind my car. I then began to observe them more closely, and observed the Black male on my rear passenger side lift up the front of his shirt and pull out what appeared to be a black, semi-automatic handgun and pass it to the other Black male who was closest to my rear driver's side trunk area. The male closest to me then put the handgun in his front, right pocket. There was a very brief conversation between the two men after the other placed the gun in his front pocket. During that extremely brief conversation they were having, I was thinking of a way to stay alive, because I knew I was about to be the intended victim of a car-jacking, if not something more serious!

My training kicked in right away and, just that quick, I came up with a way to escape the danger. Since my driver's door was still halfway open, I discreetly put my car in reverse, but kept my foot on the brake. In that moment, I had already committed to running both men over with my car as violently as I could have possibly done, to keep that gun from being pulled on me.

Keeping my door partially open, I held on to the door handle for dear life, and steadied the door in that position with my foot. By doing this, I knew that I could run the gunman over and pin him either under my door, or under my car, simultaneously running the other man over by pinning him under the rear of my vehicle. By the sheer grace, mercy, and favor of Almighty God, there was some divine intervention that saved all three of us from an early grave!

Before the male with the handgun started to walk by my driver's side door, I heard the alarm of the parked car right next to me go off, and the doors being unlocked. It was a lady who was returning to her car with a bunch of items in her hands. When she put the items in her car, she put them in on her rear passenger side door, unknowingly stepping right in between me and the armed suspects. As she got in

TRAINING & WORK EXPERIENCE

her car and prepared to drive off, she had no idea that she had just foiled an armed robbery already in progress.

Ultimately, the two men simultaneously walked from the rear of my car towards the front bumper of my car and kept on going, eventually making their way out of the parking lot on foot, but headed for CityWalk. If the male walking along my driver's side would have stopped and said even one word to me, my plan was to immediately take my foot off the break and floor it in reverse to stop the threat against me. Thankfully, he kept walking.

I immediately locked my car and began crawling through the parking lot on my hands and knees, looking up to peek through the windows of parked cars, every few seconds, to see if I could locate the security jeep that was assigned to patrol that parking lot while also maintaining a visual of the two armed men and their last known direction of travel. Moments later, as I'm still crawling on the ground to get to the other side of the next parking isle, I noticed a white security jeep slowly approaching my location. I frantically waved my arms at the officer driving the jeep to get him to notice that I was a fellow, off-duty security officer. I then advised him that I needed his hand-held radio immediately, so that I could put out an emergency broadcast. As soon as he handed me his radio, I told him to get out of the area as fast as he could, and slammed his passenger door shut so he could leave the area—he followed my directions to the letter!

Now armed with a way to communicate directly with emergency personnel, I called the CityWalk security dispatcher by stating, "81... this is Officer Wroe!! I'm off-duty in the Z-Lot, and I need you to clear all radio traffic, right now, and stand by for a 417 (man with a gun) broadcast!!" At my command, the CityWalk security dispatcher came on her radio and advised all tours and lower lot security personnel to stay off the radio and stand by for emergency traffic, then she came back to me and cleared me to begin broadcasting my emergency radio traffic. For purposes of identification over the radio, as best as I can remember it, that radio traffic sounded almost exactly like this...

46: 46 to 81, start me some 95 units (sheriffs) to the Z-Lot NOW!! Two males tried to car-jack me and are now headed into CityWalk on foot from the Z-Lot. Once the light turns green, they'll be crossing the street with other pedestrians, going towards the Odeon Plaza. The male with the firearm is a male black, white short-sleeves over blue jeans. Copy?

81: 81 to 95, 95... be advised two male blacks are heading towards the Odeon Plaza, one male carrying a handgun in his front, right pocket... 95, do you copy?

95: 95/Collins from the substation in less than two... 46, what's your 20?

95: 95/Gross from Tram Road in less than one.

TRAINING & WORK EXPERIENCE

46: 95/Collins, be advised I'm still in the Z-Lot, observing the suspects from a distance. Both suspects are now in the crosswalk, crossing the street mixed in with other pedestrians. [Break] The Black male with the handgun is halfway across now... white over blue jeans, and at the far end of the crosswalk, furthest from the intersection.

95: 95/Collins copy! Be advised, West Hollywood units are responding Code 3.

Just as Deputy Collins had told me that West Hollywood units were responding to my location with lights and sirens, almost immediately, I could hear a faint sound of sirens coming from a great distance. The radio traffic then went uncomfortably silent, for what *seemed* like five minutes or more. During the silence, and as all of the pedestrians were almost across the street, I got on the radio and advised Deputy Collins that the suspects were directly in front of him, about to step up on the sidewalk. He never got back on the radio to acknowledge my radio traffic. I suddenly heard Deputy Collins start yelling at the two Black males at gunpoint, "Get your damn hands up, now!!! Get down on the ground!!! Do it now!!" Not realizing what was going on, the other pedestrians quickly ran for cover and got out of harm's way by continuing to run towards CityWalk.

As uniformed and undercover deputies converged on the intersection to overtake the armed suspects, the unarmed Black male got down on the ground immediately! The Black male with the handgun in his front, right pocket wasn't so smart. Before the armed male got down on the ground, he reached into his pocket, pulled out the handgun, and tossed it into some nearby bushes. Little did he know, there was another deputy already positioned near those same bushes, taking cover behind a large, street light controlbox, ready to shoot the suspect if he made any overt attempts to fire his handgun. After the suspects were taken into custody by sheriff's deputies, I advised the security dispatcher that both suspects were in custody, and that is was okay to resume normal radio traffic. As luck would have it, I still made it to my girlfriend's job on time to have lunch with her during her break… give or take four or five minutes. God definitely had a guardian angel watching over me, because, had it not been for that female employee arriving at her car when she did, to put those boxes in her car during the car-jacking attempt, this situation could have had a terrible ending for me.

A few days after this event, during our morning briefing at the beginning of our shift, I was told by my supervisor that I had received a commendation by our American Protective Services Project Manager, Tom Ralphs, for my assistance in taking the armed suspects into custody without incident. In a formal, companywide memorandum, dated August 28, 1994, Tom Ralphs described the incident in his own words.

TRAINING & WORK EXPERIENCE

"On August 26, 1994 at 2030 hours, Officer Wroe had just driven his private vehicle into the Z-Lot and parked. He was in soft clothes, as he works in a plainclothes assignment, and was not recognizable as a security officer. As a safety precaution, Officer Wroe checked his vehicle mirrors prior to locking his car and observed two males approaching his vehicle from the rear. Realizing a potentially dangerous situation developing, Officer Wroe left his car engine running and continued to observe them. As they were standing behind Officer Wroe's vehicle, he observed one of the males take a handgun from under his shirt and give it to the other male, who placed the gun in his pocket. Officer Wroe immediately placed his car in reverse to escape the volatile situation. The two males began to walk away in an obviously aborted robbery attempt. Officer Wroe secured his vehicle and went to the vehicle gate where he borrowed an APS radio from another officer. Officer Wroe immediately took control of the situation by utilizing the radio in clear, concise instructions. He began by identifying himself, his plainclothes attire, his location and that he was following two men with a gun. He requested LASD to respond.

At this point, it should be noted that all air traffic with APS officers ceased, allowing Officer Wroe and LASD to correspond without interference. Officer Wroe began following the two males, who were heading towards the Odeon Plaza. He continued by broadcasting an accurate description of the suspects, which suspect had the gun and the location the gun was carried. With controlled diction and calmness, Officer Wroe continued to follow the suspects and direct responding LASD units to safely intercept and arrest the suspects without incident. The gun was retrieved and found to be a .9mm semiautomatic handgun, loaded with six (6) live rounds. One of the arresting deputies made the statement, 'I may have shot him (suspect) when he reached for his wallet, except that Officer Wroe had given such a precise broadcast and exact location of the gun. He was so calm and cool on the radio and his description so accurate that it gave us that extra edge for safety.'

Officer Wroe is to be commended for his *expert* assessment of a dangerous situation and the presence of mind to remove himself from that peril. Of equal importance was the flawless way he handled the radio transmissions with calm, clear and accurate statements. He has displayed bravery,

TRAINING & WORK EXPERIENCE

common sense and excellent judgement. His tenacity in the face of danger is exemplary. Your fellow officers and supervisors recognize and respect you. Again, thanks for an outstanding job."

For those people in society who look upon security officers as rent-a-cops, wannabe cops, or any other derogatory terminology they can use to belittle the security profession, look what I had to go through as a former security officer to ensure that other people, who probably resented my profession, could have a safe, enjoyable, and violence-free experience at CityWalk. Because of my skill, observations, and knowledge of the law as a security officer that many people resent, a person with a loaded firearm and an appetite for crime was not allowed to go into CityWalk and victimize anyone else, and was taken to jail where he belonged!

Who would have ever imagined that a security officer would have experienced as much as I had experienced, and would have witnessed as much as I had witnessed during my first few years of joining that workforce? There's no possible way that I could capture 12 years of being in the private security industry in just one book. However, there are things that I have seen over the course of those years that I may never be able to unsee... physically, emotionally, and psychologically. As you will see later on in subsequent chapters of this book, my experience, my authority, and my legal judgement regarding my use of deadly force was called into question during a high-profile, prejudicial, slanderous, and politically motivated murder trial, in which I was the defendant.

At the time of my commendation shown above, I was only 23 years old when the person who wrote that commendation identified my abilities as having an "expert assessment of a dangerous situation." How could I possibly possess the ability to have expert decision-making skills at 23 years old, but not have those same expert abilities at 32 years old, when my life depended on those same skills all over again? Let that sink in for a moment! You can't make this stuff up, especially when there's this much documented proof that supports my expert ability to make life or death decisions under extreme mental stress!

Before my time had ended with APS Security, at the Universal Studios entertainment center, I had personally responded to and secured some very unusual crime scenes. One of the most memorable incidents I had ever responded to was when an emergency radio call went out, just as I was about to turn in my equipment and get off duty. The call was regarding a man standing on the "inner" railing of the fifth level escalators next to the parking structure, threatening to jump! My partners and I grabbed our radios back from the dispatcher and took off running to the Odeon Plaza escalators, where the jumper was located.

As we were all running to the scene to identify the jumper and begin negotiating with him to get down off the rails, I got on the radio and instructed our dispatcher to call the valet parking office and tell them to have all of their em-

TRAINING & WORK EXPERIENCE

ployees stay away from the subject until we got there. Unfortunately, by the time we arrived on scene, the man had already jumped to his death. His lifeless, purple body laid permanently still where he came to rest, and it was obvious that he suffered multiple broken bones and disfigurement, as a result of his jump. This incident haunted me for many years, and I carried around the guilt of not getting there fast enough to save the man from himself.

I later learned that the man who jumped to his death was a part of an adult daycare group that was there visiting CityWalk. Somehow, the man managed to stray away from his group and, for whatever reason, felt the need to jump to his instant demise. In my heart of hearts, particularly due to the excessive amount of training I already had, I felt like I could have talked the man out of jumping, but I would never get that opportunity to even try, and that disappointed me for quite a long time.

Not long after that incident, while mid-way through my day shift, another terrifying call came out over my radio. Our dispatcher put out an emergency broadcast one day, informing us that an unknown female had just been seen standing on the Universal Studios Boulevard bridge, and she looked like she was attempting to jump off of the bridge. Still to this day, the only thing underneath that bridge is the 101 freeway. By the time that myself and two other plainclothes security officers had jumped in the security jeep and sped down to the bridge to intercept the woman, she had already jumped off of the bridge and onto the 101 freeway, ending her life.

The unknown woman was immediately struck by a few vehicles but, by the time we got there to investigate, the woman had been run over by several more vehicles. It was a scene that I hope to fully forget one of these days. Not only did we have to write an incident report about the jumper, we also had to photograph the point of impact on the freeway where the woman jumped from our bridge. Most people would never imagine that a security officer would ever have to deal with situations of this magnitude, but this was my reality while working in the security department at Universal Studios Hollywood back in the early 90's. Sometimes I wonder if my mind's eyes will ever unsee some of the awful things I've had to witness, or protect others from. I've seen things with my naked eyes that I would never wish on others. Some of those traumatic images never seem to go away. They go away just long enough for me to feel like a normal, unbothered human being but, at some point, they resurface again when I least expect them to.

Whenever I wasn't working plain-clothes details, I was in my regular security uniform, just like many of the other officers I used to work with, who never got a chance to be an active part of the exciting assignments that I was fortunate enough to have worked. Based on my excellent work performance that I demonstrated while being a member of the SPU Team, it only elevated my work ethic once I began working with the Citywalk Suppression Unit (CSU). The CSU Team was formed primarily to be proactive against underage curfew violators, and to detergang activity. There was a total of about 10 to 12 CSU members that patrolled

TRAINING & WORK EXPERIENCE

CityWalk on any given weekend. For our entire shift, we would walk around in pairs of two, routinely switching up our patrols so that we made sure patrons always saw that we were there if anything jumped off. If there were concerts going on during the weekends, then those concerts drew in a lot of extra foot traffic, so we would pair up in three groups of four officers per group. When CityWalk had officially opened up to the public, it became the night-life that people came from all over Los Angeles County to be a part of, even gang members. Our busiest times where CityWalk saw the most traffic was on the weekends.

Everything was going rather smoothly on the weekends and then, all of a sudden, the security department began to see an increase in radio calls for fights breaking out. Most of the fights we broke up were gang members who had crossed paths on our property. Anytime we were able to arrive on scene and make a determination as to who was fighting, those people were arrested and escorted upstairs to the sheriff's substation to be booked. Since CityWalk attracted families with small children, and people in general who just wanted to come spend money and enjoy the entertainment that CityWalk offered, we did not tolerate fighting in any form or fashion!

When it was time to start doing curfew sweeps, the entire CSU Team would meet up at the far end of CityWalk, closest to the main entrance to Universal Studios, and start asking people for ID if they looked like they were younger than 18 years old. Once we began our walk down towards the opposite end of CityWalk, enforcing the 10:00pm curfew, at least four deputies of the Los Angeles County Sheriff's Department walked right behind us, as reinforcements for anyone who did not want to comply with our orders.

As divine intervention and God's timing would have it, I came across yet another impressionable document during my research in writing this book. Immediately upon reading this two-page document, dated December 9, 1993, I vividly recalled this incident as if it were just yesterday. This MCA Interoffice Memorandum was a formal commendation addressed to myself and several other security officers who ended up arresting a burglary suspect during a live taping of the Billboard Awards being held at the Universal Amphitheatre. In his own words, describing the incident in specific detail, John Colella wrote the following narrative report below.

> "On 12-8-93 at 1930 hours Lieutenant Derrick Thompson responded to a burglary call at the trailers behind the Amphitheatre. At that time the 'Billboard Awards' were in progress inside the Amphitheatre. Lt. Thompson was met by Judy Chabola from FYI Productions. Chabola advised Thompson that a computer and computer equipment had been taken from her production trailer. The on duty Sheriffs responded to the scene and completed a crime report.
>
> On 12-8-93 at 2300 hours Ronald Martinelli from Fox Square Productions was behind the

TRAINING & WORK EXPERIENCE

Amphitheatre, approaching the communications trailer, when he observed an unknown male black inside the communications trailer. Martinelli entered the trailer door and could observe that the trailer had been ransacked. Martinelli could also observe that the male black had two radios inside of his jacket pockets. The male black walked out of the trailer and attempted to leave the location. Martinelli requested a staff member, Pam Duckworth, to call the police. While attempting to stop the male black, Martinelli and another witness Wylleen May became involved in an altercation with the male black. The male black was able to free himself from both witnesses. The male black began running from the location.

Officers Dameon Wroe and Magiting Daw is were responding to the disturbance call when they observed the male black running on Tram Road. Wroe and Dawis were joined by Officer Jim Chatel and Lt. Thompson. During the foot pursuit the officers could observe the male black throwing objects on the ground. The male black was apprehended at Lot W Road. Following the male black's apprehension, Officer Chatel conducted a search of the vehicles parked on Tram Road. Chatel found a white Nissan that contained numerous stolen items including several computers.

A subsequent investigation conducted by the Sheriff's Department revealed that the items found in the Nissan were in fact the items taken from the two trailers. Articles were found in the Nissan that identified the male black as Deyon K. Davis M Black 26 yrs. In addition to the Billboard pass Davis had several other passes including an American Music Awards pass. A total of $10, 985.00 of stolen property was recovered. An investigation is being conducted to ascertain if Davis has been involved in other crimes on Universal Studios Hollywood property.

Lieutenant Thompson and Officers Chatel, Wroe, and Dawis are to be commended for their attention to duty, ability to remain calm during an excitable situation, investigative techniques, and their tenacity."

Words alone are just not enough to describe how grateful and honored I was to have worked for the Universal Studios Hollywood entertainment center, and to have been trained by certified experts in the private security industry, all of which had commendable careers in law enforcement as some of the greatest who had ever done it. Before leaving that job and continuing my journey in life, it touched my heart to see that my name was featured on a wall in the

TRAINING & WORK EXPERIENCE

executive security office, along with many other security officers who had fearlessly provided a high level of security and protection to all of the patrons who visited our entertainment center to make memories with their family and friends. However, once I began to feel as though I had done all that there was for me to do for APS Security, during my time at MCA/Universal, it was time for me to start seeking out better employment opportunities that allowed me to grow and move up the corporate ladder with the gifts and talents that I knew were within me.

3
★ ★ ★ ★ ★

AN UNDISPUTED WORK ETHIC

After my time at APS Security had ended, I somehow ended up working for another security company called Langner and Associates, Incorporated. Although their corporate offices were based out of Long Beach, California, they had many accounts that serviced shopping malls and strip plazas within the Greater Los Angeles area. By this time, it was somewhere between late 1994 to early 1995 when I began working for Langner and Associates in their retail mall division. Upon being officially hired by the company, I became the newest security officer assigned to the Baldwin Hills Crenshaw Plaza (BHCP), most commonly referred to by the community as the Crenshaw Mall.

During the first week or two that I started working with the company, I felt as though I had been given a fresh, new start. My supervisors would assign a few of my more seasoned co-workers to me, to take me around the entire property to start showing me around. These select few co-workers, and supervisors alike, would educate me on the history of the mall property where certain types of crimes or disturbances would take place. During my first few weeks of working at the Baldwin Hills Crenshaw Plaza (BHCP), I became very impressed with how the security department was ran, and how well-organized the day-to-day operations were. We even had our own locker rooms for members of our security staff.

Once I was able to start moving all of my extra uniform pants and shirts into my own locker, I was starting to feel more and more like I was really starting to fit in, and be openly accepted into being a valuable part of the team. Little did I know at time, the positive and inviting feeling of fitting in would ultimately be short-lived among the other officers I worked with. My continued training and experience with Langner and Associates was so extensive, there's no possible way that I can capture it all in just one chapter and expect you to fully digest it, so I will jump right into describing my most memorable incidents that I was involved with that quickly afforded me ongoing opportunities to earn the respect of my co-workers and superiors.

When I first started with the company, I recall being a bit frustrated and unappreciated, because I was always being assigned to patrol areas outside, rather than inside. Whenever I was assigned to a post outside, it was either too hot or too cold, obviously depending on the time of year. Since I already knew that I wanted to move up the company ladder as soon as humanly possible, I knew that my opportunities to work better assignments and positions would be dependent upon how well I knew the property. At that time, the Baldwin Hills Crenshaw Plaza was in a fairly rough part of town, situated right at the corner of Crenshaw Boulevard

AN UNDISPUTED WORK ETHIC

and Martin Luther King, Jr. Drive. One of my greatest challenges with this new security company was responding to what was known as *merchant assists*. The thing that made it difficult for me to respond to merchant assists, or even other security officers calling for backup, was because I was new, and I didn't know the exact location of most of the stores that I was advised to respond to.

At the Baldwin Hills Crenshaw Plaza, we took merchant assists very seriously in the security department! Whenever our dispatcher would send us to a merchant assist, called in by one of the businesses on the mall property, we responded to those calls with a defined sense of urgency. Whenever a merchant had a need to call into our security office to ask for assistance, we immediately stopped what we were doing at that time, and started running over to that merchant's store to fix whatever their problem was. Within the security department, a merchant assist was almost the equivalent of a resident in the community calling 911 for help. Once we got there to investigate the nature of the merchant assist, it was typically regarding an irate customer who had been asked to leave the store, but was refusing to, and possibly becoming combative with a store employee. Other times, the merchant assist was regarding a store patron who was seen shoplifting.

The most common stores that our dispatcher called merchant assists for, *inside* of the mall, were Wilsons House of Suede & Leather, KB Toy Store, Macy's, Sally's Beauty Supply, Malik Books, and the food court on the first floor of the mall. As for our merchants on the *outside* of the shopping mall, our most problematic areas during those times were Taco Bell, the Magic Johnson Theatres, Subway and Lucky grocery store.

It's important to know that my probationary period with Langner was for an initial period of 90 days. Within those first 90 days, I was becoming more and more accepted by the security team, and nearly everyone seemed friendly towards me, and always had something comical or polite to say to me whenever I came to work. After about 60 days, it seemed like nobody wanted anything to do with me anymore! My co-workers didn't stop talking to me because I did anything to them, they stopped talking to me because, 60 days into my 90-day probationary period, I became their supervisor. Yes, you read that correctly. Before my 90-day probation period expired, I was promoted to the position of corporal. My new radio handle… 30 Charles (30C).

In all honesty, it didn't take me very long to know ahead of time that I would excel in my work performance and start to show my leadership abilities. I will never forget the time, prior to my promotion, when one of my supervisors, a sergeant, made me partner up with him for the day so that I could shadow him, going all around the mall property for my entire shift. About halfway through my shift, as I was walking on the second floor of the mall, just above the food court, a call came out over the radio of a 415 (fight, California Penal Code 415) in progress.

Once our dispatcher gave us the location of the 415, my supervisor takes off running towards the downstairs escalators, and tells me to follow him. As we were on the escala-

AN UNDISPUTED WORK ETHIC

tor going down to the first floor, my supervisor is advising other units to also respond to the location of the fight, but makes the mistake of saying, "417 in progress!!" At the exact moment that I heard him say, "417," I immediately stopped running, and looked at him like he was crazy, as he continued running towards the disturbance with me way, way behind him. After the problem was resolved, my supervisor pulled me aside and asked me why I didn't respond to the fight call with him. I politely said to him, "I was with you when the initial call over the radio came out as a 415 but, when I heard you say 417, I stopped running because, in my past experience of training I received in the sheriff's academy, 417 means *man with a gun*... and I was not about to show up to a gun fight with a PR-24 (side-handle baton)." Once I explained this to my supervisor, he was obligated to explain this to our lieutenant and our captain, as they were expecting periodic updates on my work performance.

Not long after that incident, I was afforded many more opportunities to demonstrate my knowledge of the law and enforce policies that the mall management offices were expecting us to enforce. It wasn't long before the next merchant assist came into the security office. This time, the merchant assist was at the Sally's Beauty Supply store on the first floor of the mall, right across from what used to be Sears. A woman entered the beauty supply store and, for some unknown reason, got into a shouting match with the owners of the store. At some point, the store owners asked the woman to leave the store, and she refused to leave. Since the lady was refusing to leave the store, and was continuing to cause a loud disturbance in the presence of other store customers, we finally arrived to assist the merchant.

This time, Lieutenant O'Neal and I took the call, assisted by one other security officer. When we entered the store, I observed both of the store owners arguing with the customer loudly. As Lt. O'Neal was talking to one of the store owners, I took the initiative to separate the verbally combative customer from the female store owner. After politely trying to calm the angry customer down, she remained adamant that she was right and the store owners were wrong. I then explained to her that, as a merchant in the state of California, the merchants have the right to refuse service to her for whatever reasons they decided not to service her. I went on to educate the irate woman that the store owners do not necessarily have to have signs posted inside of their store that display this admonishment, and I then advised her to leave the store.

After explaining these facts to the irate customer, she then took her aggression out on me! As I saw Lt. O'Neal attempting to intervene, I waved him off and advised him that I could handle the situation. I then asked the woman to leave again, and she refused. I then asked the woman to leave a third time, and she refused again. At this time, I warned the woman that I was only going to ask her to leave one more time and, if she refused again, she'd be placed under arrest for trespassing (602 PC). I recall asking the woman to leave one final time and, as luck would have it, she refused to leave, yet again. As I reached behind me and unsnapped my handcuff case, the woman had an immedi-

AN UNDISPUTED WORK ETHIC

ate change of heart and decided it was time for her to leave. She gave me the cursing of a lifetime as we were escorting her out of the mall but, at the end of the day, the problem was solved and the merchant was able to resume business.

Looking back at that incident, I don't think the irate woman truly meant to go off on me, I believe her ego was bruised a little bit because, at the time of this encounter, she was old enough to be my mother, yet she had to be escorted off of the property by someone like me, who was young enough to be her son. Sometimes, this type of dynamic can make an otherwise cordial person act like a complete fool in public. Nevertheless, after that incident played itself out in front of my lieutenant, it was only up from there for me.

Fast forwarding to a couple of months after this incident, I came into work one day ready and equipped to face whatever the day was going to throw at me. That's one thing that I loved about doing security work... it was never the same, boring routine each and every day. I never knew what the day was going to bring my way when I clocked in for work to start my shift. Little did I know, this particular shift would be the ultimate test of my professionalism, my ability, and my work ethic.

In various areas of the mall property, at the Baldwin Hills Crenshaw Plaza, we had security observation towers in various areas of our parking lots. These observation towers were placed there to discourage and prevent crimes from happening in those areas. During our morning briefings, at the beginning of our shift, I would personally assign each officer a specific area of patrol where I felt they would be most useful and/or effective. Halfway through our eight-hour shift, it was customary that, after four hours, officers would be rotated to work a different area for the remaining eight hours of their shift.

On this particular day, one of our newest security officers was assigned to work in an observation tower that faced the Wells Fargo bank parking lot. I vividly recall the observation tower being placed in between the Wells Fargo bank and Macy's department store, facing Crenshaw Boulevard. Approximately two to three hours before my shift was about to end, our dispatcher called me on the radio and advised me that a mall employee had come to the security office to report that her vehicle had been broken into, and that her pull-out car stereo was missing.

When I had finally arrived at the scene where the mall employee's car was parked, it became evident to me that the point of entry to her vehicle was via a bashed in window. Another strange detail about the scene was the fact that, upon my arrival, there was no security officer standing in the tower. It was very disturbing to me, and equally suspicious, that this woman's vehicle was broken into while parked in the parking space right next to the base of the security observation tower! I immediately went into investigation mode, thinking to myself, "How on earth was this incident reported to our office by the victim before it was reported to us by the security officer who was assigned to be standing in that tower?"

I got on the radio and asked our security dispatcher to send the captain to my location, which she did. When my captain arrived at my location, his suspicions were the same

AN UNDISPUTED WORK ETHIC

as mine. As we began to examine the rest of the vehicle, I noticed traces of fresh blood around the immediate area of where the car window was smashed in. Looking down at the ground, I told my captain, "Whoever did this was bold enough to do it in broad daylight, and stand here in this exact spot for at least a minute or more." When my captain asked me why I was so sure of my statement, I explained to him that the blood spots on the ground were speaking to me. I told him that the person who was bleeding stood stationary right where the window was broken, because the blood stains on the ground all had the same pattern of nearly perfect circular stains… which indicated the bleeding person was standing still, at least momentarily.

Once I started paying closer attention to the blood stains on the ground, I noticed that the other blood stains all had small lines attached to only one side of the blood stains. The lines on the blood stains were pointing towards the mall entrance at the opposite end of the parking lot. It was at this time that I knew we would soon find out who stole the woman's car stereo.

As my captain and I continued to follow the blood trail, we noticed that the person bleeding entered the mall at the same mall doors that we exited at to respond to the original call, based on the mall employee's complaint. When we followed the blood trail through the interior of the mall, the trail led us to a nearby set of double doors, which was a service corridor used primarily by employees of the mall's janitorial department, and also served as an access route for deliveries to various stores. It was heart-breaking to find that the blood trail ultimately led to the entrance door of our own security office.

Once I opened up the door to the security office, I was able to find just a few drops of blood on the carpet in our office, one of which was directly underneath the time-clock. Starting from the bottom to the top, I examined each and every employee's timecard very carefully. By the time I got halfway up to the top of the timecards, I found a single timecard that had traces of blood smears on it, and that timecard belonged to the very security officer who had recently been assigned to work in the parking lot observation tower directly next to the woman's car that got broken into.

Once I had identified the security officer who had blood on his timecard, the next order of business was to find him. We did not know where he was because he was not at his post, and he was not responding to his radio. Once our security dispatcher was finally able to pull the officer up on the radio, I instructed her to have the officer return to the security office. Little did he know, my captain and I had already planned on giving him the interrogation of a lifetime, but I respectfully asked my captain to let me handle it once the officer made it back into the office.

When the officer entered the security office, I asked him why he had not been responding to his radio while we were trying to call him. He advised me that he had been in the restroom, at which time I noticed an unnecessary amount of paper towels wrapped around his hand that he was holding in place. I asked the officer why he had paper towels wrapped around his hand. His response was that he acci-

AN UNDISPUTED WORK ETHIC

dentally cut it on the observation tower as he was climbing down to go on his lunch break. I let the security officer make as many excuses as I could stand to listen to, and then I told him that my captain and I followed his blood trail from the vehicle with the broken window all the way back to the time clock in the security office. When I showed him the blood stains on his timecard, he ultimately admitted to taking the car stereo from the mall employee's car.

He further explained to me that he initially wrapped a t-shirt around his hand before punching through the woman's car window, so that the glass would not make much of a sound once the window broke. He stated that, even though he had a shirt wrapped around his hand, he was still cut by parts of the window that did not shatter, once he stuck his fist through it. Listening to every detail of his story, I made the determination that the security officer broke into the mall employee's car with the intent to commit petty or grand theft. After making those statements to me, in the presence of my captain and our dispatcher, I arrested my subordinate officer for 459 PC (burglary from motor vehicle), a felony, as he was still in full uniform.

Shortly after arresting him, my captain and I walked him through the busy shopping mall, and turned him over to the officers at the LAPD Southwest Substation, at which time he was booked. As I was taking my handcuffs off of him so that he could be handcuffed by one of the LAPD officers, I confiscated his uniform shirt and returned to my office to write my arrest report. He may not have seen things in this way but, as far as I'm concerned, that security officer who broke into that woman's car, and stole her car stereo, didn't just shine a negative light on himself, his actions reflected negatively on all of us who wore that same uniform. Because of his actions, I wanted to make it painfully clear to everyone who visited our shopping center that we did not tolerate crime of any kind, even if it was committed by one of our own. Just as swift as we were to arrest members of the community who broke the law on our property, we would also arrest our own employees if they ever decided to participate in any form of criminal activity.

As a supervisor, it was important for me to lead by example, and set a new standard of leadership and work performance among my fellow security officers, including my supervisors above me. Just as my drill instructors in the sheriff's academy had done for me, I invested that same interest in all of the security officers who worked under me in every security company that I ever worked for. I taught those officers how to carry themselves with a level of dignity, professionalism, and respect that would prove to make their jobs easier, and force the public to look upon them with a greater sense of value and appreciation.

When I first got hired to work in the security department at the Baldwin Hills Crenshaw Plaza, I noticed that many of the security officers carried themselves much more differently than I did. Never, at any time, did I act like I was better than them, but I knew that I had my work cut out for me if I was going to ultimately be the driving force behind what made the security department better than it was. As their supervisor and leader, I never felt like it was fair

AN UNDISPUTED WORK ETHIC

for me to punish or discipline my officers for doing something, or failing to do something, the right way, especially if I never made sure that they had the proper training.

There was a particular point in my employment at Langner that made me deeply reflect on why so many of my officers were having so many of the same problems in their assigned patrol areas. It seemed like my officers were always getting on the radio calling me over to their area, due to them having ongoing confrontations with mall patrons or suspects on our property committing crimes. In many of those cases, once I arrived on scene, the person who was being detained didn't have a problem with the fact that my officers had asked them to leave the property, their biggest issue was based on how my security officers came at them. If a mall patron felt disrespected by one of my officers, based on how my officer spoke to them or treated them, that mall patron made my officer's job much harder than it needed to be.

In every salty encounter that my officers were having with uncooperative mall patrons or suspects, the primary complaint I was getting from my officers was, "I asked them to leave the property, and they wouldn't leave." This is when I started getting more aggressive with training my officers on how to handle these situations and do their jobs with a more defined level of dignity. It wasn't long after this that I began to implement the *'Ask, Tell, Make'* technique, and taught my officers how to carry themselves a lot more professionally during their shifts. In those days, the surrounding areas near the Baldwin Hills Crenshaw Plaza were quite rough, so there were times when we had to go hands-on with some of the neighborhood's most combative and criminal-minded characters, some of which were gang members.

Back in the mid 90's, the mall management company at BHCP had a zero tolerance policy for gang members coming into the mall sagging their pants, hanging red or blue bandanas out of their back pockets to promote their gang affiliation, or even walking in mob-style groups throughout the mall. Many of these behaviors made it uncomfortable for many other mall patrons in the community to shop or be in the mall while these types of individuals were roaming around freely, displaying intimidating behaviors. This is when the *'Ask, Tell, Make'* technique became effective. If we were to encounter a gang member, walking through the mall with a red or blue bandana hanging out of his back pocket, we would immediately approach that individual and advise him of our mall dress code policy against gang attire.

We would then explain to the gang member that, if he wanted to stay in the mall, he would need to put his bandana completely in his pocket out of public view. If the gang member refused to abide by our dress code policy, we would *ask* the gang member to leave the property. If the gang member still refused to leave the property, we would assertively *tell* the gang member to leave. If the gang member continued his refusal to leave the property, we would *make* him leave the property, by using any reasonable amount of force necessary to remove the gang member from the property, or arrest the person for assault or battery, if they tried to physically fight us.

AN UNDISPUTED WORK ETHIC

Once I was able to demonstrate the effectiveness of this approach to my subordinate officers, they began to utilize it at their discretion, with successful results in subsequent encounters with gang members when necessary. The next biggest thing I trained my officers on was how to be more conscious about how they carried themselves while working with the public. My primary objective in how I was going to train my officers on this principle was to show them that how the public reacted to them was largely based on how much they first respected themselves.

During our morning briefings in the security office, when all of my day shift officers were present, I would make all of them line up from left to right, so that I could inspect their uniforms and give them some constructive criticism about their appearance before going out into the field. The very first time I held uniform inspections with them, I didn't hold back my first impressions of them and their appearance.

"What I want you all to do is turn to the left and look at the person next to you, from head to toe, and tell me what you see. Look at their appearance, look at their cleanliness, and look at the quality and care of their uniform, and tell me what you see," I would tell them.

After we broke the ice with this manner of instruction, each of my officers took turns giving me their feedback. Upon taking their feedback into consideration, I ultimately told them the reasons why we would be doing uniform inspections more frequently. "So many of you guys have called me on the radio for assistance because you told someone to leave the mall property and they didn't leave. The reason why they didn't leave is primarily based on the fact that they don't respect you! Look at yourselves. Look at how your uniforms look. Look at how beat up your shoes look. Some of you have food stains on your uniform shirt.

Some of you guys have dirty, wrinkled up pants that look like you just took them out of the laundry basket and put them on as is. I want you guys to understand that if you don't start respecting the way you look when you come to work, the public isn't going to respect you either! If I was a mall patron, and one of you guys walked up to me and tried to kick me out of the mall, I wouldn't leave the mall either, because I wouldn't respect the way you carry yourself. If you don't respect yourself enough to come to work looking more professional than how you look now, why should I have to respect you?"

I was not the type of supervisor who sugar-coated the things that I told my officers. I said things the way they needed to be said, and I did things that needed to be done… things that other supervisors were not capable of doing. Myself and many of my subordinate officers carried batons as part of our equipment. Based on our certified training that allowed us to carry this type of weapon, it was our responsibility to know *when* and *when not* to use it in the performance of our duties.

One day I heard a call come out over the radio that one of my officers across the street, assigned to the Bank of America parking lot area, was reporting that a person trespassing was refusing to leave the property, and was trying

AN UNDISPUTED WORK ETHIC

to fight him. As I took off running across the street to assist my officer, I could see from a distance that the male subject who was trespassing had a skateboard in his hands, cocked back over his right shoulder in a fighting stance, ready to take a swing at my officer. As I got closer to the confrontation, the subject had actually swung the skateboard at my officer, striking my officer with the skateboard. I immediately took out my PR-24 baton and yelled at the subject to drop the skateboard.

The subject then took a fighting stance with me, in an effort to defend against being arrested, and I was able to strike him with two to three quick blows of my baton, tactfully blocking his skateboard with the longer portion of my baton. As other security officers arrived, we were eventually able to take him into custody, at which time I arrested him for 245 PC (assault with a deadly weapon). We then escorted the suspect down to the LAPD—Southwest Division substation, where he was booked and prosecuted for his crime against my officer and I. I was later informed by an LAPD officer that the suspect ended up receiving jail time for his actions.

Other training methods that I implemented within my security team at BHCP included hands-on training about the importance of protecting themselves while on duty, simply by being overly observant of people or situations that could potentially harm the public or one of us. As a supervisor, it was up to me to always know where my officers performed best. Their attention to duty, coupled with their ability to proactively solve problems in those areas, usually determined what areas I assigned them to. Officer Bowens was one of my more reliable officers. Because of the thorough ways in which he did his daily patrols, I typically assigned him to be the officer who had roaming privileges to patrol the entire interior of the mall, both on the top level and the bottom level.

The biggest challenge I would constantly have with Bowens was that he was always talking to the ladies too much. Whenever I would come out of the office to do my own random patrols, to check on my officers, I would always find Bowens inside of one of the businesses talking to one of the attractive employees who worked in that particular store. Sometimes Bowens saw me when I would walk by and notice him inside of a merchant's store, other times he had no idea that I was there. After getting tired of seeing Bowens paying more attention to the ladies, than his security duties, it was time for me to pull him aside and give him a warning.

I told Bowens that he was headed towards a write-up if I continued to see him spending too much time fraternizing with mall employees. Bowens corrected the things that I had brought to his attention and improved his work performance. Unfortunately for Bowens, he soon fell back into his old ways, and I felt compelled to teach him the lesson of a lifetime.

As I was walking back to the security office one day, from the far end of the mall, I spotted Bowens approximately 100 feet ahead of me, leaning on the railing of the second floor, talking to another female, with his back facing me. I could tell by his body language and mannerisms that he had been there fraternizing with the female for quite a while, because he looked way too comfortable. When I called him on his radio, he did not respond. When I tried to call him on his radio for a second time, he still didn't respond. As I got closer to where he was standing, the female he was talking to looked directly at me as I was creeping up behind him, at which time I put my index finger over my lips and gestured for the female not to alert Bowens that I was coming. As the female continued talking and laughing with him, I noticed that Bowens had both of his arms on the railing, as he became seemingly more comfortable chatting it up with the unknown female.

Seeing that the handle of his PR-24 was facing me, and unsecure in his baton holder, I snuck up behind Bowens, rapidly snatched his PR-24 baton out of its holster, took a few steps back, and swung his own baton around into a *ready* striking position, as he could do nothing except look on in disbelief. In a very calm, polite tone of voice, I then said to him, "When you finish your conversation, 10-19." In essence, I was politely telling Bowens to return to the security office once he was finished doing the very thing that I had been warning him to stop doing.

When Bowens returned to the security office, I did not hesitate to explain to him that I would be writing him up before the end of his shift for losing his weapon, and for failure to patrol his assigned work areas. As soon as he sat down at the office table, I was very direct with him. "Bowens, I have repeatedly warned you about getting caught fraternizing with these females all over this mall, and you're still doing it! The female you were talking to saw me coming and didn't even warn you that she saw me creeping up behind you. By the time you heard your baton coming out of your baton ring, it was already too late because I already had full control of it. At that point, you became helpless. What if I wasn't your supervisor in that moment? What if I was that gang banger that threatened your life a few weeks ago because you kicked him and his homies out of the mall? If I was someone who had previously threatened you, I could have beaten you to death with your own weapon, all because you let your guard down to try to get at some female. That could have ended very badly for you... you're just lucky it was me!"

One thing that I admired about Bowens is that he didn't even argue the point, or try to make excuses. He knew he got caught slippin' and, as his supervisor, he knew that I had to do what I had to do, with regard to writing him up. We never lost respect for one another and, thankfully, Bowens never had those same issues with me ever again. I was glad that he learned a valuable lesson from that surprise encounter with me, because that type of mistake could have cost him his life. Although a PR 24 baton is not a firearm, it is still legally defined as a deadly weapon because, in the hands of someone with criminal intentions, it can still cause great bodily injury or death with the appropriate amount of force.

There came a time, not long after this incident with Bowens, that our corporate security office sent out a formal, company memorandum to our post at BHCP. I don't know the exact circumstances that led up to a particular incident,

AN UNDISPUTED WORK ETHIC

but the memo was directed to all mall security personnel. The memo stated that, effective immediately, no security personnel was to physically restrain and/or search any mall patron who was under the age of 18 years old.

Once I had come to work and read the memo, it bothered me that we could no longer physically restrain or search minors, because many of the minors who visited our mall on a daily basis were known to carry weapons, and sometimes drugs. During my time at BHCP, I personally confiscated brass knuckles and knives from minors. Every once in a while, I even searched minors and found them to be in possession of marijuana, which was illegal at that time. Quite a few subjects that we came in contact with back then were known to carry weapons, and they wouldn't hesitate to use them against us if given the right opportunity.

This company memorandum was not in existence for a full 30 days before our corporate security coordinator, Mr. Lee Kingsford, gave me his blessing to completely disregard the memo.

Whenever anyone had to be called into Lee Kingsford's office, it was usually because some sort of employee disciplinary measures were coming down from our corporate office, and Lee Kingsford was the on-site, corporate security coordinator that shared office space within our security department to oversee the daily security operations on the mall property. Mr. Kingsford called me into his office one day, and specifically wanted to meet with me to speak to me about the details of the memo. In that meeting, Mr. Kingsford had expressed to me that he overheard several of the security officers, including myself, openly talking about the pros and cons of what that memo meant to us if we were to ever encounter more confrontations involving minors on our property.

Lee Kingsford made it crystal clear to me that the memo did not apply to me, as far as he was concerned. He expressed to me that he had been very discreetly monitoring my work performance, and he was very pleased with my knowledge of the law, my ability to lead others in a professional capacity, my ability to move others into action by always demonstrating to my subordinate officers that I was always willing to teach them how to be more effective security officers, and he was also impressed with the fact that my work ethic always achieved desired results. Also during our impromptu meeting, Mr. Kingsford made mention of the fact that he really enjoyed watching me grow with the company. He was specifically impressed with how articulate I was, and how my written and oral communication skills allowed me to achieve things that other supervisors and subordinate officers before me struggled to even grasp or understand.

One of the last things I remember Mr. Kingsford saying to me in that meeting was, "Don't do anything differently than what you've already been doing! With your knowledge, ability, expertise, and communication skills, if you ever have to put your hands on any juveniles for any reason, I'm confident that you will be able to fully articulate *why* you had to do it, and that you will back it up with solid, written documentation that will not expose the company to any liability." Being a young, 25-year-old Black man at that time, those words gave me such a sense of self-worth and dignity, coming from someone like Lee Kingsford, a retired, *White* police officer. His

AN UNDISPUTED WORK ETHIC

belief in me and my abilities gave me a renewed measure of confidence and courage to continue doing what I had already been doing since day one.

Looking back on my 12-year, intermittent work history in the private security industry, I can say with every degree of assurance that I have truly enjoyed all of the times that I was able to protect the public from people who get enjoyment from breaking the law and victimizing others. I have truly enjoyed sharing some very intense experiences with all of my former co-workers because, in all of those interactions, there was a valuable lesson that I learned from those encounters, which allowed me to grow personally, professionally, and sometimes even spiritually.

I feel extremely blessed that God was able to use me as a vessel to teach others in the security industry things that they may have never learned in life if we had not crossed paths. I have immensely enjoyed arresting all of the people that I witnessed using violence, fear, and intimidation against others, for their own self-gratification and entertainment. Even considering all of the people that I could have arrested, but chose not to, I'm grateful for those interactions as well, because it gave me an opportunity to show that my work ethic has always included grace, mercy, and a willingness to give second chances to those who were deserving, including those who were not always so deserving.

I feel so honored and fortunate to have worked under people like Mr. Lee Kingsford, Lt. Anthony O'Neal, Mr. John Colella, and a select few of the seasoned, veteran detectives of the Los Angeles Police Department's Special Investigation

Section. Between the young ages of 23 to 25, I could have never, single-handedly orchestrated all of the things that I experienced in the security and/or public safety arena. The ongoing training and priceless lessons that I learned from all of these high-ranking veterans, afforded me to survive several life or death situations. Those lessons also allowed me to be a better judge of character, when needing to make split-second decisions during the course of my employment, and discern whether or not my life was in danger. Another one of my most epic resume accolades, while working at the Baldwin Hills Crenshaw Plaza, was the opportunity that I got to work security for the late rapper, Tupac Shakur, for his video shoot he did for his song *"To Live And Die In LA."*

Just like it was yesterday, I can very vividly recall showing up to work one morning and, as soon as I walked into the office, my captain called me into his office with a sense of urgency! He leaned back in the chair at his desk and says to me, "You won't believe who's gonna be on the property today!!" After it became obvious that neither one of my guesses were accurate, he hands me a printed copy of a memo that he had received before I arrived at work. After reading the memo, I responded to him by telling him that the memo simply stated that there would be a film crew on the property that day, but the memo didn't specifically state *who* would be on the property. He then told me that Tupac Shakur would be on our property, filming his video for his song *"To Live and Die In LA,"* and that the majority of the filming would take place on the first floor of the mall, inside of the food court area.

AN UNDISPUTED WORK ETHIC

Although the mall management office delegated my captain to oversee the security detail for Tupac's video shoot, he made me his right-hand man, and delegated me to select a few more officers to place in strategic locations to ensure that Tupac had protection while on location in our food court. It was a blessing for everyone who was inside of the mall that day being showcased in the food court scenes of Tupac's video because, not long after we starting filming, the atmosphere around Tupac reached a boiling point that could not be tamed!

As more and more people from the community found out that Tupac was physically up at the mall shooting a video, the more people from all over the Baldwin Hills area continued to pile into the mall. While the cameras were turned on, filming Tupac lip-sync the words to his song, he remained very professional at all times. However, whenever the director would yell, "Cut!" it was evident to me that something was really bothering Tupac, and he was becoming increasingly annoyed by something or someone. Since I was so close to him when the cameras were turned off, I quickly determined that there were a few guys in the crowd who were getting under Tupac's skin because they didn't like him, so they started *set-trippin'* with him. When a person starts set-trippin', what they are actually doing is purposely trying to provoke a violent, or otherwise explosive situation with someone else by announcing their gang affiliation to intimidate the other person.

Well, these unsavory individuals were finally able to get what they were asking for, but it didn't go in their favor. Each time the cameras were turned off, I could hear Tupac talking to one of his personal bodyguards, asking the bodyguard to give him enough space so that he could punch the trouble-maker in the face, just one time. "Just please let me swing on this nigga just one time and knock his ass out," Tupac said in desperation. Each time Tupac asked to engage the trouble-maker in a fist fight, the bodyguard kept on telling Tupac that the guy wasn't worth it, yet Tupac continued to insist.

By this time, the person in the crowd, who was actually holding an infant in his arms at that time, provoked a back and forth shouting match with Tupac. At some point, the man holding the infant yelled out a volley of gang slurs, vehemently yelling out and announcing his gang affiliation to Tupac. Almost immediately, Tupac yells back at the guy by stating, and I quote, "Fuck yo hood, nigga… this Thug Life!! What you wanna do?"

When Tupac said this to the Black male in the crowd, the man showed obvious signs that he was ready and willing to fight Tupac, and I knew that we were about to have a huge problem. As the man began to take a fighting stance, an old lady in the crowd yelled out, "Don't fight that boy with that baby in your hands! What's wrong with you?" I will never forget the words spoken that day, during those hostile moments inside of our shopping mall. As my adrenaline level began to reach its peak, I feared that a fight was about to jump off between the gang member and Tupac, as the gang member had at least five to six goons with him, and Tupac had my security staff and his own personal bodyguards to back him up if anything jumped off.

AN UNDISPUTED WORK ETHIC

Finally, after the elderly woman gave the hostile troublemaker that admonishment, the crowd around Tupac and the other male began to open up, and everyone began to take giant steps backwards, because we knew that a fight was inevitable. I immediately got on my radio and advised my dispatcher to turn all video surveillance cameras in the exact location of where Tupac and I were standing, which was right in front of the elevator doors on the first floor, right across from what used to be Mrs. Fields cookies. Simultaneously, I heard Tupac's bodyguard discreetly say to him, "Hit this nigga one time and let's get up out of here!" This was music to Tupac's ears.

The mouthy gang banger passed the infant in his arms off to an unknown female standing next to him, without ever taking his eyes off of Tupac. The Black male ran up on Tupac and took two swings at him, that had absolutely no effect on the icon. As soon as the Black male ran up on Tupac, I immediately got on my radio and advised my dispatcher that a 415 [fight] was in progress, and to contact the LAPD—Southwest substation to get some officers down to our location immediately. When the male initially ran up on Tupac, Tupac took a few quick steps back, and delivered an incredible punch to the man's jaw with his right hand, knocking the man down with such force, that the man staggered into the elevator doors and ultimately fell to the ground.

When all of the other men who entered the mall with the neighborhood thug saw that Tupac had nearly knocked out their homeboy, they all came to his aid and tried to rush Tupac, to overtake him in the fight, but we did not allow that to happen. Between keeping Tupac protected, and fighting multiple people in between, I managed to get another call out over the radio and requested EVERY security officer to my location to assist with the fight in progress. As soon as Tupac was finally able to hit the guy, and nearly knock him completely out, I observed his bodyguard literally pick him up from behind and turn him in the direction of the escape route that we had already staged for him, in case something like this was to happen.

While my captain and I followed behind Tupac and his security team, as they were headed for the rear delivery corridors to usher Tupac to safety, my remaining subordinates stayed at the scene of the fight to detain the guy who swung on Tupac, pending the arrival of officers already responding from the LAPD—Southwest substation. We finally got Tupac back to his trailer, which was stationed in the south side of Sears, which the production company for the video had blocked off the entire south side of the Sears parking lot, just for Tupac. Once we got him back to his trailer, we didn't have to worry about anyone else trying to get to him to provoke another fight, because there was a small army of uniformed, LAPD motor officers posted all around the perimeter of his trailer where we knew he was safest.

When the huge fight was over, and my captain and I had escorted Tupac back to the area where his trailer was located. We stayed outside of Tupac's trailer, just enjoying being in the atmosphere that Tupac attracted during those previous moments of excitement. My captain wanted to take a picture with Tupac, but he was too afraid to knock on Tupac's trailer door to ask for a quick photo op, so he asked me to do it. I fearlessly walked up to the trailer door and knocked to get Tupac's attention. When

AN UNDISPUTED WORK ETHIC

Tupac finally opened up the door, the first thing that I saw was a huge cloud of weed smoke come out of the trailer. When the smoke started to disappear, I could see a large table behind where Tupac was standing, where several Black males were sitting but, at that time, I did not know who the males were. I then asked Tupac if my captain and I could take a picture with him. He then told me that he would be out in a few minutes and that we could take a picture with him at that time.

When he finally exited the trailer, I noticed that he had a very large, freshly rolled blunt in his hands that he was smoking. He walked right by where we were standing and started digging through a large ice chest filled with drinks provided by craft services, but didn't seem to like the beverage options the ice chest had to offer. As he was walking back towards where myself and my captain were standing, an unknown Black female asked him if she could take a hit of his blunt. Tupac then took a long, slow drag of the blunt and, while trying to hold the smoke in as long as he could, told the woman, "Here... you can have it!" I couldn't believe it! Since marijuana was not legal back in 1995, I couldn't believe that Tupac was walking around in front of so many uniformed LAPD officers while smoking weed, and no one dared to say anything to him about it. Then again, that was just Tupac!

Tupac finally obliged us and took individual photos with my captain and I. The picture was taken with an old-school polaroid camera. Once the photo had fully developed, Tupac was gracious enough to autograph my picture with the caption, "West side IV Life!" That photograph that I took with Tupac became the coolest piece of memorabilia that I ever received while working security, that I carried it around in the shirt pocket of my uniform for months. When the autograph on the photo began to fade away, due to me handling the picture so much, I eventually laminated the picture to keep it as preserved as possible. Still to this day, I have that same photograph in its original laminate that I had done many years ago.

Not long after Tupac's video shoot was over and done with, my captain and I began to grow apart on a professional level. Once Lt. O'Neal had been promoted to the position of captain, and transferred to the Burbank Media Center Shopping Mall, I began to lose my interest in remaining at the Baldwin Hills Crenshaw Mall. I got tired of working with officers who showed no interest in bettering themselves. I got tired of fighting random people in the community who showed no respect for themselves or the community by how they conducted themselves when they visited our property. I got tired of the mall management politics that, near the end of my time at BHCP, made it harder and harder for my staff and I to effectively do our job. Additionally, I got tired of working under a captain who was only looking out for his own best interests, when it came to better job opportunities to elevate from where I was already at.

When it became clear to my captain that I no longer enjoyed working under his leadership, he began to make my time at Baldwin Hills Crenshaw Plaza very unbearable. This was the same captain that, months before this point, had promoted me and had also recognized me on several occasions with *Supervisor of the Month* certificates. I personally felt his

AN UNDISPUTED WORK ETHIC

behavior towards me had changed because I was beginning to outshine him on the job.

My captain had also expressed to me his intentions to transfer out of BHCP to go work at a different account. On the day I told him of my desire to transfer to the Burbank Media Center Shopping Mall to work with Captain Anthony O'Neal, he said to me, "Nobody is going to transfer out of here before I do." Prior to making that statement to me, I don't think my captain took into consideration how much dirt I had on him, if anyone from the corporate offices were to find out all of the things he had been doing on company time. Initially, I thought my captain's dismissive comment towards me was just him being his usual, sarcastic self but, as weeks turned into months, I knew that he was serious.

While focused on his own goals, and next-level opportunities for himself, he made no effort to even talk to me about what steps I needed to take to even be considered for a transfer to another account. Rather than continue to butt heads with my captain, I did what God gave me a gift and a talent to do… I started writing, and documenting a paper trail that I knew would follow my captain right on out of the company's front doors. When a person maliciously and intentionally hinders or tries to sabotage someone else's opportunities for advancement, they deserve to be held accountable and face every possible consequence that comes along with that behavior.

That statement made me so angry that, one day after getting home from work, I got on my computer and drafted a formal, eight to twelve-page, written complaint against my captain. In the written complaint, I disclosed very vivid, descriptive details about everything that my captain was involved in while on company time. The complaint also itemized specific incidents that my captain was involved in while in uniform, on duty, and also talked about occurrences that involved my captain taking the company vehicles off of the mall property to conduct his own personal business during working hours, in which he was still on the clock getting paid. Initially, I was hesitant to say too much about the fact that my captain was taking the company vehicle off of mall property because, in some of those instances, I was also in the company vehicle with him. In my complaint, I admitted the few times that I was riding along with my captain, but I also mentioned the fact that, as my senior officer, I should have never been allowed to do some of the things that my captain approved of me doing.

I had earned so much respect with my higher-ups at BHCP that, if I were to come up to the mall on my days off, and I saw any of our officers doing things they should not have been doing, I could literally write them up, and the write-up would have the same effect as if I had written them up while I was on duty. I only exercised that privilege two or three times but, for those few times, the officers that I had written up truly deserved it because they had been violating officer safety rules that the company allowed me to put in place.

After my written complaint was completed, signed, and mailed out to the Langner & Associates corporate office, the avalanche began to fall... and it was headed right for my captain!

AN UNDISPUTED WORK ETHIC

Somewhere between seven to ten days after I had mailed my complaint to our corporate office, I was contacted by a corporate security representative by the name of Kevin Collier. Kevin eventually contacted me and informed me that he had received a copy of my formal complaint, and that he had been tasked with investigating my allegations against my captain. During the initial phase of that investigation, I was assigned to work at a different post. Mr. Collier felt that, based on the severity of the allegations contained in my formal complaint, I would be safe during the investigation by working at the Watts Willowbrook Shopping Center.

In all honesty, I didn't really like working at the Watts Willowbrook Shopping Center because it was in a really rough part of town, and I wasn't overly confident that it was an area in which I felt I could thrive and take advantage of better opportunities. I was tired of chasing people off of the property and getting into physical confrontations with random people in the neighborhood who had nothing better to do than to come up to the shopping center and cause problems. I wanted to get up out of the hood. The good thing about the move was that I still had my rank, and officers still respected the fact that I was their new supervisor. It only took a couple of days for Kevin Collier to come and visit me at my new work location to fill me in on what was happening since I had been transferred out of the Baldwin Hills Crenshaw Plaza.

The first thing that Mr. Collier told me was that, as a result of my written complaint, my captain, Captain Moore, was placed on a five-day suspension, pending further investigation. I was also advised that Captain Moore had been given very specific instructions to stay off of all properties where Langner & Associates, Inc. was contracted to provide security services. He was also told that he was prohibited from calling up to the BHCP to speak to any security officers and, equally, all security personnel at all locations were advised not to speak to my captain for any reason, to maintain the integrity of the company's investigation into my allegations.

At the conclusion of the five-day suspension, the company found that my allegations against Captain Moore had been substantiated, and he was ultimately terminated as a result of *his* actions. Shortly after his termination from the Baldwin Hills Crenshaw Plaza (BHCP) security department, I finally got my chance to transfer to the Burbank Media Center Shopping Mall to work with Captain O'Neal. Even though the company had authorized me to transfer to our Burbank office, I couldn't leave the BHCP until I took care of an unforeseen problem, and that problem went by the name of Detective Greg DeMirjian.

4
★ ★ ★ ★ ★

MALICIOUS PROSECUTION—1995

Thanks to a couple of incompetent employees of a Little Caesars Pizza in Sherman Oaks, California, Francis Pijano and Ernie Amato, who apparently think that all Black men look alike, I was falsely accused and arrested by the Los Angeles Police Department—Van Nuys Robbery Division for two counts of armed robbery, compliments of Detective Greg DeMirjian. As the history of the LAPD continues to repeat itself, even in the 21st Century, it comes as no surprise that, back in 1995, I was falsely arrested for two felony counts of armed robbery that I had no knowledge of, and that I absolutely, unequivocally did not do!

At this point, I can only imagine what you're thinking, based on what I have already shared about my Taco Bell incident in the previous chapters, when I was only a kid. Little Caesars has the most god-awful pizza on the face of the earth! For that reason, I would never have entertained the idea of setting foot in any of their establishments, neither in 1995 nor in the present time. As you will soon see, in the following information below, the follow-up police report, written by Det. DeMirjian, pointed more towards my innocence rather than my guilt.

Back in 1995, at the time I came under investigation for this robbery allegation, I had no motive whatsoever to have committed a robbery of any kind, let alone at a Little Caesar's. Things in my life at that time were the most stable that they had ever been. I was gainfully employed, and I was not hurting for money to even entertain the idea of robbing anyone. Let's get to it! If you don't already despise the LAPD, you likely will by the end of this chapter, after I reveal to you how recklessly and negligently they treated me in their extremely sloppy investigation.

Back in June of 1996, myself and a high school buddy of mine decided to go visit a popular nightclub, hoping to hook up with some cute girls after the club let out. It was the typical nightlife at the club we ended up at, but we made the best of it and actually had a great time while we were there. Approximately an hour or two before the club was going to close, my pager when off at several different intervals. Each time I looked at the numeric display on my pager, I saw that it was my mother trying to contact me. After about the third time she paged me, I finally stepped outside of the club to return her phone call to see what she wanted. When my mother answered the phone, she asked me, "Are you in some kind of trouble?" With a shocked, confused look on my face, I responded with, "What do you mean? Why would I be in any trouble?"

She went on to explain to me that she received an Investigator Contact Card in the mail from a detective of the Los Angeles Police Department in Van Nuys, by the name of Detective DeMirjian. She further stated that it was regarding an incident involving a license plate number associated with the vehicle I had at that time. When I asked her more information regarding what was on the contact card, she simply gave me the detective's contact information and admonished me to call him as soon as I possibly could. My mother proceeded to inform me of the license plate number that the detective had mentioned to her when she initially called him to find out what this was all about. I specifically remember telling her, "Mom... I don't even have those letters on my license plate, so they probably have the wrong person."

Once I began walking out to the parking lot after the club started to shut down, I walked over to my car and looked at the license plate number. To my surprise, the license plate number that the detective had given to my mother was in fact my license plate number, but I still could not make sense of why a detective was trying to contact me. According to my copy of a follow-up police report, Detective DeMirjian paged me on June 15, 1995, at about 1:30pm. Per the report, I returned his phone call within 30 minutes. The detective told me that he wanted to speak to me, and asked me if he could come to my apartment on June 19, 1995 to speak to me in person at 7:00am. Since I had absolutely nothing to hide, I agreed to the in-person meeting and voluntarily gave him my address.

On the morning of June 19, 1995, DeMirjian and his partner, Detective Moran, showed up to my apartment to advise me that two employees of a Little Caesars Pizza place saw me and my car in the same shopping center parking lot where they worked at that time, and that I was the person that robbed them on 05-24-95, stating that they were *positive* of the car and me! From this point on, it is very important that you stay focused on the fact that the detective said that the witnesses were *positive* of my car *and me,* because I am about to prove his statements to be a total lie! I want you to follow his statements in this chapter very, very closely, because they will be proven to be false and misleading statements.

When the detective told me this nonsense, I immediately became upset that I was being accused of a crime that I had nothing to do with, nor did I have any knowledge of. To prove that I had nothing to do with this crime that the detectives were there to question me about, I offered to follow the detectives over to the pizza place so that the alleged witnesses could see that I was *not* the person who robbed them, but I was not allowed to do so, for reasons that were never shared with me. At some point, Detective DeMirjian asked me if I owned a gun, at which time I told him that I did own a gun. Once I told the detective that I had a gun, he asked to see it, and I took him directly to where I stored it in my locked bedroom… no questions asked, and with no hesitation or reservations! He took a few photos of my gun, and also took a polaroid picture of me. After taking pictures of me and my gun, DeMirjian also wanted to know if he could see my car. Once again, without any hesitation or reservations, I took him outside to where my car was parked on the street. He then started taking pictures of my car.

Per the follow-up police report, the detectives met with the witnesses of the robbery the very next day and showed each witness what is called a *six-pack photo lineup* to see if they could identify the person who robbed their pizza restaurant.

MALICIOUS PROSECUTION—1995

Per the report, one of the witnesses identified me immediately, and the other witness stated that he was 99% sure that I was the person who robbed them. This is where the police report starts to lay a foundation for being more and more ridiculous and inaccurate! On that same day, 06-20-95, the detectives pulled up in front of my apartment building again to question me, as I was putting my work gear into my car to get ready to go to work at the Baldwin Hills Crenshaw Plaza (BHCP). When the detectives approached me, I was dressed in my navy blue, Class A uniform pants, my black, Magnum work boots, and my white, crew-neck T-shirt, with my bullet-proof vest obviously protruding from underneath my T-shirt. Detective Moran never really did any of the talking during any of my conversations with the police, it was always Detective DeMirjian. DeMirjian told me that they had just come back from interviewing the witnesses to the robbery and they both identified me as the suspect.

After adamantly denying the allegations, I continued to tell DeMirjian that I would do whatever I needed to do to prove that my accusers were wrong about identifying me, and that I had frequented that same shopping center ever since I had been living in that neighborhood. I further explained to him that the only businesses that I had ever patronized in that strip plaza were Mail Boxes, Etc., El Pollo Loco, Thrifty, and a neighborhood dry cleaners that was located right next door to Little Caesars. Never in this lifetime could I ever be hungry enough to eat at Little Caesars Pizza. The fact remained... never at any time did I ever step one foot into that place!

After speaking to me for about five to ten minutes, Det. DeMirjian asked me if I would take a polygraph test. I initially told him that I would cooperate and take the polygraph test because I had nothing to hide. During our interaction, prior to me getting into my car to go to work, I was so angry that I was being investigated for a crime that I didn't commit, that I became very emotional and somewhat tearful. Seeing how upset and emotionally spent I was, Det. DeMirjian asked me if he could take my gun out of my apartment, because he felt that I was distraught, and did not want me to hurt myself.

Even though I agreed to let him take my gun, I knew that he wasn't taking it because he was concerned about my well-being… he was taking it so that he could book it into evidence and try to build a case against me. Although I should have probably cared more than I did at that time, I really didn't care, because I was confident that the investigation would ultimately be dropped once the police could see that I had nothing to do with the crime that took place. When I had finally updated my mother on what was going on with the investigation, and that I had told Detective DeMirjian that I would voluntarily submit to a polygraph test, my mother suggested that I first talk to an attorney. My mother just so happened to know of a former co-worker of hers who left the company she was working for to become a defense attorney. She set up a meeting for us to go down to his office to inform him of what Detective DeMirjian had been questioning me about. By the time we walked out of his office, we signed a retainer agreement for him to represent me and speak to the detectives on my behalf.

MALICIOUS PROSECUTION—1995

One thing I remember about our meeting with my attorney, Daniel Ramirez, was the fact that he was very shocked why Det. DeMirjian had not arrested me, if he had so much concrete evidence against me.

Mr. Ramirez added that, if Det. DeMirjian was going to keep on making me such an active focal point in his investigation, without arresting me, then DeMerjian was simply harassing me!

On a much more personal note, now that I had retained an attorney to represent me, I asked Mr. Ramirez if he could possibly get his hands on a copy of Det. DeMirjian's police report regarding the alleged robbery at Little Caesars. Using the gift that God gave me to be an excellent writer, I knew within myself that I could eventually find holes in these malicious allegations if I could just get my hands on that police report. My attorney informed me that I would not be privy to getting a copy of any police report(s) *unless* I had been taken into custody for the alleged crime. At the conclusion of our meeting, my attorney advised me that he did *not* want me to take a polygraph test.

Detective DeMirjian's follow-up report also mentioned that he spoke to the Van Nuys District Attorney, Ed Abla, on 08-08-95, at which time it was determined that there was sufficient evidence to arrest me for two felony counts of armed robbery. Prior to arresting me, Det. DeMirjian still continued to ask me if I would take a polygraph test and, additionally, asked me if I would come down to the station to allow him to take my fingerprints. Apparently, as mentioned in the poorly structured follow-up report, the person who *actually* robbed Little Caesars left a fingerprint on the countertop the day of the robbery. When I saw this documented in the police report, a sense of happiness and joy came over me, because I knew that fingerprint would prove that I was not there on the day of the alleged robbery! On or about 08-08-95, my attorney continued to inform me that he did not want me to take a polygraph test, but he did *initially* agree to allow me to go down to the police station to allow the detectives to take my fingerprints.

By the time I heard from Det. DeMirjian again, it was August 21, 1995. He paged me from his office, and I returned his call relatively quickly, as I had always done. He asked me again about coming into the station to have my fingerprints taken. It was at that time that I told him that my attorney had advised me not to have my fingerprints taken, and to stop communicating with him altogether. Shortly thereafter, Det. DeMirjian and Det. Moran returned to my apartment and falsely arrested me for two felony counts of armed robbery.

Fortunately, my time in custody was short-lived, because I was bailed out much sooner than I thought I'd be able to get out. When I was finally back home and awaiting my trial, that's when I put my blinders on and went straight to work. Detective DeMerjian told me not to go back to the strip plaza where the robbery happened, until his investigation was over, but I defiantly disregarded his admonishment and continued to frequent the strip plaza to start building my own defense against what I felt were racist allegations. The only thing that I was guilty of was being a Black male in

MALICIOUS PROSECUTION—1995

the wrong place at the wrong time, especially knowing that I was in a predominantly White neighborhood.

When I got bailed out of jail, the first thing I did was urge my attorney, Daniel Ramirez, to get me a copy of the robbery report. Once I had finally gotten a copy of the report, I read it in its entirety, and the flagrant inconsistencies documented by Det. DeMirjian *literally* began to jump off of the pages at me! At the next meeting that my mother and I had with my attorney, Mr. Ramirez, I pointed out to him all of the inconsistencies that I found in the report. Mr. Ramirez showed very positive signs that he was going to be able to use my findings as a means to eventually get the case dismissed, and stated that he would ask the court for a continuance at our next hearing. This would buy me even more time to continue working on building my defense.

By the second time I began to read DeMirjian's report again, I decided to take a red ink pen and start circling and underlining every detail in the report that had absolutely nothing to do with me! By the time I was finished fact-checking the 25-page report, I had identified nearly 30 inconsistencies that had nothing to do with me. Also in these inconsistencies, it dawned on me that some of the things that Det. DeMirjian was telling me in-person contradicted what was written in his follow-up report. Based on the follow-up report alone, the Van Nuys District Attorney's Office should have NEVER made a decision to arrest me! The following statements below reflect the *actual* inconsistencies that I found in the follow-up police report. It is important to note that *my car* is what triggered me to be completely engulfed in this ridiculous robbery investigation, not my personal, physical description. On page 12 of the robbery report, the narrative states that, on 06-01-95, one of the employees of Little Caesars was driving into the strip plaza parking lot, coming to work, when he observed the same sky blue Mustang that the suspect drove away in after the initial robbery on 05-24-95.

The employee (witness) went on to say that he saw me exit the Mustang and go into the Thrifty ice cream store. While I was inside of the Thrifty ice cream store, purchasing a few rolls of 35mm film to take on our scheduled family vacation to Hawaii, the employee (witness) who was allegedly robbed walked up to my car after I got out and wrote down my license plate number on a paper napkin and called the police on me. The report goes on to say that, by the time the police arrived on scene, I had already left the area. That's how this whole case got started. It wasn't because I robbed Little Caesars, it was because I was seen driving a similar *type of car* that the alleged robbery suspects were seen driving away in on the day of the actual robbery.

The preliminary investigation report stated that the suspect's height was 5' 7" with a weight of 140 pounds, yet the follow-up police report listed the suspect's height to be 5' 5" with a weight of 130 pounds. Back in 1995, I didn't weigh 130 pounds with all of my work equipment on, including my body armor. Additionally, when Detective DeMirjian spoke to my mother over the phone, not long after she received the Investigator Contact Card, Det. Demirjian documented that my mother told him that my height was 5' 4".

MALICIOUS PROSECUTION—1995

The preliminary police report *and* the follow-up police report both identified the suspect's vehicle as being a *sky blue*, Ford Mustang and, in actuality, the vehicle I had at that time was a *royal blue* Mustang. Clearly a few people didn't learn their colors in elementary school. The preliminary police report and the follow-up police report state that the suspect's vehicle went northbound on Fulton Avenue from Riverside Drive, yet, when I spoke to Det. DeMirjian at my apartment, he told me that my car was seen driving away from the robbery location, eastbound on Riverside Drive from Fulton Avenue towards Coldwater Canyon Avenue. The police report described the suspect as being left-handed. I have never been left-handed. In one section of the police report, the suspect was described as having a shaved head. In a different part of the same police report, the same suspect's hair description is listed as being a natural or an afro! The police report described the suspect as having a dark completion. I have never had a dark complexion.

The police report described the suspect as having a long nose. I do not have a long nose… not now, and not back then. The police report described the suspect's shoes as being slip-ons. Now listen… what type of idiot wears slip-on shoes in the commission of an armed robbery? Based on all of the training and experience I've shared about myself in the previous chapters, does it make any sense that I would show up to a robbery wearing flip-flops or slip-ons, let alone be participating in a robbery at all, while in the process of trying to get hired by the same police department that investigated me? It just literally doesn't make any sense to any reasonable person. As documented in the police report, both witnesses, Francis Pijano and Ernie Amato, both wrote statements on their individual Photo Identification Report form.

Francis Pijano wrote, "When I flip the 6 pack picture I recognize photo No. 5 right away that rob Little Caesar's. I'm positive." Here is why Francis Pijano's statement on the Photo Identification Report should have caused the case to be dismissed. If anyone were to physically see a copy of the police report, it is plain to see that when Pijano wrote the number five, he wrote it extremely dark with an ink pen—the kind of dark ink that a person makes when they have made a noticeable mistake! If you were to look at the number five even more closely, you would see a non-bold number three underneath the number five.

The reason why I focused on that mistake so intensely is because, within the follow-up police report, Detective DeMirjian referred to me as *"Dameon Weaver."* After all of the times he had previously been to my house, or talked to me over the phone, why would he make the mistake of referring to me as Dameon *"Weaver?"* For as many years as DeMirjian had already been on the police force, that was such a rookie mistake! The last name *"Weaver"* is not even similar in spelling to the last name *"Wroe."* This made me conclude that the last name of the person positioned in photo number three more than likely had the last name of *"Weaver."* Contained in the follow-up police report, Detective DeMirjian writes, "I 'paged' Dameon Weaver, on 6-15-95, approx 1330 hrs. He returned the page, within 30 mins. I told him I wanted to talk with him, in person & asked if I could come to his apt on Monday, 6-19-95, 0700 hrs.

MALICIOUS PROSECUTION—1995

He agreed." Still, some twenty-nine years later, I can't help but wonder what the last name is of the person positioned in photo number three! Considering the fact that I ended up teaching report writing classes on my days off, at the Burbank Media Center Shopping Mall security department, I was all too familiar with abbreviations used in police reports and other legal documents.

The word *suspect*, or *suspects*, in the body or narrative of a police report is abbreviated as [susp] or [susps]. On one page of the police report, documenting the alleged robbery at Little Caesars, the report states, "Upon arrival susps were GOA." Based on the fact that the plural abbreviation for the word suspects was used, this has always led me to believe that, somewhere documented in the original police report, the robbery was done by more than one suspect. If this report was written by a seasoned officer of the Los Angeles Police Department, then it is no mistake that the report very clearly stated that the *suspects* were GOA [Gone On Arrival].

The preliminary police report shows that the date and time of the robbery was on 05-24-95 at 11:10 in the morning. However, pay close attention to this part, the date and time that the robbery was actually *reported* was on **05-24-95 at 11:40 in the morning.** Read that one more time... and then read it again! The date and time of the robbery was on 05-24-95 at 11:10 in the morning, and was not reported to police until **after** an entire thirty minutes had gone by! Who in their right mind calls the police thirty minutes *after* a handgun is put in their face during an armed robbery? Does that sound logical to you? If you came home from work and saw someone breaking into your home, as you were pulling into your driveway, would it take you thirty minutes to dial 911 to get the police there? I think not, but the case got even more sinister once my trial started.

Once my mother and I saw a pattern that my initial attorney, Daniel Ramirez, was filing continuance after continuance, so that we would continue lining his pocket with non-productive legal representation, we had talked about firing him and obtaining a better lawyer. Prior to terminating the services of Mr. Ramirez, he had received a formal letter from the supervising latent fingerprint specialist of the LAPD. In that formal letter, the fingerprint specialist wrote that my *known* fingerprints were compared to the fingerprint that was lifted from the countertop at the scene of the Little Caesars robbery, and the conclusion was that my fingerprints were *not even similar* to the fingerprints lifted at the crime scene! Even though the fingerprint comparison proved that I was not the one who robbed the Little Caesars pizza place, located at 13351 Riverside Drive, Sherman Oaks, California, the district attorney, Ed Abla, prosecuted me anyway… exposing me to an unjust and malicious prosecution, and a potential prison sentence of 30 years.

Knowing that I was desperately looking for a new attorney, a good friend of mine at that time told me that a girl he was dating had a father who was an attorney. He told me that the girl's father was already helping a client with a big case, and was not available to assist me, but also mentioned to me that her father had a mutual friend who may be able to take on my case for representation.

MALICIOUS PROSECUTION—1995

The phone number that my friend eventually passed on to me was that of a Mr. Donald J. Calabria. My friend at that time didn't have very many details to pass on to me about Mr. Calabria, he just told me that Calabria was a Criminal Specialist and that he had helped eight people get off of death row. I knew this had to be the guy to represent me, because my need was substantial. By the time I was able to speak to Donald J. Calabria over the phone, I was already well on my way to building my own defense. In the interest of time, I explained to Mr. Calabria how I was building the foundation for my case.

By the time Mr. Calabria was able to spend some quality time listening to all of the inconsistencies that I had already found in Detective DeMirjian's police reports, he was very impressed with my findings and determination to fight the malicious charges against me, he agreed to represent me. Donald Calabria was so upbeat about all of the information that I was able to share with him about the case, he felt very strongly that we would have enough leverage in court to likely get the case dismissed altogether, and he urged me to continue gathering defense criteria for our case, and I did exactly that!

Even though Det. DeMirjian told me to stay away from the strip plaza where Little Cesars was located, I intentionally drove down there anyway, in my *royal blue* Ford Mustang, to start taking pictures of all access points into and out of the strip plaza, to challenge the information DeMirjian wrote in his bogus, prejudicial police report. A few days prior to me driving down to the shopping center, I bought myself a disposable, panoramic camera. I then stood on the far south side of Riverside Drive, facing north, and began taking pictures of the strip plaza. My objective was to have my new attorney, Donald J. Calabria, use these photos to show the jury the businesses that I frequented during the time I lived in that neighborhood. Of all the businesses in that strip plaza, I would never have gone into Little Caesars pizza when there was a perfectly good El Pollo Loco restaurant less than 200 feet away.

Once I was satisfied that I had taken enough pictures to show the jury, it was equally important that I be able to prove to the jury that I had frequently patronized several of the businesses in the strip plaza on a regular basis, within a very close proximity to Little Caesars. God also gave me the insight to go out and purchase about four to six, 22" x 28" plain white poster boards. The idea I had for each poster board was to draw an oversized copy of a 1995 calendar for approximately four months. I drew an oversized replica of about four calendar months to account for two months *prior* to the alleged robbery at Little Caesars, and two months *after* the alleged robbery at Little Caesars.

By creating these oversized calendars, the jury would be able to clearly see them from across the courtroom once my trial began. I would ultimately be asking my attorney, Mr. Calabria, to admit these calendars into evidence in court. Once the calendars were complete, I took a dark colored ink pen or marker and wrote down the name of the business I had visited on a specific day of that month. I then took one gallon-size Ziploc bag and taped it to the back side of each poster board calendar so that I could secure my purchase receipts inside of each bag. If I went to buy food from El Pollo Loco on March 10, 1995, then that El Pollo Loco purchase receipt was placed inside of the Ziploc bag on the back of the March calendar. If I went to pick up my clothes from the cleaners located next door to Little Caesars on April 10, 1995, then that customer receipt from the cleaners was also placed inside of the Ziploc bag on the back of the April calendar.

During the last few encounters that I had with Det. DeMirjian, I found it rather odd that he wanted to know so much about the people that I knew, who were relatively close to me in my circle of associates. When he initially inquired about my then girlfriend, he asked me her name, phone number and her address. In all honesty, I didn't really think it was any of his damn business but, since I didn't have anything to hide, I gave him the information he asked of me. The more I moved around the city to take care of my business, and occasionally still spend some quality time with my girlfriend, I became more noticeably alert and observant to the things that were happening all around me.

My girlfriend lived right off of Whitsett Avenue, which was about three to four miles away from where I lived at the time. One day when I drove to her house to visit her, I observed something happening in her neighborhood that caught my trained eye right away, just before I made a right turn onto her street. Once I made a left turn onto Whitsett Avenue, and merged into my far right lane, I noticed that there weren't very many cars coming and going on Whitsett Avenue as usual, for that time of day. As I was monitoring oncoming, southbound traffic coming towards me, my attention was divinely drawn to a carport in front of some apartments on the west side of the street. As I took notice of all of the cars that were parked underneath that particular carport, I noticed that all of the cars were parked facing away from Whitsett Avenue in a westbound direction in the parking stall… except for one!

As I began to slow down to get prepared to turn right onto my girlfriend's street, I noticed what appeared to be a blue, unmarked police car with two people sitting in the front seats, backed in and facing in an eastbound direction toward Whitsett Avenue, seemingly monitoring traffic in surveillance mode. Rather than turning right onto my girlfriend's street, I kept on going northbound on Whitsett Avenue until I was out of sight from the obvious unmarked police car. I then turned around and began going southbound on Whitsett Avenue back towards the unmarked police car. As I started to pass the unmarked car, still sitting in the same place, the driver of the unmarked car and I locked eyes for several seconds as I continued to roll by. My eyes were not deceiving me… it was Detective Greg DeMirjian and Detective Moran.

By the time I turned around and came back to turn onto my girlfriend's street, I noticed their car was no longer there. This is when I knew they were following me, and keeping me under unnecessary surveillance wherever they thought I was likely to be. Not only were they camped out in the immediate neighborhood where my girlfriend lived, I also observed them sitting outside in their detective car on a few occasions, right outside of my apartment building. One time in particular, while looking out of my third-story window, I noticed Detective DeMirjian sitting outside of my bedroom window, across the street in his unmarked police car—just sitting there on the 12800 block of Addison Street, facing Coldwater Canyon Avenue.

At this stage in the investigation, these two detectives, obviously with nothing better to do than watch me live my life, were starting to really scare me, because I knew they were trying to frame me into being somewhere that I was never at! I can't begin to describe to you the psychological and emotional stress DeMirjian's investigation was having on me. There were nights that I didn't even want to eat dinner. Since my apartment building was at the corner of a very busy intersection, the sirens of emergency vehicles got to me the most. Every time I heard or saw an emergency vehicle going by my apartment, blaring its siren, it made me feel like it was a police car coming to my house to arrest me again and take me back to jail. Every time I heard a car turn the corner too fast outside of my window, the sound of screeching tires and engines accelerating made me feel like Det. DeMirjian and Det. Moran were about to storm into my apartment building and arrest me, even though I had done nothing wrong. Those were just a few instances of how the unfounded robbery investigation started to take a toll on my nerves. I just wanted the entire investigation to be over and done with... for good!

By the time my new attorney, Donald J. Calabria, had finally made a court appearance on my behalf, my mother had already planned a family vacation for us to go to Hawaii. Once our case was called at a subsequent court hearing in Van Nuys, Mr. Calabria had asked the court for a continuance, so that he would have a little bit more time to review some discovery documents, and also informed the court that I was planning to go on a family vacation to Hawaii. The court denied my attorney's request for a continuance. After denying our request for a continuance, the judge clearly stated, "The request for a continuance is denied. This case is the oldest case on my calendar and I want to get it off my calendar. If this trial doesn't go the way your client's planning for it to go, he's going to be going on a long vacation, but it's not going to look anything like Hawaii." When I heard the judge say that, I knew that I was in the fight of my life.

In a felony robbery trial, it is not so uncommon for a defense attorney to *not* allow their client to take the stand and be exposed to cross-examination by the prosecutor. However, in my case, Donald Calabria couldn't *wait* to put me on the stand! He would always tell me, "You're my star witness! You've already done all the work by building your own defense. I want the jury to hear what you have to say!" On the day that Donald Calabria and I went back to court to begin our ridiculous, fabricated robbery trial, we literally blew the witnesses and the prosecutor, Ed Abla, completely out of the water! The only possible way that anyone would ever believe *my* version of all the courtroom shenanigans that the prosecutor and the detectives exhibited in court, is that they would have to be *literally* sitting inside of the courtroom to witness it themselves—it was beyond terrible and embarrassing!

MALICIOUS PROSECUTION—1995

Once the trial began, I sat at the table alongside Mr. Calabria with an extreme level of anger, hatred, and resentment towards the entire Los Angeles Police Department, all because of the actions of Detective DeMirjian and Detective Moran, for falsely arresting me and trying to get me convicted of a crime that I never committed, nor did I ever have any knowledge of. The only thing I was *ever* guilty of was being a Black man in a predominantly White neighborhood! Once I started to listen more intensely to the testimony of the detectives and the witnesses, my anger, my hatred, and my anxiety started to slowly fade away, although my resentment was still there. The more the detectives and the witnesses spoke on the stand, the more confused I became.

Per the information contained in Detective DeMirjian's police reports, the two witnesses who worked at Little Caesars could have definitely identified me if they ever saw me again. The prosecutor, Ed Abla, continued to question one of the witnesses by stating something to the effect of, "Do you see the person in courtroom today that robbed your place of business on 05-24-95?" The witness on the stand, under oath, responds by saying, "Yes." The prosecutor then continues with, "And, for the record, can you please point to, and describe, the person in the courtroom that you see as being the one who robbed your store?" At this time, the witness literally pointed *at me*, yet described a completely different Black man in the courtroom, who just happened to be sitting out in the audience on the front row, directly behind me! If you don't believe me, contact the Van Nuys Superior Court Clerk's Office, and try to order a copy of the court transcript from my robbery trial back in 1995. You will see it for yourself in living color! When the prosecution's witness pointed at me and said, "The one with the stripped shirt and bolo tie," I immediately began looking all around the courtroom to see who the witness was describing, because he was absolutely not describing me!

The person that the witness was actually describing was my friend, Sterling, who came to court with me that day to show his support of me during my circus of a trial. The next words out of the prosecutor's mouth were, "Your Honor, let the record reflect that the witness is describing the defendant, Dameon Wroe." The moment I looked behind me and discovered that the witness on the stand was describing my friend, Sterling, I immediately began writing a note to my attorney. I slid my notes over to my attorney, which said, "The witness isn't even describing *me*... he's describing my friend sitting behind me!" It was all downhill for the prosecution once Donald Calabria cross-examined the witnesses. Oh my Lord! Calabria tore those witnesses a new one before they got off that witness stand.

He made those witnesses, and detectives, wish that they had never come to court. Mr. Calabria embarrassed Detective DeMirjian so badly, he had a very hard time making eye contact with me as I sat at the defense table next to my attorney. DeMirjian knew within his heart that I was not the one who committed that robbery at Little Caesars, but the reality is... he didn't care. His job was to build a case against me under any circumstance, and that's exactly what he did. Had I been wrongfully convicted of that robbery that I never committed,

MALICIOUS PROSECUTION—1995

I would have spent 30 years in prison for something I didn't even have any knowledge of... all because I was a Black man and had a blue Mustang!

Once the trial was over, and I was unanimously found *not guilty*, I remember my attorney, Donald J. Calabria, taking me outside of the courtroom and talking to me privately about all of the winning aspects of the case that I put together to defend myself. He told me that several of the jurors had come up to him after the trial was over, to express their feelings of shame and disappointment towards the prosecutor, Ed Abla,

about the trial. Calabria told me, "Many of the jurors came up to me after the trial and told me they didn't acquit you because the prosecution did not prove their case, they acquitted you because they believed that you were innocent. That statement speaks volumes about you!"

When Mr. Calabria told me that, tears began to roll down my face as I stood there and took it all in. God smiled on me all throughout that entire ordeal and, after 30 long years, I feel relieved that He has finally given me the mental and emotional strength to write about how that malicious prosecution adversely affected my mental health, and affected my life over the years. It was important to me that I finally let the public know what Detective Greg DeMirjian, Detective Moran, prosecutor Ed Abla, and the Van Nuys District Attorney's Office did to me. None of those things would have happened to me if it were not for the reckless actions of Little Caesars and their two incompetent employees, Francis Pijano and Ernie Amato.

I had to re-live a variety of terrible memories and traumatizing emotions to be able to write this story and share my testimony with the world, but I did it because I never want to see another Black man, and his family, have to go through what I went through to prove my innocence!

When the trial was over, and the courtroom was beginning to empty out, I noticed Det. DeMirjian preparing to exit the courtroom through the back door, I'm guessing it was because he didn't want to go out the front door and have to face me for the hell he and his crooked partner put me through. Before he actually turned to exit the courtroom, he and I locked eyes for several seconds. As he stood off in the distance in front of me, I gave him my middle finger with great pride and heart-felt disgust for what he unnecessarily put me through. I should have never been arrested… ever! I should have never been charged! I should have never been prosecuted for a crime I never committed. Never!

A few days after the trial was over, and I was acquitted with flying colors, I went back up to the courthouse to pick up my gun that Det. DeMirjian had taken from my apartment at the beginning of his investigation. The prosecutor, Ed Abla, was so angry and upset that he lost the robbery trial, he did not want to give me my gun and holster back. Whenever I showed up to his office to get my property back from him, he would not even come up to the counter and face me. I ultimately got my property back from someone else that worked in his same office, I believe it may have been his supervisor. Just another example that demonstrates the fact that, in so many cases, the White man hates to see a Black man win... but God!! God saw the integrity of my heart and He exonerated me and set me free in the presence of my enemies.

Sometimes it takes decades for people to realize that the horrible things they did to you or said about you will one day come back to bite them. All I can say is that I'm glad my family taught me about God at an early age in life, because it was God, and God alone, that got me through that emotional and psychological nightmare!

Finally winning my trial, I was so happy and relieved that I was able to go back to work. Even more importantly, I was extremely grateful and blessed that I still had a job to go back to at all. During the course of the unfortunate robbery allegations against me, I had to take quite a bit of time off from work to focus on defending myself. I was very blessed that I worked with people who had enough belief in me, and my integrity, that they supported me by finding a way to keep my job safe while I was gone, and fighting for my freedom. When all of that was finally behind me, I finally went back to work, and was subsequently able to transfer to the Burbank Media Center Shopping Mall to work with Captain Anthony O'Neal, and I was even promoted to the position of sergeant shortly after arriving there. Only God could have choreographed that victory... and I thank Him beyond measure.

Once I took on my new role at the Burbank Media Center shopping mall, still with Langner & Associates, I hit the ground running by building a solid rapport with my new team of officers. My work ethic and my work performance at the Burbank Media Center shopping mall was no different than my work performance at the Baldwin Hills Crenshaw Plaza. In fact, being in a much better area around a totally different community of people made me relax enough to be able to notice better opportunities around me. I still kept my head on a swivel while I was doing my job, but I was able to do things at the Burbank Shopping Mall that I was not able to do at the Baldwin Hills shopping mall.

As I would review the daily activity logs of my officers, I noticed that many of them did not know how to write very well. In all honesty, this was a very sad reality for me because many of my officers were much, much older than me, and I would have expected them to at least know basic grammar, punctuation, and sentence structure, but that was not the case. Not long after noticing this, I approached Captain O'Neal with a proposition. I told Capt. O'Neal that if he would allow me to come in on one of my two off days, I would teach a report writing class to all of our officers for free, for up to four hours. Since we had a tendency to make occasional arrests at the mall, the people we arrested would eventually have to go to court, and our report(s) would be relevant in the evidence that the court would ultimately hear in regards to that arrest.

I explained to Capt. O'Neal that, unless our officers knew and understood the dynamics of how our arrest reports would aid in the conviction of an arrestee, the person we arrested would likely go unpunished.

O'Neal contacted our corporate security office to run the idea by his bosses and, before long, I got the okay to start conducting the report writing class on my off day. I im-

MALICIOUS PROSECUTION—1995

mediately created a sign-up sheet and passed it around the office to my officers during our shift briefings, to see who would be interested in signing up. Surprisingly, I ended up with more sign-ups than I thought I would get, and I began teaching the class. Even though I had offered to teach the classes for free, the company ended up paying me for it anyway. I was very grateful that Langner & Associates saw enough value in me to start paying me for my report writing classes, even though I still would have done it for free.

Successfully implementing all of these positive changes at Langner & Associates, both at the Baldwin Hills Crenshaw Plaza and the Burbank Media Center Shopping Mall, made me feel incredibly good about myself as a leader, and gave me a greater sense of accomplishment to continue adding to my resume but, once again, it was time for me to move on.

After my robbery trial came to a close in my favor, and ended the only way it was supposed to end, Donald Calabria and I kept in touch for a very long time. I told him that I would forever be indebted to him for saving my life, and keeping me from going to prison when I did nothing wrong. We oftentimes hear people around us talk about how *guardian angels* have appeared in their lives during some of their darkest storms. Donald Calabria was my personal guardian angel. God allowed us to cross paths at a time in my life where evildoers were trying to railroad me into taking the fall for something I did not do.

For many, many years after my robbery acquittal, I would always send greeting cards to Donald Calabria for holidays and special occasions. Showing up in Donald Calabria's life, by way of text messages or occasional greeting cards, was always my way of reminding him how thankful and how grateful I was that he believed in me enough to represent me. From that moment forward, my family and I didn't see Donald as just a defense attorney… we saw him as an extended family member, for saving my life. Never would I have ever imagined that God would reunite Donald Calabria and I once again but, unfortunately, under all-too-familiar circumstances.

5
★ ★ ★ ★ ★

MY SECOND SHOOTING INCIDENT

By 1999, I began working for an entirely different security company, Airtight Security, Inc. What attracted me to want to work for Airtight Security was the fact that they looked like a security company that took pride in how they presented themselves to the public. Once they saw the experience that I had on my resume, I was hired relatively quickly. Airtight Security, Inc. had a contract secured with Edwards movie theaters in various locations around Southern California. Although my primary post was at the Edwards movie theater in West Covina, on Lakes Drive, I periodically worked at their other locations in Southgate, Ontario Mills, and La Verne.

Whenever I was assigned to work the Ontario Mills and West Covina locations, my primary duties consisted of maintaining a high visibility to deter any potential crimes that may have been occurring on the property, and also to keep patrons from sneaking into movies that they didn't pay to see. Whenever we stopped people for attempting to enter a movie theater without having a valid ticket for that show, most of the time, they didn't resist us or give us a hard time. When we asked them to leave, they left without incident. Every once in a while we encountered that one person in a particular group of patrons who decided to act a fool, but we dealt with them accordingly, and we saw to it that we maintained order on *our* terms, not theirs. Whenever I was assigned to work at the Southgate location, my duties were the same, but I would oftentimes provide armed escorts to and from the theater box office for the armored car companies who would come to pick up large bags of cash from the theater.

Since it was subsequently called into question during an unforeseen, high-profile trial in 2004, this chapter will also contain an abundance of information that pertains to my work ethic, as well as how I used many years of training to handle two separate, deadly confrontations while being employed by Airtight Security, Inc. back in January and June of 2000.

It was January of 2000 when all hell broke loose during my shift at the Edwards movie theater in West Covina, California. During this time, the movie theater was debuting the release of the movie *Next Friday*. Since this movie had been receiving a great deal of hype and publicity during that time, we were already expecting large crowds and sold out showings of this film. We were also expecting this movie to attract a large presence of people from the hip-hop community, primarily from the black and brown communities.

On the day that Next Friday debuted at the Edwards movie theater in West Covina, I was working that day, and assigned to work in the Wells Fargo parking structure for the first half of my shift. I was in charge of patrolling the en-

MY SECOND SHOOTING INCIDENT

tire parking structure and the open parking areas surrounding the parking structure. After the first few showings of the film, it was business as usual. People exited the theater and headed back to their vehicles, often talking out loud about how they liked or disliked the movie they had just watched. However, as the evening hours slowly began to grow closer, all hell broke loose!

One minute I was walking around the parking lot area, just to the east side of the Wells Fargo parking structure, then, without warning, the radio chatter erupted and alerted me that chaos was about to break out! As one of the last showings of *Next Friday* had ended, and people were pouring out of the theater, my supervisor came over the radio and alerted all outside security personnel that a fight was about to break out in front of the box office between two groups of Hispanic patrons. By the time I ran over to the box office from the parking area, I heard Lieutenant Grant come over the radio in a panic and shout, "Shots fired... shots fired!!!" Even though I had no firearm to protect myself at that time, I still ran over to the location where the shooting was happening to get eyes on the suspect doing the shooting. By the time I located the shooter, all I could see was him running with his arm extended out in front of him, shooting at someone from the rival group, as they fled into the north parking structure on the far east side of the property. The person who was with the shooter fled in the same direction, but closer to the west side of the north parking structure.

As I chased the second suspect on foot, northbound through the parking lot, along the west side of the north parking structures, a West Covina police car came from the back side of the north parking structure and cornered my suspect between the sidewalk and the parking structure. The officer slammed on the brakes, quickly jumped out of the car with a shotgun, and ordered my suspect to the ground at gunpoint. Unarmed, I backed off and continued to monitor my radio traffic to see if the actual shooter had been taken into custody yet. Apparently, while the initial fight was just beginning to brew in front of the box office after the movie originally let out, West Covina Police Department had already been called regarding a fight that was about to break out. By the time the police arrived, the shooting was already happening.

By this time, Lakes Drive was crawling with West Covina police cars! Shortly after my suspect was taken into custody, I ran over to the parking structure where the actual shooting occurred. Once I arrived there, I asked a few of my fellow officers to stand at opposite ends of the entrance that led out to South Glendora Avenue so that I could start setting up the crime scene of the shooting, so that officers from the West Covina Police Department could see the exact location of where the shots were fired. I then got on my radio and asked another officer to bring me about 7-10, red water cups from the concession stand area. Once the red water cups were brought out to me, I began placing the water cups upside down, covering all of the shell casings I found that were left behind by the shooter. By this time, West Covina Police Department had taken over the scene, and our work as security officers was done.

MY SECOND SHOOTING INCIDENT

If I can just continue being honest and transparent, this shooting incident really scared me! It allowed me to witness the fact that anything could happen at any given time... without any prior notice. The incident took me back to 1989 when I was in the L.A. County Sheriff's Department Deputy Explorer Program, when our drill instructors taught us to, "Always expect the unexpected." Once the dust from the chaotic event had settled, I realized how dangerous it was for me to be chasing an armed suspect without having a firearm of my own to fight back if that suspect would have turned around and decided to engage me. Just a few short months after this incident had occurred, I took the advice of my supervisors at Airtight Security and started making plans to apply for my firearm permit.

For obvious safety reasons, it was important to me to get my firearm permit to protect myself but, at the same time, the guys that I was working with at that time also told me that having a firearm permit would give me an opportunity to earn higher pay, because armed guards typically make more money per hour. After successfully completing all required testing and training, I was issued a permit to carry an exposed firearm while on duty. My firearm permit was issued in March of 2000, and I was required by law to requalify with my firearm every six months to keep my permit valid. My firearm permit allowed me to carry my choice of four different calibers of weapons (.38, .357, 9mm and .40). I could finally breathe a sigh of relief knowing that, if tragedy ever struck at work again, I would at least be able to defend myself.

My godfather, John M. Lawrence, was a former Chief of Police from New York. Whenever I had a day off, I would go with him to the shooting range whenever he wanted to shoot, because he knew the owner of the gun range in Burbank, California and wanted to introduce me to him. There were plenty of times where I didn't even need to qualify to keep my permit valid, I just used my godfather as an excuse to take a day off so that I could be with him at the outdoor shooting range.

It was incredibly peaceful up at the range, and it also gave me an opportunity to learn some new tactics, considering the owner of the shooting range was a retired police officer himself. The range master taught me how to shoot very proficiently, utilizing several different styles of shooting. Each style of shooting that he taught me was representative of potential scenarios that could play themselves out while I was working in the capacity of security officer. He taught me how to shoot better with one hand, he taught me how to shoot with my weak hand (left hand), he taught me how to shoot using the double-tap method, and also how to shoot from hip level, after immediately pulling my gun out of its holster.

Another cool thing I got a chance to do while I was up at the outdoor shooting range with my godfather, was watch the LAPD "Metro" SWAT Team do their training on the other side of where we were shooting. Watching the SWAT team train was nothing like what you see on television. To see and hear how they communicate with each other and feed off of each other's energy and body language while

MY SECOND SHOOTING INCIDENT

they are approaching a potential threat was so unexplainably eye-opening. If these guys ever show up to your house for any reason, **please just comply, because you are 200% not going to win against them!** I was really fascinated by them in the few minutes that I got a chance to watch them train. As my range master advised me, SWAT guys do not allow people to watch them train, so it was a blessing that they allowed *me* to watch them for the few minutes that I stood there, without them asking me to leave. It was training like this that would give me yet another chance to escape another deadly confrontation while on duty with Airtight Security, Inc.

During the time I worked for Airtight, our corporate office called me and asked me if I'd be willing to cover another officer's shift at the Edwards movie theater in the city of La Verne, California. After offering me the night shift at the La Verne work site, the gentleman who called me could obviously tell that I was quite hesitant to accept the schedule at the other theater. To sell me on the offer, our scheduling manager tells me, "This is a very laid back post. It's in a quiet, upscale area of La Verne… where nothing ever happens." I ultimately accepted the shift, but the scheduling manager could not have been more wrong about his description of the environment at the theater!

The evening of June 16, 2000 was a Friday night, so I was already expecting it to be pretty busy at the theater. To my surprise, the movie theater atmosphere was relatively busy, but not as busy as I had imagined it would be for a weekend. Operating primarily on the training from my days in the LA County Sheriff's Department Deputy Explorer Program, I was extremely intentional about my patrols on that night, as I had always been. For the majority of my shift that night, I was the primary security officer on a roving patrol of the entire property. Although there was another officer at the theater with me that night, I wasn't counting on him to really help out with anything that might have happened on our shift. The other officer on duty with me that night had a reputation throughout the company for being very lazy! His laziness will prove to be validated later on in this story.

Every 30 to 60 minutes, I would make it a point to switch up my patrol patterns to make myself more visible and more alert to everything that could potentially be happening all around me, not only for my own safety, but for the safety of all theater patrons as well. Since I had never been to this particular theater location before, I spent a great deal of time outside patrolling the parking areas to familiarize myself with the entire property. While doing my outside patrols, I quickly learned all of the entry and exit points. Just in case something bad were to happen there while I was on duty, I felt that it was important for me to know the fastest way onto and off of the property, just in case someone were to try and rob the box office. No matter what theater location I was assigned to, there always had to be an armed guard assigned to stand within close proximity to the entrance of the box office, because that's where all of the theater's cash was kept. This was the standard at every movie theater location.

Whenever I worked inside of the movie theater, it was common for me or other officers to personally escort the

MY SECOND SHOOTING INCIDENT

movie theater management team to and from the concession stands, as they would frequently pick up excess cash or give change to the cashiers at all concession areas. If nothing was going on outside in the parking areas, or inside of the main theater lobby, I would randomly go inside of the actual movie theaters to make sure that there was no one either sneaking in without a ticket or causing a disturbance while the movie was showing. Sometimes, if I felt like the showing of a particular film was going to likely attract a rowdy crowd, I would walk into that theater before patrons were allowed to come in, and I would literally stay posted up behind the movie screen, out of sight, in case there were any unruly outbreaks during the movie.

Once I identified the people causing the disturbance, I was at an advantage of being able to see exactly where the unruly patrons were sitting, and they never saw me until it was too late. Once I called for additional security officers to enter the theater I was in, and saw them walking into the theater, I would come from behind the movie screen and walk directly to the seats where the unruly patrons were sitting and eject them from the theater. Sometimes they got their money back, sometimes they didn't. Sometimes they went peacefully, sometimes they wanted to fight. Always being alert and always relying on my training is what constantly gave me the edge to protect myself, the movie patrons, and my fellow security officers.

As the night began to fall, I eventually made my way out to the front of the theater to make sure that I was visible to theater patrons coming into the parking lot to catch their evening movie. Finally getting tired of pacing back and forth in front of the entire movie theater from one end to the other, I decided to take a walk up and down each isle of the front, northeast parking lot area for a quick patrol.

While patrolling, I observed a male and a female standing outside of their vehicle talking. It appeared to me that they were either waiting for their movie to start, or just coming out of their movie to eventually go home. I then went back to my observation post, along the red curb east of the box office entrance. After about 20 to 30 minutes, I could still see the same couple standing outside of their vehicle still talking, but this time, the couple was hugging each other, and seemingly not paying too much attention to their surroundings. After about 15 minutes from this point, my attention was immediately drawn to a vehicle that was driving around our parking areas, blasting the music from their car extremely loud.

The first time the vehicle passed by me, I didn't approach them to ask them to turn their music down because I felt they might just be looking for a parking spot so they could come watch a movie. The vehicle then went around the southeast corner of the building towards the parking lot exit at the back of the theater, out of sight. When the sounds of the loud music went away, I knew the car was gone. Approximately 10 minutes went by, and I observed that same car drive right by me again, still blasting their music as if they didn't even see me standing there. This time, the vehicle made a left turn in front of me and drove to the far north end of the isle and made a quick right. After the car

MY SECOND SHOOTING INCIDENT

made that right turn, I never saw it make another right turn to start going southbound down the next isle. It didn't take long for me to grow increasingly suspicious about this vehicle because, if they had really been there to watch a movie, they passed up several empty parking spaces closest to the theater entrance, if that were the case.

I then stepped off the sidewalk and began walking northbound down the first isle to investigate and see what they were doing. I then observed that the car had pulled into a parking space momentarily, with the front of the vehicle facing Foothill Boulevard. By the time I got halfway to where the car was parked, I noticed the reverse lights on the car come on, and saw the car backing out of the parking space. The car then proceeded to make an immediate right turn down the next isle over, headed right in the direction of the couple who had been standing outside of their vehicle for nearly an hour.

When I saw the car driving slowly down the next isle over, in a southbound direction, I was in the parking isle just to the west of the couple's vehicle, when I observed the headlights on the approaching car turn off while still in motion. I knew right then and there that something bad was about to happen. Making myself even with the couple's vehicle, I immediately took cover behind a parked minivan and got on my radio to call for the armed security officer inside of the theater to come out to my location. I used the vehicle closest to me as cover and concealment, and continued to monitor the robbery in progress through the vehicle's back window.

As soon as I keyed my mic to talk to the other security officer, a red indicator light on my radio began to flash rapidly, letting me know that my battery was dead, and that I could not broadcast any radio traffic. By this time, I observed the passenger of the suspect vehicle jump out of the car with a mask over his face and what appeared to be a black, sawed-off, pump shotgun in his hand. The armed suspect then told the male victim, "Give me your fucking wallet or I'll blow your head off!" As soon as I heard that statement, I pulled my gun [9mm Ruger P89] out of its holster and prepared to confront the armed suspect, in an effort to keep him from harming the two victims.

Since I felt confident I would have a clear shot, my first reaction was to pop out from behind the parked vehicle I was hiding behind to order the armed suspect to drop the gun immediately. In just a matter of a split-second, I decided against that option because I felt like I would spook the gunman, causing him to panic and shoot both victims and kill them. Since I could hear the two victims cooperating with the gunman, and following all of his orders, I gave him a chance to get back into his vehicle and leave the victims unharmed. Once he got back in the car, the driver of the suspect vehicle looked as though he was going to continue driving southbound through the parking isle, and possibly exit the property via the south exit, located directly behind the movie theater. This is when I came out of my hiding place and began to run southbound in the isle that I was in, to maintain a visual of the fleeing vehicle.

By the time I saw the suspect vehicle turn right to come back towards the front of the box office, I then heard an ex-

MY SECOND SHOOTING INCIDENT

tremely loud bang as I ran across the parking isle to intercept the fleeing vehicle at the main entrance. There was a short pause for a few seconds, and then I heard approximately two more very loud bangs as I ran to the opposite side of the parking isle to take cover behind some large palm trees. Once I made it to the opposite side of the parking isle, I stepped off of the sidewalk and immediately engaged the driver of the fleeing vehicle by *screaming* commands at him, at gunpoint, to stop the vehicle. Even though it was the passenger who was shooting at me, he wasn't shooting at me as the vehicle attempted to exit the property via Foothill Boulevard. The getaway car began to slow down, just long enough to make me *think* he was about to surrender. Almost immediately, the driver then aimed the fleeing vehicle directly at me and accelerated the vehicle directly at me as he got closer to the Foothill Boulevard exit.

Just as I was about to put a few rapid fire rounds directly into the driver's side of the front windshield, I quickly noticed the front seat passenger turn his back towards me and position his knees facing the back seat. I could tell that the passenger was trying to stabilize himself in the seat so that he could try to shoot at me a few more times before reaching Foothill Boulevard. I continued to shout at the driver as loud as I could for him to stop the vehicle. As the suspect vehicle got closer to me, I noticed what appeared to be a large, black shotgun barrel come out of the passenger window, at which time I immediately opened fire on the front passenger.

With many, many years of firearms education and training, I knew that if that passenger would have had a chance to fire at me in that moment, at such a close range, my chances of survival would have been minimal to none! The moment I began firing at the suspect in the passenger seat, I instantly heard a calm, reassuring voice in my head that whispered to me, "If you stop firing your gun, you're going to die." Just as the vehicle was passing by me, within about four to six feet, the passenger tried to pump a new round into the chamber and fire at me one last time but, instead of the gun firing, it ejected the intact shotgun shell onto the ground near where I was standing. The vehicle then made a right turn onto Foothill Boulevard and continued eastbound at a high rate of speed and out of my sight.

Once the two suspects were taken into custody by La Verne Police Department patrol units, several of those patrol officers, along with members of the La Verne Police Department Detective Bureau, returned to the crime scene at the theater and began to interview me and the other two victims. By the time police started returning to the scene of the shooting, I had already began placing red water cups on the ground for identification purposes, to allow detectives to see where all of the shell casings fell during the shootout, including the location of the ejected, unfired shotgun round that the shooter left behind before fleeing the scene.

When the officers asked me how many rounds I fired, I recall saying, "Ten or eleven." In actuality, I was so distraught and traumatized by what had just happened that the investigation revealed that I had actually fired a total of six rounds at the suspect who tried to kill me. Two of the patrol officers involved in the short vehicle pursuit of the

MY SECOND SHOOTING INCIDENT

suspect vehicle gave me some very hair-raising information pertaining to the shooting. I remember the conversation like it was yesterday. One of the patrol officers told me, "When we heard the first bang, we were right next door, sitting in the drive-thru at In-N-Out ordering some food. When we heard the second bang, we thought it was a car backfiring… and then we heard pop, pop, pop, pop, pop, pop!" I then replied, "Yeah… that was me returning fire." The patrol officer went on to explain to me, "After we heard the volley of gunshots, we put our overhead lights on to get the cars in front of us to move so we could respond. As we approached the intersection of Foothill Blvd. and D Street, we saw a vehicle traveling eastbound at a high rate of speed on Foothill that ran the red light right in front of us. When the vehicle went through the intersection, we knew that was the car involved in the shooting because we noticed a bunch of bullet holes in the passenger door."

The officer went on to explain to me that they immediately fell in behind the vehicle, which took them on a short pursuit, and ultimately took both suspects into custody without incident. The officer went on to advise me that, once they began searching the suspect's vehicle, they ultimately found the property of both victims, and also the black shotgun. The officer told me that the shotgun they found in the trunk, wrapped up in a hooded sweatshirt, was exactly as I had described it to the 911 dispatcher. When I arrived at the police station after the suspects were taken into custody, the detectives informed me that the shooter was sitting in their interview room laughing about the whole encounter, thinking it was all a game. He went on to tell me that the shooter was informed by police that, if one of my rounds that hit the door was about two to three inches higher, my bullet would have likely struck him in the neck and killed him instantly, but the shooter continued to laugh it off like it was all a joke.

The way I looked at the whole situation… it just wasn't his time to go. God spared both of our lives that night, and I hope that he turned his life around by now and is a more productive member of society, because he was lucky to have been given a second chance of that magnitude. Because the shooter was denying his involvement in the robbery and the shooting, the district attorney advised him that he was going to be looking at 27 years in prison for armed robbery and attempted murder if he tried to fight the case and go to trial. On the day that I showed up at the suspects' court date, with the La Verne detectives, there was a small crowd of what appeared to be the suspects' family members gathered outside of the courtroom. As I followed the detectives inside the courtroom, an older Hispanic woman came up to me cautiously and said, "I'm so sorry, sir." With tears building up in her eyes, I could tell that her apology was genuine. I simply replied, "It's okay… It's not your fault, it's your son's fault."

Once Detective Gary Mason and his partner drove me back to the police station, Det. Mason asked me how often I train with my handgun. I informed him that, at the time, I trained very often… more frequently than the mandated requalification requirement of every six months to maintain my firearm permit. He then took me outside to where they had the suspect's vehicle towed into their storage yard at

MY SECOND SHOOTING INCIDENT

the station. He showed me the passenger side of the vehicle where most of my rounds hit and told me that, based on the placement of all my shots, it was apparent to him that I shoot often. He shared with me that he was impressed with the fact that my impact groups were so close together, considering I was shooting at a target moving at a fairly moderate speed. For anyone currently working in the private security industry, I hope that my testimony of what I survived lets people know how important it is to receive ongoing training in all aspects of private security, especially firearms training, in case they ever have to make a life or death decision to defend themselves, because it's not a game! It doesn't matter if you are a police officer or a security officer, when a person is committed to the idea that they do not want to go to prison, they will do ANYTHING to get away... even if it means taking your life! Don't ever think that what happened to me can't or won't happen to you or someone you love, because you just never know! After the legal proceedings were over for the guy that shot at me, I later learned that he was subsequently sentenced to 17 years in prison for armed robbery and attempted murder. I believe the driver was sentenced to about 5 or 7 years in prison for his involvement.

In the days and weeks following this shooting incident, I took some much needed time off of work to try to mentally recover from what I had just experienced. Even while writing this book, I remember 98% of everything that happened that night as if it just happened 24 hours ago. I was in counseling for quite a while after the shooting incident, and I also received quite a bit of post-traumatic stress coaching from one of the office managers with Airtight Security, Inc., who I believe was a retired peace officer at the time. The office manager warned me that I would have bad dreams about the shooting for a while, possibly even nightmares, but constantly encouraged me to ignore them—telling me in advance that the nightmares were not real. He also mentioned to me that, if I was planning to remain in the private security business, I should upgrade my handgun to a combat-style firearm for better stopping power in case I were to ever get into another shooting.

He also told me, "If you don't have the money to upgrade your handgun, upgrade your ammunition to something with higher grains and more stopping power." The rounds that I was firing at the suspect that night were just standard 9mm parabellum rounds. At that time, I didn't have the money to upgrade my handgun, so I upgraded all of my ammunition to a 9mm hydra-shock round for increased stopping power to protect myself. Due to the violent nature of my shoot-out with the robbery suspect, I went from carrying 31 rounds of ammunition on my Sam Browne duty belt to carrying 46 rounds of ammunition. I was preparing myself for worst case scenario if I were to ever get into another gun battle again because, when the robbery suspect and I were exchanging gunfire in the movie theater parking lot, the armed security guard inside of the movie theater NEVER came outside to help me fight for my life... I was on my own!

About a month or two after the shooting, my supervisors were asking me if I had planned on attending the company picnic. I had never really been thrilled by attending

MY SECOND SHOOTING INCIDENT

company picnics or other events, so I declined the invitation several times. I eventually got a personal phone call from the owner of the company to attend the company picnic and, reluctantly, I agreed to go. Midway through the company picnic, the owner gathered everyone together and spoke in detail about the importance of being alert while on the job, as well as taking training very seriously to protect ourselves and others we were hired to protect. After explaining the details of my shooting incident to all of my other co-workers, the owner of the company presented me with a commendation that was professionally engraved onto a wooden plaque. With my first and last name displayed at the very top of the plaque, the commendation stated the following...

> "In recognition, admiration and respect we herebycommend you for your heroic actions on June 16, 2000 at the Edwards La Verne theater. On that date you placed your life in jeopardy to protect innocent customers from harm. You met force with force and with God Almighty on your side, overcame and survived. Your actions protected the innocent and apprehended the guilty. For this we at Airtight Security, Inc. salute you and say job well done."

To this very date, this plaque still hangs on the wall in my home as a reminder of God's love, grace, and mercy for always keeping me protected in the face of danger, on multiple occasions. This plaque also serves as a reminder to me not to ever go through this life thinking that tragedy can never land at my doorstep.

For anyone interested in confirming any of the details related to the shooting incident described in this chapter, contact Detective Gary Mason or Lieutenant Rick Aragon with the La Verne Police Department Detective Bureau.

6
★ ★ ★ ★ ★

RAILROADED

This chapter is the very reason why I felt it was necessary for me to finally write this book! This chapter is also the reason why it has taken me more than 20 years to tell *my* story. My *Road to Redemption* over the past two decades has been extremely overwhelming, psychologically taxing, emotionally painful, periodically depressing, and filled with constant reminders of the tragic events that unfolded in Rancho Cucamonga, California on the evening of January 1, 2004, as I was at work minding my own business, doing what I was supposed to be doing, at the very place I was supposed to be doing it at. I didn't go looking for trouble that night... trouble came looking for *me!*

For the past 20 years, the San Bernadino County District Attorney's Office, the Inland Valley Daily Bulletin newspaper, the LA Times, and the San Gabriel Valley Tribune newspaper, have wrongfully and maliciously slandered my name and damaged my reputation by constantly publishing biased, one-sided perspectives of the events that led up to the unfortunate shooting of Michael Krause, Jr. at the Sycamore Springs Apartments. Now, the time has finally come for me to share *__the real story__* with the world, so that everyone interested in the truth can see that I was maliciously and unfairly prosecuted as retaliation for the poor choices that Michael Krause, Jr. had been making all day long on January 1, 2004.

If you can righteously proclaim that you are a reasonable person, I am more than confident that, by the time you have finished reading this book in its entirety, you will conclude that I was railroaded by the San Bernadino County District Attorney's Office, the family of Michael Krause, Jr., San Bernadino County

Deputy District Attorney Jeremy Carrasco, the judge who presided over my preliminary hearing, the judge who presided over my murder trial, the Rancho Cucamonga Voice newspaper, and a host of hostile, White residents of the Sycamore Springs apartment complex. I can assure you in advance that it is *not* going to take a PhD in Psychology to figure out that I was railroaded, and that I did **not** get a fair trial—this is not my opinion, this is a fact!

In this chapter, I am going to share with you the cruel, terrible things that I had to go through in order to prove my innocence, while I was incarcerated at West Valley Detention Center (aka: Stress Valley Detention Center). However, I am also going to share with you how God's hand was in every encounter that He allowed me to endure and overcome while I was incarcerated, fighting to get back home to my friends and my family. There is no possible way that I could have come out of that situation the way I did, had it not been for God surrounding me with a *legion* of His best angels! He is the reason that I am even alive today to tell this story all these years later... and to Him be the glory.

Before I begin to tell the *true version* of what happened on the night of January 1, 2024, I first want to publicly offer my sincere condolences to the family and friends of Michael Krause, Jr. Some people who read this book might feel like it's weird of me to offer my condolences to the friends and family of a man who tried running me over with his pickup truck but, as for me, I still feel in my spirit that it's the right thing to do... it speaks to the true nature of who I am, and I feel like it's a gesture that God is pleased with and expects of me as a Christian. This story is not a fairytale. This is not a fictional depiction of a blockbuster movie. What I am about to describe in the forthcoming pages happened in real life.

Although I am going to describe a great deal of malicious, terrible, unfair treatment that I received after being charged with murder, I want every person who reads this book to keep an open mind in understanding that this was a devastating situation that adversely affected multiple families, not just one. There were no winners in what I am about to describe to you, because two families suffered a great loss, as every life is precious and valuable. Although some of what I am about to disclose may periodically sound harsh, keep in mind that, in order for me to paint a vivid and clear picture of truths that the public has never heard before, I must re-live some extremely traumatic events. I assure you that, from January 1, 2004 to now, this book is the truest version of this story that the public will ever be told and, even after the publication of this book is complete, I have a plethora of documented **evidence** to back it up that was never allowed to be considered in court during my trial, because *documentation* beats *conversation* every day of the week!

I am not offering any of this information for the truth of the matters asserted, I am offering the forthcoming information as *my personal perspectives* of the details that I am sharing, as I have either witnessed them first-hand, or I have, at some point, been told much of this information by multiple third party supporters in my circle. By the time you reach the end of this book, I will have given you enough documented information for *you* to research on your own, and form *your own* opinion as to what YOU believe to be factual or vicious lies that were told on me, in an effort to destroy my integrity and my character.

I used to always wonder why many of my Black friends and associates would always refer to Fontana, California as *"Fontucky"* and Rancho Cucamonga, California as *"Rancho Klu-camonga,"* until I maliciously became a defendant facing a biased and fabricated murder charge! In the Black community, these are our nicknames for Fontana and Rancho Cucamonga, because it serves as a warning sign for other people of color that many of the residents and public servants in the judicial system in these places have a White privilege, Klan-like mentality towards Black and Brown people. I also want to make it painfully clear that all of the so-called witnesses against me, who lied to investigators about what they allegedly witnessed, were also White—that's how this story begins.

So that you can better understand all of the slanderous lies that were told about me in the public eye, I am now going to share highlights with you from various front-page newspaper articles that painted a one-sided narrative about me, and about my character, that made Michael Krause, Jr. look like a saint. So that you can follow this story in chronological order, as events began to unfold from beginning to end, let me first share these *allegations* that were told to me by my former employer, Southwest District Patrol, and various other third parties that supported me throughout my criminal trial.

It was alleged that Michael Krause, Jr. was the son and grandson of a very wealthy, White family with much of their wealth coming from their well-known, family furniture store known as Krause's Sofa Factory. I personally believe this allegation to be credible. It was alleged that several patrol deputies of the San Bernadino County Sheriff's Department were very familiar with who Michael Krause, Jr. was after the shooting at Sycamore Springs Apartments, because he had been a familiar face at more than one or two calls for service in the community. Allegedly, deputies had to be called out to break up loud music at residential parties and Krause was oftentimes found at these parties being "mouthy" with the cops. Based on how disrespectfully Krause spoke to *me* during my encounter with him, I personally believe this allegation to be credible.

It was alleged that, when Michael Krause, Jr. was between 16-17 years old, he totaled a BMW as a result of his unsafe and/or reckless driving. Based on Krause's behavior while interacting with me at the Sycamore Springs Apartments that fateful night, I personally believe this allegation to be credible. It was alleged that the father of Michael Krause, Jr. oftentimes played golf with the judge that presided over my murder trial, Judge John Bunnett, and possibly Deputy District Attorney Jeremy Carrasco, along with the judge that presided over my preliminary hearing, Judge Joan Borba. Based on how the San Bernadino County District Attorney's Office and the San Bernadino County Superior Court handled my case, I personally believe this allegation to be extremely credible.

It was alleged that the reason why I was prosecuted for murder, even though the San Bernadino County Sheriff's Department's Detective Bureau ruled my shooting to be justifiable homicide in self-defense, is because the Krause family had close friends, political ties, or possibly even family members who worked in the DA's office, and that I was prosecuted as a *favor* to the Krause family, in *retaliation* for the death of Michael Krause, Jr. Based on how I was treated throughout my entire court case, I personally believe these allegations to be extremely credible.

It was alleged that the Krause family's wealth and influence on pressuring the San Bernadino County District Attorney's Office to prosecute me for murder was possibly due to the family making campaign contributions to all of those who had a hand in getting me arrested, and aiding in my malicious prosecution. Based on how I was treated from the moment I turned myself in to authorities, coupled with the fact that I was prosecuted during the 2004 local election period, I believe these allegations to be extremely credible!

It was also alleged that one or more of the writers for the Inland Valley Daily Bulletin newspaper had close, personal ties to the Krause family by way of multiple, mutual friends and/or associates. Based on the fact that Inland Valley Daily Bulletin Staff Writer Rod Leveque had written at least six different biased and slanderous articles about me, I wholeheartedly believe this allegation to be extremely credible! Based on the repeated stories published about my case in newspapers circulated all throughout San Bernadino County, the jury already had a tainted perspective about me long before my trial even began. Based on all of the negative, unfavorable newspaper coverage my case got in the community, many of the jurors who ultimate voted to convict me of something, had convicted me way before my trial began!

One of the most disrespectful things that was done in my case was the fact that the San Bernadino County District Attorney's Office went against the findings and recommendations of the San Bernadino County Sheriff's Department, and unfairly prosecuted me for murder and manslaughter, when the sheriff's department detectives had already concluded that the deadly confrontation between Michael Krause, Jr. and I was determined to be justifiable homicide in self-defense! The very first newspaper article that came out after my shooting incident that involved Michael Krause, Jr. and Scott Martinez ended up cultivating a very high-profile case that was *constantly* showcased in the public eye long before I ended up going to trial.

The front-page article that backs up this statement was published in the Inland Valley Daily Bulletin on January 3, 2004 under the heading

> Teen Killed by Security Guard: Officials Believe it was Self-Defense.

The article was very up-front in saying,

> "Sheriff's spokesman Chip Patterson said detectives believe the incident to be an act of self-defense, and are not pursuing it as a criminal homicide. However, the case has been passed along to the District Attorney's office for review. Asked if the guard was permitted to carry a firearm in the course of his duties, Patterson said he believed that was allowed, mainly because the guard had not been arrested."

I want to make it painfully clear that my case was not a high-profile case because it should have been a high-profile case, it was a high-profile case because a Black man working in an upscale, White community shot a young White man who came from a wealthy, White family.

It doesn't take a rocket scientist to figure out that no portion of my incident would've been publicized if the story was about a Black man who shot and killed another Black man, and that's a fact that even some of my very close White friends have agreed with, and I have plenty of White friends who I love very much for also supporting me through this horrific ordeal! If the person who died trying to run me over was *Tyrone Jackson* or *Darnell Crawford*, none of these awful things would have ever happened to me... it would've simply been looked upon as just another Black man dead—no big deal. A documented statement, later made by Jeff Weaver, civil attorney for the Krause family, is going to prove my point regarding my theory.

Now let's dive right into the second, front-page newspaper article published in the Inland Valley Daily Bulletin newspaper on February 19, 2004 with the heading,

Guard surrenders to authorities,

written by Staff Writer Melissa Pinion-Whitt (continued on page A6). Also plastered on the front page of the same aforementioned article, was another article within the article, written by Staff Writer Rod Leveque with the heading

Jailed guard is published poet

(also continued on page A6).

> "San Bernadino County Supervising Deputy District Attorney Joe Gaetano said charging Wroe was 'a careful, thoughtful decision. After looking at the physical evidence and the independent witnesses, we do not believe he had a right of self-defense under these circumstances,' Gaetano said."

Now that you've heard that angle of *their* narrative, pay very close attention to this next quote, because this is where the attorney for the wealthy, White family begins to speak out for his *privileged* clients, setting the stage to eventually sue for the alleged wrongful death of Michael Krause, Jr. The newspaper went on to say,

> "Jeff Weaver, an attorney speaking for the Krause family, said the Krauses were relieved the District Attorney did not believe the guard's account. 'His statements were patently false and a wrongful attempt to shift blame away from him in making false allegations agains Mikey,' Weaver said."

The newspaper article rambled on by stating,

> "Krause's family believes Krause was honoring the guard's orders to move his truck when the guard opened fire.

The extremely lengthy article went on to describe what two other White, teenage witnesses allegedly saw on the night of the shooting. Once I describe to you what the witnesses could not have possibly seen, you will better understand later in the book why the testimony of these very same witnesses was not admitted into evidence during my trial. In a way, I was happy after listening to their testimony at the preliminary hearing, because I knew that their testimony *helped* my case rather than hurt it, because it was not physically possible for them to have seen what they said they saw from that great of a distance, *and* at that angle. In my opinion, any reasonable person should immediately rebuke the testimony of an adult man who saw it plausible to be dating a then 17-year-old (minor) and calling her his girlfriend! The article stated,

> "The witnesses, a 19-year-old man and his 17-year-old girlfriend had just returned from Disneyland when they saw the guard talking to Krause, according to court documents. The male witness told detectives he saw Krause pull his Chevrolet truck out of the parking space. The security guard got into his own vehicle and followed him to the gate. At the gate, the guard got out of his vehicle and stood about a foot from the truck, pointing his 9mm Ruger P89 towards the driver's side window, according to court documents. 'As the gate opened, the green truck started to leave very fast and (the witness) saw the security guard fire four shots at the green truck,' the reports said."

Now, I want you to pay very close attention to this next colorful section of the same newspaper article mentioned above, that describes the sequence of events leading up to the actual shooting, as told by Scott Elliot Martinez, the *so-called friend* of Michael Krause, Jr., and front passenger in the truck with Krause. In the haste of trying to paint a reckless picture of *my* actions against Krause, I really don't think that Scott Martinez, even 20 years after the fact, realized that what he told detectives that night actually substantiated *my* version of what happened, and his statements in the article proves my point.

The article continued with,

> "Krause's passenger, 21-year-old Scott Elliot Martinez of Alta Loma, told detectives he and Krause had bought and smoked marijuana before going to the apartment complex to see a friend. Martinez described the conversation between the guard and Krause, saying the guard told them they were not allowed to park at the complex because they were not residents. Krause agreed to leave and pulled out quickly. Martinez told detectives they were trying to avoid being harassed by the guard. As they pulled out of the parking stall, Martinez was not sure if the vehicle hit the security guard, but as they drove away, Krause reached out of the driver's side window to pull the driver's side mirror back into position," detectives said. The guard followed them to the front gate, got out of his vehicle and walked up to the truck, according to Martinez's account. Krause told the security guard, 'Move the hell out of the way,' and then noticed they had enough room to get out of the gate."

The defamation of my character didn't stop there! Another two residents of the apartment complex seized their opportunity to avail themselves to tell the investigating detectives yet another fabricated lie about *me*, the Black security guard in the predominantly White apartment complex! The Inland Valley Daily Bulletin's slander continued with,

> "Deputies later interviewed two residents of the apartment complex who said they had a run-in with the same guard on Christmas Eve. Chad Barker was walking his friend, Shalene Villela, home to her apartment when they were confronted by Wroe. Wroe said there had been a lot of break-ins and that they matched the description of the people he was looking for, according to court documents. Wroe told them he would be watching the two of them and stood in front of them with his hand on his holstered gun, Villela told detectives." Are you ready? Here comes the most ridiculous part of the article, "He said he had a gun and a permit to use it and was not afraid to use it," according to court documents."

This very last statement I just mentioned, made by a White person against a Black person is the very reason why Black men are sitting in prison to this day—innocent as the day they were born, but God had my back!

Now that you have seen all of the exact words that were said about me in the above article, you will better understand why the jury was ultimately compelled to vote for acquittal of murder, in my favor, and also deadlocked on the lesser charge of manslaughter, also in my favor. The newspaper's version of events that were disclosed above, was the constant and universal theme of lies that were told about me throughout the ENTIRE prosecution process, but now I'm about to show you how **God** turned it all around for my good!

I actually agree with the statements made by San Bernadino County Supervising Deputy District Attorney Joe Gaetano, but for much different reasons! From my perspective, it was *a careful, thoughtful decision* because, as you will see later in the book, his office was getting *pressured* by the family of Michael Krause, Jr. to prosecute me for murder. It was *a careful, thoughtful decision* because the malicious strategy of the prosecution team was to make it look like I was this rogue security guard who was coming to work looking for trouble every day, but their plan failed miserably. It is common knowledge in the Black community that the conviction rate in San Bernadino County tends to be higher for Black people than it is for any other race. Based on this factor alone, do you think it would have ever been probable that the San Bernadino County District Attorney's Office would believe *my* version of events over the statements of a group of privileged White people? I think not!

Going into *their* witch hunt of an investigation, I already had three strikes against me, simply because I was a Black man in a predominantly White community. Joe Gaetano and his team of prosecutors may not have felt like I had a right or a reason to defend myself but, at the end of the day, the jury saw it much differently, and I thank God for *their* belief in my innocence.

Truth be told, the statements made by attorney Jeff Weaver were totally predictable, because he represented the Krause family in a civil, wrongful death lawsuit, so he had no incentive to believe *my* account of the incident. In wrongful death lawsuits, lawyers who litigate those types of cases have a clear picture of how much money they stand to gain by representing families who will likely win big settlements against large companies or corporations, and that's exactly what happened in my case. As I will show you evidence of this later on in this chapter, the Krause family was awarded a civil judgement against my former employer, Southwest District Patrol, in the amount of $6,018,912.46, which I did not know about until I started doing my research to write this book!

Even before my acquittal, I always felt like Jeff Weaver had already been a long-time personal friend of the Krause family so, to me, it felt like he was simply showing his privileged allegiance to the Krause family for what had happened to their son. To prove my theory, I'd like you to focus on his statements in the above newspaper quote. In his statement, he references Michael Krause, Jr. as *Mikey*.

> "His statements were patently false and a wrongful attempt to shift blame away from him in making false allegations against Mikey," Weaver said.

To any reasonable person, that is a very affectionate name to use in place of an individual's real name. The use of such an affectionate nickname typically suggests that there was an existing, intimate connection or relationship between Weaver and the Krause family.

In my opinion, people who come from wealthy backgrounds tend to protect those in their circle who also come from a family history of also having wealth. In my wrongful and malicious prosecution, I was not just fighting a bunch of White people from the community who were telling lies about what they *allegedly* witnessed, I was also fighting a wealthy White family who had enough money to make sure I was unfairly prosecuted, but God was my real attorney, and He did not allow the devil nor his helpers to have any victory over me. With God on my side, I was being protected from evil people who clearly wanted to see me suffer at any and every cost.

In response to the Krause family's *belief* that Michael Krause, Jr. was *simply* honoring my orders for him to move his truck, that is a complete and utter fallacy that never happened, and the following statements will prove that I *never* ordered Krause to either move his truck *nor* leave the property at the time that he initially and violently backed out of his parking space and struck me with his vehicle's side mirror, then attempted to flee to avoid being arrested. In order for Michael Krause, Jr. to have been following my orders, I would have had to *first* give him the orders to follow! Michael Krause, Jr. and I *never* got that far before he struck me with his truck the first time, and the conversation shown below, which is also on file with the Bureau of Security and Investigative Services, will prove my point beyond *any* shadow of *any* doubt.

With regard to the White couple that was returning home from Disneyland on the night Krause struck me with his truck, the story that the male witness told investigators about what he witnessed literally made no sense whatsoever! The male witness told investigators that he saw me fire four shots at Krause's truck. With the male witness and his girlfriend at the far south end of the alleyway, and Krause's truck already facing the main entrance/exit gate, the only vehicle both witnesses could have visibly seen at the far north end of the alleyway would have been *my* vehicle, as Krause's truck was completely out of sight at that distance and at that angle.

It is the pure grace of God that, when these two witnesses testified to this in court at my preliminary hearing, my attorney, Donald J. Calabria, argued that their testimony should not be allowed at trial because it was humanly impossible for them to have seen how far away I was standing from Krause's truck when any shots were fired, because they factually did not even have a visual of Krause's truck from where they were located… not to mention that the alleyway was not very well lit at that time of night. Just so that the world can see how these biased witnesses told recurring lies on me, let me shine an even brighter spotlight on how badly these witnesses contradicted themselves to investigators, and to the court.

In yet another slanderous newspaper article about me, as published in the Rancho Cucamonga Voice on March 12, 2004, the article clearly states,

> "Two other witnesses—a teenage couple who entered the complex that night—testified they saw Wroe shoot four times at the driver's side of Krause's truck. However, Wroe's attorney, Donald Calabria, challenged the teenagers' testimony, citing the parking lot's dim lighting and their distance from the confrontation."

If their testimony was factually accurate, then the evidence at the scene should have substantiated their claims, but it didn't. Prior to the initial statements that these two witnesses made to investigators, it had already been established that Krause's pickup truck had bullet strikes in a few different areas. If I would have just ran up to the driver's side of Krause's truck and fired four rounds into his truck, as the witnesses lied about, then Scott Martinez would have likely been struck by gunfire as well, and possibly fatally injured right along with Krause—he would have been in my direct line of fire. Surprisingly, the judge ultimately granted my attorney's motion to have their testimony thrown out, making their fabricated testimony inadmissible. Next, let's extinguish the lies told by Sycamore Springs residents Chad Barker and his sidekick, Shalene Villela.

I had the total displeasure of meeting resident Chad Barker almost immediately upon working at the Sycamore Springs Apartments. During my patrols of the complex, my attention was *always* drawn to Chad Barker because he was always speeding up and down the alleyways of the complex like he had completely lost his mind. On several occasions, I stopped him and told him to stop speeding up and down the alleys before he hits someone stepping off the sidewalk to go to their car or something. He didn't like me from day one, because he did not strike me to be the type of person who appeared to like Black people, people of authority, or both.

By the way he carried himself every time I saw him, Chad Barker seemed like a snotty-nosed little White boy who was mad at the world because he had a badly deformed face. I never knew what happened to him that caused his facial deformities, but I just recall him being a very angry person every single day that I saw him… he just looked disappointed with his life in general, and he seemingly wanted to make everyone else around him just as miserable as he was. He was an extremely rude, smart-mouthed person who didn't like being told what to do, especially by a Black security officer. Within an eight-hour shift, I would sometimes have to talk to him about his reckless driving on the property more than several different times but, of course, he never listened.

After Chad learned that I was the one who was involved in the shooting incident with Krause and Martinez, he couldn't wait to jump at the opportunity to talk to investigators and make up lies about me, but it wasn't because I was guilty of doing anything wrong, it was because he didn't like me. Chad and his little female friend, Shalene Villela, told investigators that I mentioned to them that there had been a lot of break-ins on the property, and that they had fit the description of the people I was looking for. First of all, when I initially started working at the Sycamore Springs apartment complex, nobody from Southwest District Patrol had *ever* given me a description of *anyone* who may have been responsible for breaking into garages or residents' vehicles, so that was the biggest lie ever told... it just factually never happened.

The two liars went on to tell investigators that, as I was standing on the premises talking to them, I had my hand on my gun. They went on to add that I had told them that I had a gun, and a permit to use it, and I that I was not afraid to use it. Let's be very clear here—if I was standing in front of someone like Chad Barker and his little 15-year-old female friend, there's no reason why my hand would have ever been on my gun during our brief conversation. With my background in martial arts, coupled with my training in self-defense techniques, Chad Barker wouldn't have been stupid enough to try to get crazy with me—he wasn't even a threat to me like that. He was all bark and no bite!

He seemed like someone who just wasn't ever playing with a full deck, so it makes no sense, even 20 years after the fact, that I would have ever had to threaten someone like Chad Barker or a 15-year-old little child. Give me a break! Once again, after these two liars came to court and testified against me, stating the same nonsense they originally told investigators, their testimonies were also thrown out. As my attorney argued in court, they were just in their feelings because I spoke rudely towards them after they first spoke rudely to me, and that triggered them to come forward and make false statements to investigators about me.

Prior to me accepting the security job at the Sycamore Springs Apartments, my supervisor, and owner of the company, Robert Zablockis of Southwest District Patrol, had informed me that residents of the property had been reporting that their garages and vehicles had been getting broken into on occasion by unknown subjects finding their way onto the property. So, naturally, I was always on the lookout for anyone who appeared to *not* belong on the property. With my long history of training and experience, I was confident that I would eventually catch the people sneaking onto the property to commit crimes against the residents and, on the night of January 1, 2004, Michael Krause, Jr. and his passenger, Scott Martinez, by their own actions, fit the profile perfectly... they stood out like two sore thumbs!

When Michael Krause, Jr. first came onto the property of the Sycamore Springs Apartments that night, I was sitting in my personal vehicle, backed in to a frequently empty handicapped parking space, in an effort to monitor vehicle and foot traffic that was coming in and out of the property via Archibald Avenue. During my observation of the main entrance gate at the front of the complex, I observed a pickup truck with two male occupants enter the property and pull up to the main entrance gate and just sit there. From the looks of their actions, the driver, later identified as 19-year-old Michael Krause, Jr., appeared to be trying to enter a gate code several times, but the gate did not open. I then observed an unidentified white male, approximately in his early 40's, walk up to the main gate and enter a code into the key pad, at which time the gate opened immediately.

Once the gate started opening up, the unknown White male walked through the gate and then motioned for Krause to proceed through the gate at will, which he did. As Krause's truck entered the gate, another vehicle entered the gate behind him. Since my suspicions were that Krause was likely not authorized to be parking on the property behind the main gate, I followed both vehicles through the gate in order to observe where Krause was going. Once I made a right turn to drive southbound down the alley, I observed Krause's truck pulled over to the left side of the alley, facing south in a northbound lane of travel. This behavior continued to heighten my suspicions as to Krause's reasons for being on the property.

During this exact moment of observation, I noticed that Krause's passenger, later identified as Scott Martinez, had his window down—waving cars behind the truck to go past them and keep driving forward, as they continued to sit there facing the wrong direction. Once I drove past Krause's truck, I intentionally drove by him very slowly, so that I could look back at his truck to see if there was an authorized parking sticker displayed anywhere on his windshield to let me know if he was a resident. I did not see a resident parking sticker on his windshield when I drove by him. Since the alleyway was rather long, I continued to monitor Krause's truck via my rear view mirror to see if perhaps he was picking up a resident, and would quickly end up leaving shortly thereafter.

Considering all of the attention that Krause had already drawn to himself from the time he initially drove onto the property, I had seen everything I needed to see to reasonably conclude that it was likely that Krause and his passenger had no business being on the property. Knowing that I was eventually going to be making contact with Krause to find out why he was on the property, I made a left turn at the far south end of the alleyway and then made a U-turn to go back and speak with the driver of the truck, Krause. By the time I turned around and started driving northbound back up the alleyway, I noticed that Krause was no longer parked off to the east side of the alleyway where I last saw him.

Almost directly across from where I last saw his truck positioned were three parking spaces. Krause ended up parking in one of the three parking spaces, but never exited his truck. What drew my attention to the far right parking space where Krause had parked, was the fact that his brake lights on his truck were still illuminated when I turned the corner to start driving back up towards the main gate where I saw him enter the property. Before making contact with him, I intentionally pulled my car over to the west side of the alleyway (facing north) and sat in front of a garage door, approximately three to four garage lengths away from Krause's truck, and continued to observe the activity in that area. After about five minutes or so, Krause nor his passenger ever got out of the truck to go into any apartment on the property, nor did any resident of the property ever come out to greet them at Krause's truck.

My many, many years of training and experience began to make me further conclude that Krause and his occupant may possibly have been the ones who had been breaking into people's garages or vehicles, because they just seemed to be too out of place for that time of night. This is when I knew it was time for me to approach Krause's truck and investigate further. It was after 10:00 p.m., which is a time that most residents are in their homes for the evening, and not likely to come back out until early the next morning to go to work. The cover of night has always been the most opportune time for potential criminals to strike.

Since I already knew that there were two existing cars parked in the parking spaces just to the left of where Krause had parked, I thought maybe he and Scott Martinez were sitting in the truck to see how long it was going to take for someone to realize that they were sitting in the truck. I ultimately exited my vehicle and left it where I parked it after making my U-turn. As I began walking northbound up the alleyway towards Krause's truck, the only thing I had in my left hand was my compact flashlight. Considering that my gun holster was secured to the right side of my duty belt, my right hand was completely empty.

By the time I reached the far, left-hand parking space near the section where Krause was parked, I stood out of sight at the edge of a nearby garage to observe what Krause and his passenger were doing before I made contact with them. From where I was standing, it appeared that Krause and Martinez were possibly preparing to consume some alcoholic beverages, or possibly rolling up a blunt (marijuana joint). What led me to this conclusion was the fact that Krause's driver side window was raised almost all the way up, give or take an inch or so, and I could hear them laughing unusually loudly. Furthermore, they both had their heads completely fixed in a downward position just prior to me approaching the vehicle. This is why I thought they might be rolling a blunt, because, in order to roll a blunt, one must have their head at a downward angle for an extended period of time to focus on rolling the blunt correctly. I thought they might already be drunk or high, by the manner in which they were laughing and acting inside of the truck.

Since Krause already had his window cracked about an inch or two from the top of the window frame, I believe he heard me coming, as I stepped away from the garage and began to get closer to his truck. As I got closer to his truck, I immediately noticed that Krause was staring at me through the side mirror of his truck, while appearing to be making movements with his right arm, indicative of a person trying to stash or hide something, or possibly be *retrieving something*. As soon as he fixed his eyes on me, I immediately shined my flashlight beam directly into his side mirror to keep him at a disadvantage for my safety, in the event that he had a weapon within his immediate reach.

Once I shined the light into his side mirror, he then began looking at me over his left shoulder, at which time I shined my light beam directly into his eyes, also to keep him at a disadvantage for my safety. Prior to going into my investigation with Krause as to why he was even on the property, I asked him if he had any weapons in his truck. Keeping in mind that I had been involved in a violent shootout with an armed robbery suspect just four years before crossing paths with Krause, my main concern was finding out if there were any weapons in his truck. Krause indicated to me that he did not have any weapons in his truck, but I could still sense that something just wasn't right with him! At this very moment, my gun was still fastened securely in my holster. As documented in an incident report filed with the Bureau of

Security and Investigative Services, the following dialogue reflects my initial conversation with Michael Krause, Jr.

Wroe: How are you doing tonight, sir? Do you happen to live here by any chance?

Krause: Yeah, I do!

Wroe: What unit number do you live in?

Krause: Well, my girlfriend lives here.

Wroe: Just a second ago you said that *you* live here and now you say your girlfriend lives here. Which is it?

Krause: What? I never said that!

Wroe: Yes you did, sir. What is your girlfriend's apartment number?

Krause: I'm not sure. It's somewhere over there (pointing in an easterly direction).

Wroe: How did you even get inside the gate if you don't live here?

Krause: It was already open.

Wroe: Well if that's the case, who was the guy who accessed the front gate for you and signaled for you to come in?

Krause: It was already open.

Wroe: Would you happen to have any ID on you that I can see?

Krause: You know what... fuck you, dude, I don't have to answer any more of your fucking questions anymore!!

At this point, Michael Krause, Jr. started up his truck very quickly, put the truck in reverse, and began to *voluntarily* leave the location. As you can tell by our conversation above, never at any time did I <u>*ever*</u> give Michael Krause, Jr. an order to leave or relocate his truck. He left on his own free will because he was angry, and he was tired of me questioning him. He knew that I was onto him and, in that very moment, he became very irate that I had been asking him so many questions. He knew that he could not out-smart me and get past my line of questioning. As Krause pulled out of the parking stall, as I was still trying to talk to him, the side mirror of his truck violently struck me in the left (upper) arm and then he sped away towards the same exit gate that he initially drove into. Before I continue, here is where I want to point out to you that Scott Martinez contradicted himself in his initial statement that he originally gave to detectives, as mentioned in the above newspaper article.

> "As they pulled out of the parking stall, Martinez was not sure if the vehicle hit the security guard, but as they drove away,

Krause reached out of the driver's side window to pull the driver's side mirror back into position, detectives said."

How could Scott Martinez *not* have been sure that Krause's side mirror struck me, yet he was *positive* that he saw Krause reach out of the driver's side window to pull his driver's side mirror *back* into position? That statement begs the question, "What event took place prior to Krause having to pull his driver's side mirror *back* into position?"

After Michael Krause, Jr. struck me with his side mirror and backed completely out of the parking space, we locked eyes for a few short seconds, at which time I rapidly walked over to his truck with the intention of snatching him out of the truck and arresting him right then and there for ADW (245 PC), at the location where he first struck me. However, as soon as he saw me coming up to his door, he immediately pulled the truck's gear handle downward, put the truck in drive, and sped away toward the main exit gate at a high rate of speed. **Never**, at *any* time, did he stop to see if I was okay after he violently struck me with the side mirror of his truck…. he just sped away. I have already established proof that Michael Krause, Jr. knew that he struck me with his vehicle, that's why he had to readjust his side mirror, because the force of his side mirror striking me forced his entire side mirror assembly to be pushed backwards towards the front of his truck, making it impossible for him to continue driving and still see out of his side mirror!

When I saw Krause speed away towards the main exit gate, I ran back to my car in order to chase after him and arrest him for striking me with his vehicle and fleeing. By the time I got to my vehicle, Krause's truck had already made a left turn at the far north end of the alleyway we were in, and I could not see his truck anymore. However, I was confident that I could catch him before he exited the property, because the entrance/exit gate opened very slowly. As soon as I started up my car to chase after him, I attempted to make an emergency broadcast using my company issued radio, to inform any other units near my location that I had just been struck by a truck, and that the vehicle was fleeing from the property.

When I keyed the mic on my radio to put out my emergency broadcast, the red indicator light on my radio would not hold a solid red color, letting me know that my battery was either dying or already dead. In any event, my radio did not have enough of a charge on it to allow me to put out the broadcast. So, relying on my training and experience, I attempted to take Michael Krause, Jr. into custody at gunpoint for ADW, a felony, pending the arrival of sheriff's deputies. For my safety, since I was the only security officer on duty at the Sycamore Springs Apartments that night, and I was dealing with two hostile suspects in the same vehicle, it was also my intent to handcuff and detain Scott Martinez, also pending the arrival of sheriff's deputies.

As I reached the far north end of the alleyway and made a left turn to exit the gate and follow Krause, I immediately noticed that the gate was still closed, and Michael Krause, Jr. was, once again, lying in wait to see if I was going to pull up behind him, which I did. As I came around the corner, I noticed his truck stopped a considerable distance away from the gate and looking at me intensely through his side mirror again. The feeling that came over me in that very moment was that I was possibly walking right into some sort of ambush attempt, because the gate should have already been opening by then if he was truly trying to leave the property. A person adamant about exiting the property would not have been sitting a considerable distance behind the gate sensors. My training kicked in again and told me to prepare to defend myself against a possible ambush, still not aware if Krause had a firearm in his truck or not.

After pulling up a safe distance behind Krause's truck, I immediately exited my vehicle, drew my weapon, and ran up to the driver's side of his truck to begin giving him verbal commands to turn off his truck and exit his vehicle with his hands in the air. It must be made clear that the exit gate was still *not* beginning to open yet, because Krause's truck was still not close enough to the gate to trigger the sensor(s) that prompt the gate to open. Once I got even closer to Krause's truck, that is when he pulled forward a few more feet, at which time the gate had started to slowly open up.

It was at this point that I let Michael Krause, Jr. know that he was under arrest. For the first time in more than 20 years, I want to make it painfully clear that my reasoning for immediately unholstering my gun was *not* to actually shoot at Krause! My reasoning for immediately taking my gun out was because, in the heat of that moment that I pulled up behind Krause's truck, **if** he would have had a firearm within his immediate reach, and a desire to fire it at me, he had a position of advantage over me because I was in the *kill zone*.

If Michael Krause, Jr. did in fact have a firearm in his truck that he intended to use against me, so that he could ensure his escape from being arrested, all he would have had to do is open his driver's side door just a few inches in order to get a few shots off at me as I was approaching his truck from the rear. That is why I felt I was running into an ambush when I initially turned the corner of that alleyway and saw him just sitting in his truck, waiting patiently for me to come around that corner and approach him!

In that scenario, if he would have opened up his door at any length, everything and everyone *behind him* would have been in the *kill zone*... so it was imperative that I maintained the upper hand in an effort to prevent that potential fight! Once I arrived at Krause's driver's side door, I trained my gun directly on him, pointing directly into his driver's side window, and began to yell commands at him at the top of my voice, so that it was clear to him that he was under arrest and not free to go at that point... he did not comply! I continued to repeat verbal commands at Krause for him to turn off his truck, show me his hands, and exit the vehicle with his hands in the air... he continued to be non-compliant! During the first two times I shouted these commands at Krause, I observed he and Scott Martinez laughing and talking among each other, as if it were all a big joke.

About the third time I shouted commands at Krause, for him to shut off his truck and show me his hands, I noticed Scott Martinez lean forward in the passenger seat and look directly at me through Krause's driver's side window, as I still had my gun trained on Krause. Once Scott Martinez leaned forward, my training kicked in once again to alert me that Scott Martinez was in my direct line of fire. Since Scott Martinez was not my immediate threat, I quickly repositioned myself at the front, driver's side quarter panel of Krause's truck and continued to loudly shout commands at him to turn the truck off. Though I could not hear what they were saying to each other, I continued to observe Krause and Martinez talking back and forth with each other, while still laughing and treating the situation like it was all fun and games.

By this time, I felt that I was starting to make progress with getting Krause to turn off his truck and surrender peacefully, as I noticed him raise his left hand just slightly above the outer edge of the steering wheel. With his left hand slightly raised, he would look at Scott, then he would look at me… he would look back at Scott, then he would look back at me… still talking to Scott Martinez and laughing during the entire encounter. He then looked at me and locked eyes with me for a few seconds. This is the moment where I felt it was all about to come to an end, and that he was going to give up and exit the truck. Before I could repeat the commands any further, I observed Michael Krause, Jr. take his left hand down, regain control of the steering wheel, and turn the steering wheel to the left where I was standing, at which time we locked eyes for the last time. I recall looking directly at him and saying to him, "Don't you do it!!!" Without any warning whatsoever, Michael Krause, Jr. floored the truck in my direction, prompting me to begin firing my weapon in self-defense. Once the gunfire erupted, all that was previously funny inside of the truck was suddenly no longer funny… reality had quickly set in for all of us!

As the truck suddenly began to accelerate in my direction, I felt the front of the driver's side quarter panel make contact with my left arm, and I fired a single shot into the truck's windshield to try to defeat the threat, and to keep from ending up under Krause's truck. According to the aforementioned newspaper article, Scott Martinez told detectives that Krause felt he had enough room to drive out of the gate, but I *vehemently* reject his statements to detectives! If Krause already had enough room to get out of the gate, before I ever fired my first shot, there was no reason for him to have turned his steering wheel to the left, toward the immediate area where I was standing! If Krause had enough room to exit the gate, all he would have had to do is drive *straight* out of the gate and make a slight right turn to exit the property and turn onto Archibald Avenue.

Krause did *not* have enough room to exit the gate. He knew that I was going to place him under arrest for assaulting me with his truck, so he *forced* his truck out of the portion of the gate that was opened on the side where I was standing so that he could continue evading arrest. In the process of me beginning to fall backwards, still in fear of my life, I fired two rapid fire rounds at the side of the truck, in an effort to force the truck away from me. I could hear the engine on Krause's truck just fully open up, as he attempted to squeeze his truck between me and the edge of the gate, which was still in the process of opening, and that's when I fired an additional round.

I am certain that, had I not fired those rounds at Krause's truck in that moment, the two left tires of Krause's truck would have run me over. In the moment that I fired my first three rounds, I just wanted to live... I was not ready to leave this earth with so many goals and aspirations in life still unfinished. Prior to going to work that night, I had spent the majority of my evening with my then girlfriend and her son, who was only three years old at the time. Prior to leaving her house to go to work, I suited up into my uniform and said my goodbyes to her. The last thing I recall her saying to me as I walked out of her front door was, "Be careful at work, babe! Call me when you get home so I know you made it back safely." My response to her was, "I will... I promise!"

During my trial, my attorney, Donald J. Calabria, DESTROYED the entire prosecution team, and every witness that they called to testify against me, when he explained to the jury that Michael Krause, Jr. had exited the main exit gate like a bat out of hell, laying nearly 30 feet of skid marks on the asphalt as he fled out of the apartment complex! A vehicle that lays 30 feet of skid marks on the asphalt is not consistent with an innocent, law-abiding person who is *simply* honoring a request to leave the property. It never happened that way. Never! That ideology will just never make any sense whatsoever. As my aunt would always say, "That dog ain't gonna hunt!"

From the time I fired my first shot, to the time I fired my fourth shot, I felt like I was having an out-of-body experience that was happening in very, very slow motion. Although I had to fight to remain focused on firing my weapon to keep Krause's truck from trampling over me, I was simultaneously thinking about my then girlfriend and her son. Even while I was fighting for my life during my confrontation with Krause, all I wanted to do in that moment was hold her son in my arms again, and love on him as I had always done, because I was the only father he had ever known. I could not get the image of my girlfriend's son out of my mind at that time. It almost felt like *real life* had been placed on pause for a moment, and that I was functioning in some sort of *spiritual* realm or something. Immediately following the incident, I felt like I was in a trance.

After I fired my last round, I observed Krause's truck continue to drive away from the exit gate and towards the main entrance of the apartment complex. I then ran back to my vehicle to pursue Krause's truck so that I could at least get his license plate number and his last known direction of travel. I knew that if I could have caught up to Krause's truck before he actually exited the property, I could have made another attempt to take him into custody. Once I fired my weapon, I knew that it was my responsibility to maintain sight of the truck so that I could alert the authorities that the driver had just committed an assault with a deadly weapon, and to look for bullet defects on the exterior of Krause's truck.

Since Michael Krause, Jr. was trying so diligently to flee from the apartment complex, especially after the shots were fired, my instincts told me that he was likely going to make a right turn onto Archibald Avenue to hurry up and get to the 210 freeway, to hurry up and get out of the area as fast as possible. In all honesty, I had no idea that Michael Krause, Jr. had even been struck by one of the rounds I fired because, after the shooting stopped, I briefly observed his truck continuing to drive through the parking area at the front of the apartment complex, and his driving appeared to be consistent with someone who was still reasonably coherent and alert.

By the time I had driven to the main entrance to the apartment complex, at Archibald Avenue, I looked to my right to see if I noticed Krause's truck fleeing northbound towards the 210 freeway, but did not see him. Almost immediately, I noticed Krause's pickup truck stopped directly across the street in the Ace Hardware parking lot, south of the business and facing west (away from me). As I crossed the street to make contact with Krause again, I took notice that it appeared that his truck's brake lights were activated. Once again, this made me feel like I was possibly walking into another potential ambush, so I was prepared to defend against it if it happened.

Just as I was pulling up behind Krause's truck at a safe distance, I noticed Scott Martinez exit the passenger side of the truck and began to walk towards my car. I immediately threw my car in park, exited my vehicle with my weapon drawn, and immediately began to give Martinez commands to stop walking towards me and get down on the ground and face away from me. He continued walking towards me stating, "You shot my friend!" I continued to shout commands at him to stop advancing towards me and to get down on the ground and face away from me… he remained non-compliant. Martinez continued to step towards the front of my car, as I stood in the door jamb continuing to shout commands at him more aggressively to get down on the ground with his arms out at his sides, and to face away from me. He then told me a second time, "You shot my friend!"

He continued to ignore my orders for him to get down on the ground. As he tried walking over to me again, I told him that if he didn't stop walking towards me he would be shot. He then stopped walking towards me immediately, but he did not get down on the ground as I had instructed him to do. When I saw that he was still being non-compliant about getting down on the ground, I said to him, "If your friend is shot, I can't get help for your friend until you get down on the ground. Get down on the ground, NOW, so I can get your friend some help!" After I said those words to Martinez, he finally got down on the ground, but refused to look away from me. At that very moment, since my radio battery was dead, I took out my cell phone and dialed 911 to get emergency personnel to my location.

When the 911 operator answered the phone, I identified myself as an armed security officer from the Sycamore Springs Apartments and told her that shots had been fired at the apartment complex. I then requested sheriff's deputies and a rescue ambulance to respond to my location in the Ace Hardware parking lot, and advised her that the suspect who tried to run me over with his pickup truck had been struck by one of my rounds. I recall the operator telling me to stay on the line with her until deputies arrived, which I did. After about 90 seconds or so, I started to hear the sounds of sirens from far, far away, then getting closer and closer. When I started to hear the sirens turning off, all I could hear was the roaring engines of the responding patrol cars about to pull up behind me.

It was at that time that I knew that help had finally arrived. I told the 911 dispatcher that I was going to hang up because deputies were arriving on scene [going 97]. After hanging up with the dispatcher, I continued to train my weapon on Scott Martinez until he could be taken into custody by the deputies.

When the first two deputies came up behind me with their guns drawn, one of the deputies asked me, "What do you got?" I replied, "I got one on the ground and one down in the truck, not responding." Immediately thereafter, even more deputies began to arrive on scene. Since I already had two deputies with me at the driver's side door of my car, the remaining deputies focused on taking Scott Martinez into custody from the passenger side of my car.

As I looked over at Scott Martinez again for a brief moment, I could tell that there were at least five or six additional deputies behind me. The only reason I was able to estimate that number was because, as the other arriving deputies began to shout commands at Scott Martinez to stay on the ground with his arms out and to face away from us, I saw a bunch of red laser beams all over his head, shoulder, and back area. I recognized those red laser beams to be the laser beams attached to the firearms of the other arriving deputies, and those deputies made it very clear to Martinez not to move! Scott Martinez followed *all* of the instructions that the deputies had given him, and was subsequently taken into custody without incident. The entire time that Scott Martinez was being taken into custody, myself and the other two deputies had our guns on Krause's truck, just in case he would have suddenly popped out unexpectedly. Once Scott Martinez was handcuffed and escorted to one of the patrol cars, the other two deputies began shouting verbal commands for Michael Krause, Jr. to exit the truck with his hands up, but there was no response. We then stacked up behind each other and cleared the truck at gunpoint, approaching on the passenger side of the truck, since the passenger door was already open.

As the two deputies arrived at the passenger door, I was third in position behind them as we approached, at which time I branched outward to a wider angle of cover in order to remove the deputies from any crossfire in assisting them in clearing the truck. This is the moment that I observed Krause partially stretched over the floorboard of the truck, appearing to be trying to crawl out of the passenger door. For me, this was a very upsetting sight to see! The initial shock of physically seeing Krause down in the truck was very disturbing to me. Within seconds of seeing him down in the truck, my emotions went from professional, to empathetic and human! This was not the outcome I was hoping for during the time I was attempting to take Krause into custody for striking me with his truck.

Shortly thereafter, I began to feel an intense, burning sensation all across my lower back. When Krause initially struck me with the side mirror of his truck, while on the Sycamore Springs Apartments property, the force of the truck moving backwards so rapidly somehow knocked me against the passenger door of the car parked to the left of the space Krause was backing out of. All of the equipment on the back side of my duty belt slammed against my lower back. By this time, an ambulance had arrived on scene to treat Krause, per my request via the 911 operator. Also arriving on scene shortly thereafter was my supervisor, Robert Zablockis. The scene at the Ace Hardware parking lot was incredibly chaotic and surreal. I could visibly see things happening all around me, but I questioned if any of it was even real. During certain moments following the incident, I could vividly see people around me interacting with each other, but it felt like there was no sound that I could hear as I watched them talking to each other… I was overwhelmed by a deafening silence, trying to decide if it was all a dream.

Even now, I can't fully explain it, I just knew that I could not break my promise to my then girlfriend, because to break my promise to *her* would have been like breaking a promise to her three-year-old son. I had to fight to stay alive and get back home, because it was crystal clear to me that Michael Krause, Jr. had no regard for my safety nor for my life. He was willing to do *anything* he could do to get away and avoid going to jail. The March 12, 2004 newspaper article went on to say,

> "Martinez also testified that he and Krause bought and smoked marijuana prior to driving to the apartment complex. Marijuana and a broken glass pipe were found at the scene, court documents showed."

I knew it!! I knew my hunch about Krause and Martinez sitting in that truck possibly rolling up a blunt or possibly stashing a weapon was on point… I just knew it!

After reading this article over and over again, nearly 21 years after the incident happened, I find the article to be quite deceptive to the general public who may have read it, or who will read it in the future! I think it was very manipulative of the Rancho Cucamonga Voice to publish the fact that Krause and Martinez both smoked weed before ending up at the Sycamore Springs Apartments that night, yet they failed to disclose the fact that Martinez had also testified at my trial that he and Michael had also been driving around smoking the marijuana while Krause was operating a motor vehicle, which was a totally separate crime!

In addition, the article also conveniently forgot to mention the fact that Scott Martinez was given immunity in exchange for him testifying against me during my murder trial. Now that I've given you these parts of the truth, that the San Bernadino County District Attorney's Office never wanted the public to know, let me ask you this very important question, as you continue to ponder which side has always told lies versus which side has never had anything to hide. Why in the world would a person be offered immunity if they factually never did anything wrong in the first place?

Next, I heard one deputy ask another, "Is he still breathing?" The other deputy replied, "It seems shallow, but I think so." I was so happy to hear the deputy telling the other deputies that news, because it sounded like Krause had a chance of survival since the ambulance was on scene. However, that feeling of relief that I initially felt for a few short moments quickly began to dissipate when I started to see a deputy with a large roll of yellow tape seal off the portion of the parking lot where Krause's truck came to rest. Once I saw that yellow tape, I started to lose faith in Krause's potential survival. At a scene such as the one we were dealing with, yellow tape means one of three things. Yellow tape at a crime scene means that someone has died, someone is likely to die, or it is simply being used as a perimeter to control who is or who is not allowed to go in and out of the crime scene, in order to preserve evidence, and to maintain the integrity of an investigation.

As sheriff's deputies and Robert Zablockis were consoling me at the scene, and trying to keep me calm, it became obvious to others that my lower back pains were becoming increasingly unbearable. Robert Zablockis and one of the deputies strongly recommended that I be placed into the waiting ambulance to be transported to a local hospital for treatment and further evaluation, which I agreed to comply with. Once it dawned on me that I was the one being loaded into the back of the ambulance instead of Krause, I knew within my spirit that Michael Krause, Jr. was likely not going to make it.

After being transported to the hospital by ambulance, and staying there for several hours to receive treatment, I was ultimately discharged to go home, after receiving a prescription of medication to control any swelling in my lower back muscles. Being in the emergency room experiencing excruciating lower back pains was only one aspect of the injuries that I sustained that night. The other injuries that I sustained as a result of enduring this horrific ordeal was the psychological trauma of having to use deadly force to defend my life again, as well as the psychological and emotional trauma of learning that the man I attempted to arrest for assault with a deadly weapon had subsequently lost his life. In all honesty and transparency, that did not sit well with me back then, and it still bothers me today.

This brings me to the next inflammatory newspaper article, published in the Inland Valley Daily Bulletin, 2004, and written by Rod Leveque under the heading

Security Guard Trial Heading to Jury: Paramedic refutes Defendant's Story.

Once again, this article introduced two more White people who got on the stand to testify against me. Are you starting to see a common theme in all of the people who testified against me? Every person who lied on me and gave false information to the sheriff's department, the district attorney's office, and to Jeff Weaver, the attorney representing the Krause family, were all White! The first mistake that the paramedic and the nurse made, was that they lied under oath about me being injured at all. The emergency room doctor who treated me that night *confirmed* that I had injuries to my lower back, my arm, and my legs, consistent with my account of the events that led up to the fatal shooting.

The second mistake they made was offering testimony about my injuries as if they were there to witness everything that happened at the Sycamore Springs Apartments. My attorney had a field day discrediting them on the witness stand, and he saw right through their fabricated testimony. In part, the article written by Leveque stated,

> "A paramedic and a nurse who treated Wroe that night also testified, saying Wroe displayed no visible signs of injury. Wroe's attorney, Donald Calabria, asked Judge John Bunnett to declare a mistrial at the conclusion of testimony Tuesday afternoon, arguing that the judge unfairly limited the

defense attorney's questioning of several witnesses, including Wroe. Bunnett curtly denied the motion."

From the time I was initially arrested, to the time I was acquitted of murder, the entire prosecution team used the local newspapers as a public platform to control *their* narrative, maliciously suggesting that I was never injured by Krause's pickup truck. They maliciously accused me of lying about my injuries. Who in the world could ever fake getting struck by a pickup truck by a person who knew he was about to go to jail for using his truck as a deadly weapon? That is beyond absurd, but this is typical behavior of privileged White people! To further shed light on how baseless their lies were, it is important that the public knows that I was getting workers' compensation payments from January 22, 2004 to September 25, 2006. If all of those staff writers for the newspaper could reach all the way back into my past to talk about the fact that I was signed to Capitol Records back in 1992, I can't help but wonder why they never published the fact that I had been granted a workers' compensation award, as a result of being injured by Michael Krause, Jr., after he twice struck me with his truck!

They all lied on me from start to finish, and this book is evidence of all of their collective lies, which can no longer be defended now that the truth has been published for everyone to see and research for themselves! If my injuries that night were so minor and so miniscule, the Workers' Compensation Department of Insurance could have easily rejected my claim, but they didn't!

Now, let's fast forward to yet another hostile newspaper article plastered all over the front page of the Inland Valley Daily Bulletin newspaper on September 24, 2004, written by Rod Leveque and Jason Newell, under the heading

Guard Acquitted of Murder: Jurors Deadlock on Lesser Count.

In cases such as mine, which can potentially expose defendants to a considerable amount of prison time, defense attorneys do not typically allow their clients to take the stand and testify on their own behalf. However, my attorney, Donald J. Calabria, couldn't wait to put me on the stand, because he knew that my integrity, my honesty, my professionalism, and my ability to clearly articulate the facts of what truly happened on the evening of January 1, 2004 would all speak volumes to the jury. In the following highlights of this particular newspaper article, you will see concrete evidence of my innocence by never-before-heard statements of explanation that I will offer to help you better understand the dynamics of what the quotes in the article are saying.

The first thing that I feel is most important to share from the article truly reflects my state of mind after the verdict in my murder trial was announced. At the very moment that the court clerk began reading the verdict, I sat quietly next to my attorney, whispering Psalm 23:4 under my breath, "Yea, though I walk through the valley of the shadow of death, I will fear no evil: for thou art with me; thy rod and thy staff they comfort me." When I got to the end of the scripture, the court clerk was still reading the verdict, so I started to repeat the scripture again from the beginning. The second time around, by the time I got to, "I will fear no evil," it was at that very moment when I heard the court clerk say, "Not guilty!"

The emotions I had been holding inside of me had finally erupted. The article explained,

> "Dameon Wroe launched his hands into the air and shouted, 'Thank you, Jesus!' as a court clerk read the not guilty verdict. He then clasped his hands in prayer, sobbed wildly and collapsed into the arms of his attorney."

This was the same emotion that I experienced on the night of the shooting, at the very moment I realized why I was the one being loaded into the ambulance instead of Michael Krause, Jr. It was an extremely emotional moment for me that I just could not control. Just as I was happy that I escaped death the night that Krause tried to run me over with his truck, I was just as happy that I had escaped life in prison for simply defending myself. Anyone who truly knows me, knows that I am a giver, not a taker. I am a nurturer and lover of life, not a *taker* of life. I am an asset to my community, not a liability.

There were several reasons why I was so emotional after the not guilty verdict was announced. When I initially turned myself in, and appeared in court for my arraignment, I had a public defender, most commonly known as a *public pretender*. I did not like the fact that I had a court-appointed attorney because I felt like the attorney that was appointed to represent me was someone who may have been friends with the Krause family and, if that would have been the case, a guilty verdict would have been the only thing I had to look forward to—I couldn't afford to take that chance.

Prior to turning myself in, I had given my sister Donald Calabria's phone number, and admonished her and my family to keep trying to contact him, and to tell him that I needed him more than ever! A few weeks had passed and I had not heard back from my family to find out if they were ever able to reach Mr. Calabria. Not knowing if he was ever going to find me in time for my trial intensified my anxiety beyond measure—I was really starting to get worried, because I didn't want to end up in prison for something that I did not do. On the day I entered the courtroom to appear for my preliminary hearing, I was seated in the jury box with several other inmates, waiting for our case to be called.

While I was waiting for my public defender to come over and talk to me, I noticed the Krause family sitting out in the audience of the courtroom. The reason I was sure it was the Krause family is because I locked eyes with Michael Krause's father, and he was looking at me with a very evil, hostile look on his eyes. He was so angry, I literally watched his face turn red. When he and his family are finally able to sit down with Scott Martinez to get the *real* story about what was being said inside of Krause's truck before he tried to run me over for a second time, I hope he gives Scott Martinez that same hostile look that he gave me in the courtroom, because Scott Martinez is the one who deserves it, not me.

It is my firm belief that, if Scott Martinez was to ever have a come to Jesus moment in his heart, and tell the Krause family EXACTLY what he and Michael Krause, Jr. were discussing while I was attempting to take Michael into custody at gunpoint, he would have no other choice but to tell the truth, because his body language in that moment is not going to allow him to lie and remain believable! Just before my case was called that day, I saw the back doors of the courtroom open up. When the doors opened up, a ray of bright sunlight from outside in the hallway shined into the courtroom's double doors, and slightly obstructed my vision because of the bright glare. The light was so bright that I couldn't see the actual people who were walking in. However, when the courtroom doors had shut, I was able to see a tall, well-dressed, distinguished White man walk into the courtroom as if he had an intentional purpose... it was Donald J. Calabria. This was a major sign that God wasn't about to let me go through with a murder trial without Him sending one of His best angels to represent me and fight for me! My heart was overwhelmed with joy and gratitude.

When I saw that it was Donald Calabria walking into the courtroom, tears of joy and relief began falling down my face uncontrollably. After Mr. Calabria checked in with the court, he came directly over to me and sat next to me to tell me that my family had contacted him and retained his services to represent me at my murder trial. After the jury found me not guilty of murder, my attorney gave a statement to the Inland Valley Daily Bulletin stating,

> "This was a very big win. He never wanted (the shooting) to happen. He was just doing his job."

This statement by my attorney was very accurate. Just because it took me pulling my gun out in order to take Krause into custody does not mean that I *wanted* to use it, but Krause's continued hostility and aggression towards me left me no other choice but to match his level of aggression with that same energy.

The newspaper article goes on to describe how one particular female juror felt about the entire case.

> "A female juror, who also declined to give her name, said she voted not guilty on both counts because she felt the case against Wroe was simply weak."

The juror's exact statement to reporters was,

> "I feel the prosecution didn't prove it beyond a reasonable doubt."

This juror was truly not alone, because my family and I also felt that the prosecutor did not prove his case beyond a reasonable doubt. In all honesty, there was one particular point in the trial where God showed me in my spirit that I was definitely going to be found not guilty!

Now, keep in mind, this was a felony murder trial which could have landed me in prison for 50 years to life. As I was being questioned on the stand by Deputy District Attorney Jeremy Carrasco, he asked me a question that had zero impact on the actual murder trial. It was one of the stupidest questions any district attorney could have asked someone in my situation, but I'm grateful that he asked it. He asked me directly, something to the effect of, "Is it true that, when you first noticed Michael Krause come onto the property and try to enter the main gate, you were illegally parked in a handicapped parking space?" I immediately responded, "Yes."

He went on to question me, asking me something to the effect of, "And while you were illegally parked in that handicapped parking space, isn't it true that you were backed in rather than parked head in?" I'm not sure if the jury saw me or picked up on my facial expression or not but, when he asked me all those questions about being illegally parked in a handicapped parking space, I thought to myself, "What in the world does being illegally parked in a handicapped parking spot have to do with a motorist getting shot and killed for trying to run someone over?" When he asked me those questions, it gave me more of a confirmation that his case against me was incredibly weak. The newspaper goes on to make two very controversial and misleading statements to the public by saying,

> "Krause's family, which attended every day of the week-long trial in West Valley Superior Court, did not attend the reading of the verdict. They instead remained in the District Attorney's Office awaiting word of the jury's decision."

Imagine that! They attended every single day of the week-long trial, yet they weren't even in the actual courtroom for the official reading of the verdict? Do you want to know the truth about *why* they were not in the actual courtroom for the reading of the verdict? The reason they weren't in the courtroom for the reading of the verdict is because, since they appeared to be so privileged, and had obvious allies working within the San Bernadino County Superior Court system, they had already been made aware of the jury's decision to acquit me, long before the official verdict was even read in the courtroom. They were not in the courtroom when the verdict was read—they already knew the verdict was going to be not guilty!

See what privilege can get you? Allegedly! Sometime after my murder trial was over, and I was found not guilty, it was brought to my attention by some of my supporters that the Krause family could be out in the hallway of the courthouse, talking amongst each other, trying to convince each other that I was coached to say the things that I said on the stand when I testified on my own behalf. After everything they had already took me through, this was no shock to me. Insinuating that I was not smart enough to testify for myself, unless I was coached on what to say is utter ridiculous but, then again, this is what so many White people think about Black people and other people of color. They think they are better than us. They think they are superior to us. They think they are much smarter than us. They think that we do not deserve access to the finer things in life that they themselves often have or enjoy. They think they are more articulate and intellectual than we are. In my personal opinion, I believe what White America fears most is an educated, confident, articulate, fearless Black man!

These next few quotes taken from the same newspaper article are where the validity of my innocence gets ten times stronger, and further proves that Krause's family, their civil attorney, Jeff Weaver, and the entire San Bernadino County District Attorney's Office lied their way through my entire trial, which is truthfully another reason I was ultimately found not guilty, including the jurors being deadlocked 7 to 5, also in favor of acquitting me of the manslaughter charge. All of the aforementioned individuals blatantly insulted the intelligence of the jury, and even the jurors saw right through their lies!

While seizing his opportunity to chime in about the Krause family's reaction to the not guilty verdict, their civil attorney, Jeff Weaver, gave quite a theatrical statement to reporters by saying,

> "They were absolutely stunned during the testimony of Mr. Wroe by his lack of remorse There was no crime committed by their son. Their son is dead, and for what? Clearly this is at least a manslaughter."

I first would like to address the lie that Jeff Weaver told when he so bravely claimed that Michael Krause, Jr. had committed no crime. That statement is a factual lie because, the last time I checked, striking someone with a motor vehicle in a violent, threatening manner is a violation of California Penal Code 245 (a)(1), which is legally defined and classified as a felonious crime.

Due to the fact that I sustained injuries as a result of being struck by Michael Krause's pickup truck, coupled with the fact that Krause's conduct during our encounter was reckless and hostile, he would have wholeheartedly been arrested for a felony, had he let me take him into custody. Furthermore, Krause's passenger, Scott Martinez, would have also been arrested for illegal possession of drug paraphernalia, as described in California Health & Safety Code 11364(a). Keep in mind, although marijuana is *now* legal in California, it was not legal back in 2004. For this reason, Scott Martinez was given immunity for any charges related to 11364(a) HS, in exchange for him testifying against me at my murder trial. I'm pretty sure the Krause family and the prosecutor had no fathomable idea that the testimony of Scott Martinez would help my defense rather than harm it. God don't like ugly, and He protects His children.

So, as the world can clearly see now, I should have _never_ been arrested for murder, nor for manslaughter! Whether or not they all will ever choose to admit it, I was never arrested because I had broken the law in any way, I was arrested in retaliation for Michael Krause, Jr. losing his life, even though Michael Krause, Jr. and Scott Martinez had caused the very things that contributed to Krause being fatally injured. I was never arrested because I had broken the law, I was arrested because the friends and family members of Michael Krause, Jr. were heart-broken that he passed away, and they all wanted *me* to pay for it. Proof of this statement is also found contained within the same newspaper article, as the article clearly proclaims,

> "Jeff Weaver, the attorney representing the family, said the Krauses were deeply distraught by the jury's decision to acquit Wroe of murder. He said the family intends to press the District Attorney's Office to pursue the manslaughter case against Wroe." Need I say more?

Again, my murder case was never about right versus wrong, it was *always* about a not-so-wealthy Black man who shot and killed a White man who came from a wealthy family, in a predominantly white community were Blacks are historically not welcomed or accepted by the majority in the community. I want to be extremely clear... what happened to Michael Krause, Jr. was absolutely terrible. Even though he assaulted me, using his pickup truck as a weapon against me, I was confident in knowing that, with my training and experience, I could have easily controlled the situation and safely took Michael Krause, Jr. into custody on my own, but I could not overpower Krause's allegiance to listening to whatever Scott Martinez was telling him to do in the cabin of that truck, prior to the shooting taking place.

On the day that Michael Krause, Jr. lost his life, I was at work earning a living for myself and for the family that I was in the process of building. I was doing what I was supposed to be doing, and I was earning an honest living by working two jobs to take care of myself and my responsibilities. I did not spend my day that day by calling up drug dealers to set up drug deals, I was being a productive member of society. I was not driving around Rancho Cucamonga smoking marijuana and getting high, I was driving around my place of business and earning a respectable paycheck. My heart truly goes out to the Krause family for the loss of their adult son, but it is unreasonable for them to ever expect me to *show* or even *feel* remorse for defending myself against a legitimate attack that their son launched against me. That is just a very selfish way to look at the situation, because it suggests that their son's life was more important than mine, and that is an unreasonable way of thinking.

Even though I had a fully loaded magazine of 16 rounds of ammunition at the time I fired my weapon, to keep from getting ran over, I only fired a total of four rounds. In my unbiased opinion, and under the circumstances, I believe I showed remarkable restraint, and only fired the number of rounds necessary to overcome the threat being inflicted upon me. The lengthy article also made mention of the fact that I had just as many supporters in the courtroom as the Krause family, if not more. The article stated,

> "Wroe's family huddled in prayer outside the courtroom in the hour leading up to the verdict Thursday and exploded with relief when the decision was announced inside."

The newspaper article concluded with an additional statement from my attorney, Donald Calabria, who empathetically said,

> "I think they should let it go. It's time to move on. Everybody has been through enough in this case."

After the not guilty verdict was reached, my bail should have been lowered but, for reasons I may never know the truth about, the judge wouldn't do it. As I have already mentioned on previous pages, there was an allegation that the judge who presided over my murder trial, Judge John Bunnett, was somehow connected to the Krause family, possibly a long-time family friend or possibly a family member. The reason I have always believed this allegation to be credible is because of the fact that, while I was in jail for the murder charge, my bail was $1,000,000.00. However, when I was acquitted of murder, the only charge remaining for me to fight was the manslaughter charge, therefore, my bail should have been lowered to only $125,000.00. Even though I was found not guilty of murder, the judge refused to lower my bail, so I had to unjustly remain in custody with the $1,000,000.00 bond still hanging over my head for no logical reason, other than the possibility that he had done that as a favor to the privileged Krause family.

If the allegations regarding Judge John Bunnett are ever found to be true, I think he should still be investigated for even presiding over my murder trial at all. If the allegations against him are ever found to be true or credible in any form or fashion, it should be used as evidence to confirm that Judge John Bunnett should have recused himself and granted my attorney and I a change of venue, so that my case could be heard in a totally different court jurisdiction. Furthermore, if the allegations against Judge Bunnett are ever found to be factual, it further substantiates the fact that my attorney's motion to declare a mistrial should have in fact been granted.

In the very last section of the aforementioned newspaper article, even the reporters seem to support the allegations against the judge by publishing,

> "Calabria asked Judge John Bunnett to consider reducing Wroe's bail in light of the acquittal, but the judge refused to hear the request."

If that's not a red flag for judicial corruption and/or misconduct, I don't know what is! Hopefully, by now, you can see why I decided to name this chapter *Railroaded*. If you thought that the Inland Valley Daily Bulletin was done slandering my name, and making me seem like a monster to the community, then think again.

The malicious and unjust prosecution against me relentlessly continued. The Inland Valley Daily Bulletin published another newspaper article on October 6, 2004 under the heading

DA Files to Retry Guard on Manslaughter Charge.

Once again, this article was also written by Rod Leveque. I wonder how much money the Krause family paid him, under the table, to continue writing these baseless articles about my case! For the purposes of contrast and comparison, there were two sections of the article that would jump off of the page at anyone with half a brain. Let's start with the first part of the article that made the most sense, offered by my esteemed attorney.

> "Wroe's attorney, Donald Calabria, called for the District Attorney's Office to drop the case and release Wroe from jail at the conclusion of the first trial. He has said Wroe will again win in a retrial, and he suggested that a decision to pursue the case by the District Attorney's Office is a waste of taxpayer money."

It is my unbiased opinion that my attorney was factually correct in his statement, and in the next chapter I'm going to give you factual information to support both of our statements. In the meantime, here's the second part of the article, offered by the delusional prosecutor that made no good sense at all.

> "Carrasco said he did not believe the strategies of either side would vary drastically during the second trial. From both sides, the evidence and the arguments will probably be the same. The only difference will be the jury."

So, as my attorney had already stated, pursuing the case any further would be a waste of taxpayer money. If the jury had already acquitted me of the biggest charge, murder, and deadlocked 7 to 5 in favor of acquittal on the lesser charge of manslaughter, then why waste more taxpayer dollars on a second trial that would have also been likely to end in acquittal? In the next chapter, you will learn of a very powerful quote that came directly from the mouth of a San Bernadino County Sheriff's Department deputy who worked at the West Valley Detention Center where I was jailed for the duration of my trial. His words are just even more evidence of the fact that I **never** should have been arrested—I should have **never** been prosecuted for defending myself!

The final part of this article that I want to shed a suspect light on is regarding yet another mention of the Krause family's attorney, Jeff Weaver. The newspaper article stated,

> "Jeff Weaver, the attorney representing the Krause family, said Tuesday that the family was pleased by the district attorney's decision to retry the case."

Of course Jeff Weaver was pleased by the district attorney's decision to retry me for another crime that I was not guilty of committing—he was likely keeping his eyes on *his* cut of the money he would potentially be getting from a civil lawsuit. Why else would every other newspaper article mentioning his name need to refer to him as *the attorney representing the Krause family?*

In fact, while this book was under construction, I learned through a random internet search that Jeff Weaver and his law firm were instrumental in suing my former employer, Southwest District Patrol, and others, and getting the Krause family a wrongful death judgement award of $6,018,912.46. If you want to research or read the full article for yourself, that proves the Krause family received this exact amount, go to the Google search engine and type in *Krause v. Western Heritage Ins. Co.* and you can reach your own conclusions about everything that I've said in this book so far, that makes more than enough sense to any rational-thinking person—it's not rocket science.

I highly recommend that you Google it as soon as possible, before the Krause family, or *the attorney representing the Krause family*, pays to have it taken off the internet. Someone in their circle of friends or family appear to be well-versed in having family secrets taken off of the internet, as I will soon give you more facts that you can research using the Google search engine as well! It gets even better. Stay with me… I'm barely scratching the surface in exposing my truths.

When I was finally released from jail, I knew that, one day, I would write a book explaining all of the terrible things that happened to me as a result of being incarcerated after the death of Michael Krause, Jr., but I didn't know exactly when I would have the presence of mind or the psychological strength to sit down and start writing. After Krause's death, I would periodically Google his full name and, when I did, at least one or two pages of information came up in the search results, showing images of him and that fact that he was directly related to the many newspaper articles that had been written about *me*. Seeing that information on the internet made me feel a little bit better about information about *me* being on the internet too.

I was at least content with the fact that it wasn't just articles about me accessible for the public to see. About a year or two after I had successfully completed my probation, I learned that there were companies offering reputation protection services to the public. As I learned more about a few of these companies, I learned that, for a fee, people could pay these companies money to get negative content about them taken out of internet searches so that members of the public would not see anything negative or damaging associated with a name search. Initially, I thought about doing it, but there was something powerful that stopped me from considering it any further.

At some point, when I continued to randomly look up Michael Krause, Jr. on the internet, I noticed that the images and information that was once showing up in the search results was suddenly and mysteriously no longer showing up… yet information about *me* was showing up every time I would do a Google search of my own name. How could this be? How is it that one minute Michael Krause, Jr. was showing up in every search and, all of a sudden, only several years later, there appeared to be no trace of him any longer in subsequent internet search results? How was that possible?

Then it came to me… someone in his family or circle of friends probably paid money to have any negative content about him removed from the internet to protect his image and his reputation so that it would not reflect negatively upon his family. Still to date, there is no information that shows up about Krause in a Google search, yet when a search is done under my name, quite a bit information still comes up. It took me a long time to finally realize that this was actually a good thing, rather than something negative. You see, I purposely did not try to pay to have information about me or my 2004 criminal case removed. I knew that eventually, when I was in the right head-space to write my book, I was going to need my story to still be on the internet so that everyone else around the world could see that Michael Krause's search results were suddenly and mysteriously no longer showing up if you were to Google his name. If I would have paid money all those years ago, to have information about my case removed, I would have felt like I was hiding something from the public about what really happened that night.

    I have always believed that a person who has nothing to hide doesn't have to worry about paying money to secretly dispose of information that pertains to something that they went through. Now that I have finally come forward to tell my story, readers would have nothing to compare my story against if I would have also paid money to remove my information from the internet years ago, prior to writing this book. Since it involved the death of a young adult, deep down in my soul, I didn't think anyone would ever believe my story of innocence if I were to make an attempt to hide any details about what happened on the night of January 1, 2004. I have never had anything to hide from anyone!

    When I first learned that sheriff's department officials had been granted a warrant for my arrest, I didn't run and hide, I willfully turned myself in because I knew that I had done nothing wrong. When I turned myself in, I was scared, I was worried about my future, I honestly had no clue as to why I was even being arrested for murder. I knew that my actions that night were only a result of my training, and legitimately being in fear of my life. I knew that a fabricated case had been built around make-believe allegations that were being construed as a factual basis to try to get me convicted of murder, but God had a different plan for my life.

When I turned myself in, I was brought to the San Bernadino County Sheriff's Station by my late godfather, who was a retired Chief of Police, as well as a family friend who had known me since I was 12 years old, and was a sworn police captain with the Los Angeles Police Department. Guilty people do not turn themselves in by bringing the police with them when they surrender to even more police. Never at any time did I take *any* joy in knowing that Michael Krause, Jr. had died as a result of being shot... never! In fact, of all the investigators with the sheriff's department, and attorneys from the prosecution team, the only person to ever publicly speak to my state of mind in a favorable way was Sergeant Gerrit Tesselaar of the San Bernadino County Sheriff's Department Detective Bureau. In the aforementioned newspaper article in the Inland Valley Daily Bulletin, published on February 19, 2004, Sgt. Tesselaar said,

> "He's a very cordial young man, very cooperative. You could tell that he was upset, but he's dealing with it the best he can."

Even today, I hold a very strong level of gratitude to the detectives that investigated my shooting and determined it to be justifiable and in self-defense. No one else walking the face of this earth has the right to tell me that I was not in fear of my life! The hostile confrontation that I had with Michael Krause, Jr. more than twenty years ago was not my first rodeo—I know what imminent danger looks like when I see it. I did not get dressed for work that night hoping or expecting to shoot anyone—it was the absolute furthest thing from my mind. Next up... another front-page newspaper article written by none other than Rod Leveque.

On March 5, 2004 the Inland Valley Daily Bulletin published another newspaper article under the heading

Guard Wroe Weighs Plea Agreement: Judge Tells Him it's an Outstanding Deal.

Once I had learned that the San Bernadino County District Attorney's Office wanted to move forward with taking me to trial on the manslaughter charge, I stopped thinking about myself and thought more about what my family wanted me to do. By this time, it was apparent to everyone who came to court to support me that the prosecutor and the Krause family were doing everything they could possibly do to railroad me straight into a life sentence... I felt it deep down in my spirit!

When the judge invited my attorney and I to come back to his chambers with him to discuss the probabilities of what a new trial could bring, I knew that short meeting in the judge's chambers was a warning to me—it just didn't feel right. While we were back in the judge's chambers, he was just too overly cordial and friendly with me, and it didn't feel genuine whatsoever... it felt like I was being baited. Just listen at the chilling tone of Rod Leveque's article, which stated,

> "Prosecutors vowed to retry him on the lesser charges. Wroe faces more than 20 years in prison as currently charged. But prosecutors could enhance the charges before a second trial so that Wroe would again face life in prison if convicted. With that as leverage, prosecutors extended the plea bargain offer to Wroe on Friday in West Valley Superior Court. It would bring an immediate end to his criminal case."

This was a set-up if I ever saw one coming! If that portion of the article wasn't chilling enough for you, consider this one. The article went on to state,

> "Neither prosecutors nor Wroe's public defender would disclose the terms of the offer, but Judge Gerard Brown told Wroe it is an 'outstanding deal.'"

Imagine that—an *outstanding* deal. It was obviously an outstanding deal for Judge Brown, because Judge Brown wasn't the one who was going to be the one ending up with an undeserved felony on his record. Again, I felt like the only reason this judge was trying so hard to encourage me to take this deal was two-fold. If I were to take a plea deal to an *involuntary* manslaughter charge, that conviction would give the Krause family better leverage in their wrongful death civil case that I already knew they were going to file. When the family of a deceased person remains in denial about the fact that their loved one caused their own demise, that denial will eventually fuel a wrongful death lawsuit to make others look responsible for the fact that their loved one died.

In my heart of hearts, I did not want to take a plea deal whatsoever! However, realizing that I was being set up to get railroaded, I reluctantly agreed to the plea deal because I could not afford to hire Donald Calabria to fight a brand new trial for me, and I was smart enough to realize that it was not a good idea to go through with another trial with a public defender *pretending* to care about winning my manslaughter case. In reality, if I would have gone to trial and been found guilty of voluntary manslaughter, I would have been sent to prison, still an innocent man. In taking the plea deal of no contest to involuntary manslaughter, I would serve no additional jail time, I would be given credit for time served, I would be on probation for three years and, the best part, I would be released from jail and allowed to go home to be with my family where I had always belonged. I did whatever I had to do in order to not be taken back to that horrific jail cell; it was truly hell on earth! The final statement of the article was made by Michael Krause, Sr. He stated, **"I just want him to admit he killed my son."**

As if I had not been publicly humiliated enough, after reluctantly signing my booby-trapped plea agreement,

I had to sit there in court, in front of what felt like *all* of Rancho Cucamonga, and listen to victim impact statements from the family of the man who tried to run me over and take me away from *my* family on January 1, 2004. Of all the good things that I stand for, it made me extremely angry to have to sit there in court and listen to people who never knew anything about me, say so many negative and unfounded things about my character. How were they able to talk about my character if they knew nothing about me?

For more than twenty years, I have always asked myself, "Would they have felt any better if the person who shot their son was White? Would they have felt any better if it was an actual police officer who shot their son, rather than a Black security guard?" In no way is it my intent nor desire to make fun of their family's painful loss of their loved one but, just being transparent, these are the real questions that have plagued me for many, many years. It's a sad reality of the racial conflicts that continue to happen every day in our broken society. I mean, what really has to happen for the Krause family to know that their loved one caused his own death, because of his hostile, belligerent, *my mommy and daddy will bail me out of trouble* behavior?

At some point in time, a few of my designated supporters were able to get up on the witness stand in court and speak on my behalf as character witnesses. One of those character witnesses was a very, very close friend of mine who was a Deputy Sheriff with the Los Angeles County Sheriff's Department. When Deputy Gee took the stand, he was initially questioned by my attorney, Donald Calabria. After my attorney had completed his line of questioning, Deputy District Attorney Jeremy Carrasco got a chance to question Deputy Gee as well, and he was *extra* salty towards Deputy Gee, in my opinion. Simply relying on my memory, I do not recall the exact question that Jeremy Carrasco asked Deputy Gee, but Deputy Gee's answer was far more than epic!

In response to the district attorney's question, Deputy Gee immediately saw right through the baited line of questioning and destroyed Carrasco's plan, by saying something to the effect of, "No, but he also shouldn't be persecuted for defending himself just because he's not a police officer!!" As Deputy Gee was just about to finish his sentence, Carrasco began to object to what Deputy Gee was saying, but it was already too late! Deputy Gee continued to blatantly disregard the objection and kept on talking until what he had to say had been heard! I was beyond honored that this highly respected deputy sheriff would go to bat for me like that, and I owe him an eternal debt of gratitude for what he did for me in that courtroom. I was on the edge of my seat when Jeremy Carrasco started questioning Deputy Gee, because I knew what type of man Deputy Gee was, and I looked up to him just as much as he looked up to me, so I already knew that he was going to give the district attorney a run for the money! Deputy Gee didn't care if the objection was going to be overruled or sustained, he didn't stop standing up for me on that witness stand until he was good and ready to stop talking. Deputy Gee was, and still is, a class act!

Just as it apparently angered the Krause family that I appeared to show no remorse for the death of their son who tried to run me over with his pickup truck, it has infuriated me for more than two decades that the Krause family has never showed ANY empathy towards me or *my* family for what their son did to ME! It infuriated me to no end that their high and mighty attitudes prevented them from taking ownership of the fact that their son nearly killed a Black man who was just doing his job. From 2004 to the date of this publication, they have always maintained their belief that their son did absolutely nothing wrong.

They have believed that falsehood for so many years now, I'm sure it would be psychologically impossible for them to *now* admit that their son committed a felony when he hit me with his pickup truck, caused the injuries that I sustained, and then unlawfully fled the scene of an assault with a deadly weapon. In my opinion, they have always given me the impression that they are the type of people who are too good to ever admit that they themselves, nor their kids, EVER do anything wrong.

Since I am also a father, I have oftentimes tried to place myself in the shoes of Krause's parents. I cannot even pretend to know what their pain has been like since the night this all happened, but I am not the monster that all of them painted me to be. Anyone who truly knows me knows that I am a loving, compassionate person. I am a loyal friend and a forgiving person. I can candidly say that I know what it's like to have to bury someone you love. I stand in unwavering agreement with anyone who can mutually agree that it is a parent's worst nightmare to have to even fathom the idea of having to bury their child, regardless of their age. I get it!

As much as it still disturbs me that Michael Krause, Jr. lost his life, I cannot go back in time and change what happened that night, nor can I ever admit to *killing* Michael Krause, because he did not afford me the chance to bring our situation to a peaceful resolve. To say that I am responsible for his death is like insinuating that I am also responsible for him getting high. He made that decision all by himself. No matter how sad his loss is, the State of California recognized him as a lawful adult who was responsible for his own actions. However, I do acknowledge the family's grief, as I know within my heart that they miss their son dearly and, despite the tone of this book in some places, I am extremely sorry for their loss. It is not the fault of his friends and family members that he got high on illegal marijuana that night. If he and Scott Martinez were not high on marijuana that night, I am persuaded to believe that they would have made much healthier decisions that would have afforded Michael Krause, Jr. to still be alive today.

Since my encounter with Krause back in 2004, I myself have suffered the loss of so many people I cared for very deeply, so I sincerely understand the dynamics of missing a loved one beyond expression or comprehension. After the deadly encounter I experienced at the Sycamore Springs Apartments, more than 20 years ago, I completely lost my desire to ever pursue my childhood dream of becoming a law enforcement officer because, in that career field, I never want to be faced with the possibility of ever having to use deadly force upon another person ever again, justifiable or not. It's just not worth the mental and psychological torture of always having triggers that take me back to that night to re-live everything all over again. Although I do not personally feel or expect that the Krause family will ever forgive me, I hope that, one of these days, they will find it in their hearts to do so, as God continues to heal their emotional and spiritual wounds, and hopefully make them whole again in whatever way He sees fit.

I never thought or imagined that I would ever admit this, but the death of Michael Krause, Jr. has drastically changed my life, but in a positive way. Even though he made some poor choices that contributed to his demise, it is humanly impossible for me to get the image of his face out of my mind. I see him every day in my mind's eye, and I often wonder what he would be doing with himself today if he would have chosen not to try to run me over with his pickup truck. I feel like he would be doing something more rewarding with his life if he were here today, rather than getting high off weed or any other kind of drugs. I'd like to think that he would have seen my encounter with him as a wake-up call to straighten his life up and maybe be getting himself into position to start a family and get serious about a career field that he enjoyed or was passionate about. I see him in my mind sometimes out on the ocean, deep sea fishing with friends and partying on the beach with his family, and staying out of trouble.

Oftentimes I wonder if I will ever be able to mentally unsee the aftermath that happened that night, but there's always a reminder. There were absolutely no winners that came out of the unfortunate incident that we all experienced, I just hope and pray that God will heal the hearts of all parties involved so that we can all find a way to get over our hurt, and continue moving on with our lives the best possible way that we can, realizing that some days will be better than others. Just to be clear and transparent, I have to reasonably assume that the Krause family still thinks that I should be doing life in prison for the death of their son. In actuality, we are *all* serving a life sentence in the prison of our thoughts and our emotions, because we were *all* affected by the loss of a human life, which was in no way intentional.

In all the many years of security and public safety training I've had, dating back to 1989, there is no training in the world that teaches security officers nor police officers how to live with the aftermath and the devastation of having to use deadly force. At the end of my manslaughter case, and upon my official release from custody, my former employer advised me of a very cruel and disturbing statement that he allegedly heard from Jeremy Carrasco, the DA who unfairly prosecuted me. Out in the hallway of the courthouse, I was told that Jeremy Carrasco was heard saying, "I can justify a police officer taking a life… but not a security guard." Again, based on the way I was treated by the entire prosecution team, I personally believe that allegation to be very credible.

Any district attorney who makes a statement such as that, is basically asserting that a police officer's life is far more valuable than that of a normal civilian. Hearing that statement repeated to me made me feel like Jeremy Carrasco did not value MY LIFE the way he obviously valued the life of police officers. I sincerely hope that, after reading this book, society will stop seeing security officers as uneducated, low-life, sub-human rent-a-cops who don't know what they're doing. That is a flagrant and prejudicial stereotype that, moving forward, MUST continue to be proven wrong in our society.

When you encounter a security officer while in the performance of their duties, you have no real idea about what they know (as far as their training, powers of arrest, etc.). You don't know what adverse situations they've been through while interacting with the general public. You don't know what they are capable of, in the event that you try to challenge them, intimidate them, or put their lives in danger. Based on previous dangerous situations they may have been involved in, you have no real idea about what *their* threshold for fear may be if they feel like their life is ever in danger.

If you are a person who hates the police, security officers, or anyone else who operates in a position of authority, that hate you hold in your heart can easily cause you to fly off the handle one of these days with a police officer or a security officer in the performance of their duties. That same hate towards people in authority can get you severely hurt, and possibly killed, if you do not learn how to manage your temper or channel your anger in a more positive direction. If you ever find yourself in a situation where a police officer or a security officer is yelling commands at you, telling you to get face down on the ground… put your hands up… throw your keys out of the car… get down on your knees and cross your ankles, or even stop resisting, I am personally begging you to please just listen to those reasonable and/or lawful commands to the letter, and **just comply** without resisting. Just comply… please! Remaining non-compliant is not worth risking your life… it's just not!!

What people don't understand is, when police or security officers find it necessary to be giving these types of commands to an individual, incidental to arrest or to being detained, it is *not* a laughing matter—it's not a game! I don't care how wrong you feel like the police officer or security officer is, please just do what they're asking you to do! If you decide to physically resist a police officer, or otherwise decide that you do not want to comply with their orders, then you are potentially placing yourself in grave danger. If you should ever happen to encounter a security officer that is detaining you at gunpoint, please just listen and be compliant so that you do not bring any unnecessary injury or harm upon yourself. People need to understand that remaining compliant ensures the safety of everyone involved.

Especially when dealing with police, or any other law enforcement officer, do not try to fight them on the streets, fight them in court if you don't agree with a ticket you got, or if you want to complain about how they mistreated you while in the performance of their civil duties. If you try to fight them on *their* turf, you're going to lose every time. Even if you think you're being unfairly treated by a security officer, compliance almost always ensures your safety. After what I've been through during my past employment in the private security industry, I personally don't want to see anyone else get unnecessarily hurt, injured or killed. If you remain calm and level-headed, you can always pursue having your day in court to argue the wrongs that may have been done to you. Either way, you live to see another day! As a society, we must get it through our heads that no one is above the law. It doesn't matter if you come from a wealthy family or a family who is from the lower class, order must be maintained in our communities... it's non-negotiable.

The last newspaper article I'd like to share in this chapter has a few particular sections that I'd like to draw your attention to. This Inland Valley Daily Bulletin publication was published on November 12, 2004 under the heading

> Slain Man's Family Sues Guard, Others: Wrongful Death Alleged in 19-year-old's Shooting.

The one-sided article starts off by saying,

> "Relatives of 19-year-old Michael Krause Jr. allege the guard, Dameon Wroe, should not have been patrolling the Rancho Cucamonga apartments with a gun on Jan. 1. They claim the deadly force Wroe used to subdue Krause during an altercation that night was excessive, unwarranted and reckless."

Immediately following these statements, Jeff Weaver, *the attorney representing the Krause family,* added his two cents again by stating,

> "I'm really left to wonder what a guard at a fairly upscale apartment complex is doing walking around at night with a gun. Somebody is dead and that didn't have to happen."

Why are some people in our society so perplexed and bewildered by the fact that security officers carry guns? Like, what are security guards supposed to carry? Should I have had a fully loaded squirt gun that night instead of a 9mm handgun? I don't know about you, but when I consider this statement made by Jeff Weaver, I feel like he honestly wanted to say, "What was this *Black man* doing in an upscale, White neighborhood in the first place?" As you can tell by the tone of that statement, that's exactly what he wanted to say! Of all the residents that I encountered at the Sycamore Springs Apartments back in 2004, while I was doing my foot patrols on the property, I crossed paths with several residents. Sometimes they were just getting home from work, walking from the parking lot to their house, and other times they were just sitting in their garages doing work or just listening to music and drinking a beer. Most of the residents that I spoke to in passing did not appear to be very friendly.

It was hard to tell if they were being rude towards me because I was Black, or because I was in a uniform that represented authority in their privileged community. For the time that I worked there, I only encountered one White female who was very pleasant and respectful towards me, and she wasn't even a resident. Her elderly father had been living at the apartment complex for several years, based on what she shared with me. One night during my patrol, the woman saw me walking through the complex and approached me asking for help. She explained to me that she lived near the San Diego/Temecula area and that she drove down to Rancho Cucamonga to check on her elderly father who had not been answering his phone nor returning any of her voice messages. She advised me that she was there to do a welfare check on her father, and asked me if I would enter his home with her to witness the fact that she was entering his residence.

I followed the soft-spoken female to her father's front door, willing to assist her in any way that I could. As she unlocked the front door and made entry into the house, she called out his name several times, but there was no answer. I immediately noticed that her father was a very heavy smoker because there was an ashtray on the coffee table, the house reeked of cigarettes, and the walls in the house that probably used to be white at one time, had a yellowish color throughout the home. The first thing that the woman noticed when we entered the living room was a Christmas gift on the coffee table that had not been opened. This set off alarm bells in her soul because she said she had drove down to visit him nearly two weeks before Christmas to give him his gift, yet she could see that he hadn't opened it.

As I followed her into the bedroom area, we observed that the bathroom light was on and the door was partially open. We then discovered why her father did not answer her when she was calling out for him. We found her father lying face down on the bathroom floor, in between the bathtub and the toilet, with his legs partially in the doorway of the bathroom door—he was clearly deceased. The woman broke down in tears immediately when she saw her father laying lifeless on the bathroom floor, not responding to either of us.

I admonished the woman not to touch him or move him, and advised her that I would notify the authorities for her, so they could come out with the coroner to take custody of her father's body. Once her father was finally removed from his home by the coroner, I recall the lady hugging me and thanking me for standing by with her as she checked on her father. Even though the White woman clearly did not physically live there, she was the nicest person that I had interacted with for the entire time I worked at that complex, and I never saw her again after that night.

Furthermore, the November 12, 2004 article published in the Inland Valley Daily Bulletin continued to take shots at my credibility by telling even more lies, to cover up all the lies they told long before that. The article said,

> "According to the lawsuit, another resident of the apartment complex complained to managers a week before the shooting that, Wroe threatened him. The Krauses contend that the decision to keep Wroe on patrol at the apartment complex after the first complaint created an avoidable public danger."

I find it detestable that any White person could even fix their mouth to refer to *me*, or any other Black person, as a public danger, when in fact White people themselves are responsible for more than 400 years of slavery and inhumane treatment of Black people. Still to date, nothing has changed, yet *we* are the dangerous ones. Wealthy White people seem to have forgotten that the foundation of their generational wealth was largely built from the blood, sweat, and tears of Black people... an indisputable fact!

Just when it seemed as though I had no more evidence to debunk all of the lies that were told about me, here's another fact that no human being can ever deny! As you have already read in previous chapters, the Inland Valley Daily Bulletin constantly mentioned that Michael Krause, Jr. was at the Sycamore Springs Apartments to visit a friend, and I submit to the public that is a total and absolute lie that I hope you will research for yourself. If you find it believable that Michael Krause, Jr. was at the Sycamore Springs Apartments to visit either a friend or a girlfriend, go to any online search engine of your choosing and try to find out his or her name. From January 1, 2004, until the date this book was published, the name of *any* friend or *any* girlfriend of Michael Krause, Jr. has NEVER been disclosed or even mentioned. Never!

Nearly a dozen delusional newspaper articles have been written about me, collectively, between the Inland Valley Daily Bulletin and the San Gabriel Valley Tribune, and NOT ONE article has published the name of the actual person or persons that Michael Krause, Jr. allegedly went to the Sycamore Springs Apartments to visit. There's only one possible answer for this mystery... Michael Krause's girlfriend never existed! Whoever she was, she never came to court to support Michael Krause, Jr. nor his family, she never made a victim impact statement, and she was never quoted by *any* newspaper as saying *anything* about my case. I can't help but wonder who taught Michael Krause, Jr. how to lie so good.

On a side note, and in a surprising twist of perspectives, I actually agree with the relatives of the Krause family—I should not have been patrolling the Sycamore Springs apartment complex with a gun on

January 1, 2004, and here's why. It would be extremely negligent and irresponsible of me not to mention that, never, at any time, did my former employer, Robert Zablockis, ever come to me to inform me that the management staff at the Sycamore Springs Apartments were getting complaints about me. If managers at the Sycamore Springs Apartments were getting complaints about me back then, that I was making hostile threats of violence towards the residents there, why weren't the complaints ever validated and documented on paper? If the residents of the apartment complex were honestly living in fear that I was walking around their property threatening people, why didn't Southwest District Patrol ever write me up and/or suspend me or transfer me to another account?

Knowing how far back in my past staff writers at the Inland Valley Daily Bulletin newspaper went to tell the residents of Rancho Cucamonga about me being an Explorer Cadet for the L.A. County Sheriff's Department back in 1989, why couldn't they also publish information in any of their articles about the dates and times that residents filed written complaints against me with the apartment management office? Simple, because the complaints never happened... they just simply never existed!

More than 15 years *after* I had successfully completed my probation, I was doing some online research and stumbled across an article described as **Krause v. Western Heritage Ins. Co.,** and learned some explosive, new information regarding my previous employer that I **never** knew before! I want to make it abundantly clear that the Krause family was not awarded $6,018,912.46 because I shot their son, they were awarded that sum of money because my former employer's insurance policy had no active or valid coverage that permitted an armed security officer (such as me) to be working on the Sycamore Springs Apartments property. From my understanding of reading the entire article, that was the primary foundation and focal point for the Krause family's argument in the lawsuit. The article explaining the dynamics of the lawsuit clearly stated,

> "As of May 2003, Southwest District Patrol employed three individuals other than Robert and Jennifer. Robert was the only armed guard working for Southwest District Patrol in May 2003."

By the time I had finished reading this entire article, finding out things that I had never been told before, I was infuriated by what I was reading—I was hotter than fish grease!!

At the time I was hired to work for Southwest District Patrol, Robert Zablockis KNEW that I was armed! Not only did he know that I was armed, I had to submit a copy of my guard card, my weapons permit, and my firearms permit with my employment application! Never at any time did he *ever* tell me that I could not patrol the premises at the Sycamore Springs Apartments with my firearm on me... NEVER! In fact, the pay that I was getting at that time was slightly higher than what another guard was earning, because the other guard did not have a firearm permit and I did, which was leverage for *me* to ask for a higher wage than the other guard. I can't begin to describe how mad I was (and still am) after reading that article because, if I would have known that Southwest District Patrol's insurance policy did not cover having an armed guard on any of its contracted accounts, I would have <u>never</u> agreed to work for them. I'm smarter than that!

Additionally, statements contained in the article, made by my former employer, substantiate my injuries that I sustained that night just as I had always described them, yet the two EMT witnesses for the prosecution team got on the stand at my murder trial and went against what an emergency room doctor had already concluded about my *confirmed* injuries. The wrongful death article stated,

> "(Wroe) who was *injured* from being hit by the pick-up truck was transported by ambulance to San Antonio Hospital, and treated for his *injuries*. Robert Zablockis was told by the emergency room doctor that Wroe had sustained *injuries* to his *arm, back*, and *legs*."

This information is concrete evidence that, while the San Bernadino County District Attorney's Office, and two of their own witnesses, maliciously and unethically lied about my injuries that Michael Krause, Jr. caused when he struck me with his pickup truck, my workers' compensation documents, my documents that were submitted to the Bureau of Security and Investigative Services, and even documents outlined in the Krause's own wrongful death lawsuit <u>all support my story</u>, and further identify me as a *victim* rather than a suspect. Still to this day, I find it appalling that the Krause family felt that the force used against their son was excessive, unwarranted and reckless, yet they seemingly never felt that the force their son used against *me* was excessive, unwarranted and reckless. Is this really how privileged White people in our society think on a daily basis when things do not go their way?

I can't help but wonder if Michael Krause, Jr. learned this same mindset as he was growing up. Did the wealth of his family upbringing exempt *him* from having to obey the same laws and follow the same rules that the rest of us in society are expected to obey and follow? Why does our broken judicial system *still* continue to uphold an obvious and blatant double-standard approach to how White people are treated, versus how Black people are treated as it relates to how criminal court cases are prosecuted?

Unlike others who have persuaded themselves to believe the untruthful version that Google has been telling about me for more than 20 years, I don't have to guess about what happened that night... I was there... I saw *everything*! The tragic and unfortunate death of Michael Krause, Jr. is no longer my cross to carry, it is for Scott Elliot Martinez to carry, because he is the one who instigated the entire confrontation at the apartment's exit gate between Michael Krause, Jr. and I, and Michael Krause, Jr. is the one who subsequently paid the ultimate price for it!

Now that this book has finally been published, and my truths are finally being told, Scott Elliot Martinez must, one day, stand and face the Krause family, and explain to them why he continued to urge Michael Krause, Jr. to continue ignoring my commands and put the pedal to the metal to continue fleeing. Now that these facts are finally being released to the public, Scott Elliot Martinez has no leverage to defend himself against the truths contained in this book, because he knows within himself that he *largely contributed* to the death of his friend; some friend he is. A real friend would have told Michael Krause, Jr., "Hey man, pull over and see if that security guard is okay... you hit him with the side mirror of your truck when you backed out of the parking space." A real friend would have told Michael Krause, Jr., "If that security guard arrests you, I'll call your parents to come to the sheriff's station and bail you out... just do what he says for now."

Instead, Scott Elliot Martinez faithfully instigated the entire incident that led to Michael Krause, Jr. striking me with his vehicle a second time, just to make it through that exit gate so they could get away, and he will forever be equally responsible for the death of his friend. Moreover, though Michael Krause, Jr. was only 19-years old, he was a legal adult at the time of his death who knew right from wrong, yet chose to do wrong, and spent the better half of his day that night setting up drug deals, purchasing said drugs, driving around the city with Scott Martinez while smoking said drugs, and making poor decision after poor decision... decisions that most parents would not condone or be proud of. In my experience, a 19-year-old can kill you just as quick as a 49-year-old, and I wasn't about to take any chances to risk not going back home to my family that night.

By his own actions, and by his own obvious disregard and resentment towards authority, Michael Krause caused his own demise by not complying with orders that would have saved his life! As for Scott Martinez, if he's any kind of honest man, he is the one who owes the Krause family an honest explanation as to the exact details of the *conversation* he and Michael were engaged in at the time I was attempting to take Michael Krause, Jr. into custody at the main exit gate. Even while writing this book, a deeply-rooted anger resurfaced within me as I'm recollecting these events, because I came extremely close to talking Michael Krause, Jr. into surrendering to me and getting him to turn off his truck but, due to Scott Martinez sitting in that truck *encouraging* Krause to remain defiant, Michael Krause, Jr. sided with his friend and, sadly, he went for it and paid the ultimate price.

7
★ ★ ★ ★ ★

BUT GOD

As you will see by the end of this book, THIS CHAPTER will be my starting point for *my* road to redemption… for complete **justice** in response to the malicious and unjust things that were done to me by our broken judicial system. This journey that I am embarking upon is not a race, it's a marathon! In order for me to describe every single thing that I experienced, from start to finish, I would have to write a second or third volume to this book. In the interest of time, and being eager to finally exhale, the goal of this chapter is to share some highlights of what my life behind bars was like, from the day I turned myself in until the day that I was finally released.

Though I am going to share some very troubling experiences that I endured in jail, I'm also going to share my testimonies of how God turned it all around for my good in the midst of other inmates who were highly unlikely to ever be released back into society. I sincerely hope and pray that no other Black man in America has to go through what I went through, just to prove their innocence against a broken, biased, and systemically prejudicial justice system that unfairly targets the prosecution or overall social demise of Black men!

Just to give you a more accurate idea of how psychologically and emotionally difficult this book was for me to write, I **literally** had to do breathing exercises at times to push through many parts of my story that I knew I wanted to share with the public. There are so many portions of this book that insanely challenged my mental, spiritual, and emotional fortitude. For the better part of about three to four consecutive months, it got to a point where I had to start writing down my blood pressure readings daily, because I was having a series of migraine headaches, traumatic flashbacks of dangerous encounters, or just dealing with all of the emotional triggers that reminded me of every story I've shared within this book.

My blood pressure readings were so dangerously high at times, I had to stop writing for several weeks, intermittently, just to calm myself down and get myself back to being level-headed enough to finish this book. As I got deeper and deeper into some of the facts about my encounter with Michael Krause, Jr., that the public was never made aware of, depression got the best of me on so many occasions! There were times when I had to stop writing because I felt like I was going to have a nervous breakdown. On more than several occasions, I picked up my phone to call friends that I felt would talk me through some of the hurt that I was reliving as I was constructing this book. I can vividly recall a few close friends who took my phone calls, no matter how early or how late I called them.

BUT GOD

On one particular phone call with a close friend, she said to me, "How's it going, friend?" As much as I wanted to respond to her question, I just couldn't say anything. I couldn't get a word out to save my life. Before I knew it, I was breathing heavily and crying uncontrollably, trying my best to keep my emotions and my thoughts out of the dark corners of my mind. There are just no words that come to my mind that would adequately allow me to describe the pain I was dealing with in those moments. In most of those instances, all I could say to the person on the other side of the phone was, "This is so hard to finish! I just want my life back! I want this to be over!"

It's not because I felt any *guilt* related to the fact that Michael Krause, Jr. had lost his life by making a foolish decision to put *my* life in danger, it was literally just a demonstration of my human emotion of feeling empathy that another human being was no longer here. I do not feel any guilt about defending my life against a hostile attacker but, at the same time, I feel angry that, based on all of the training I've had in my lifetime, no one ever trained me how to recover from having to use deadly force to stay alive. How do you train another person to adequately deal with that? How do you train someone to unsee a mental event that periodically feels haunting? How do you explain your feelings to a person who has never been through those exact same tragedies that you may have experienced? How do you do it?

As a person who has always been taught to live an upstanding life, on the right side of the law, it pains me to no end that the justice system that I had always been taught to respect, turned against me and prosecuted me for doing exactly what they mandated me to have the training for. Talk about being betrayed! All of us, even the Krause family, including the entire San Bernadino County District Attorney's Office, have made mistakes in our lives that I'm sure we are not necessarily proud of but, at some point in our lives, we should all feel deserving of some measure of genuine redemption. So many people in this world who *claim* to be believers of God *want* to be forgiven, yet those same people oftentimes *show* no forgiveness. Then again, I guess the only people who could ever desire forgiveness are the people who are capable of acknowledging that they did something wrong in the first place.

On the day that I voluntarily turned myself in to the San Bernadino County Sheriff's Department, I knew that I was eventually going to beat the false charges against me, but I didn't know it was going to take the better half of a full year to do it. I was driven to the sheriff's station by then LAPD Captain Ron Marbrey and my godfather who, at the time, was a retired Chief of Police from New York. The moment we exited the unmarked police car we arrived in, several detectives from the San Bernadino County Sheriff's Department immediately approached us and introduced themselves.

While my godfather and Captain Marbrey stood outside in the parking area talking about the unfortunate set of circumstances surrounding my voluntary surrender, I was casually escorted inside the sheriff's station by another detective. The detective sat me down in a private interview room and courteously explained to me what to expect during the arrest and booking process. From what I can readily recall, the detective read me my rights [Miranda Warning] and asked me if I wanted to talk to him. Although I do not remember exactly what I said to him, I faintly recall voluntarily speaking with the detective, and answering the few questions that he had for me. I could have easily told the detective that I did not wish to make any statements, but the only reason I agreed to cooperate with him and answer his questions is because I had absolutely nothing to hide.

I knew going into this ordeal that I was innocent, and I was confident within myself that, when all was said and done, my innocence would be publicly revealed. Most people who end up as inmates in this world do not find God until they are in serious trouble, or until they learn that they may never be released from jail. I found God and accepted God into my life LONG before I knew West Valley Detention Center even existed! This factual statement was always the difference between me and other inmates at the jail.

Before I go any further, I want to make it perfectly clear that, from the time I surrendered to authorities, to the time I arrived at the West Valley Detention Center for processing, members of the San Bernadino County Sheriff's Department treated me with a great deal of professionalism and respect. If there was anything hostile, or inappropriate, or crooked that they had done to me, I would have definitely disclosed it in this book. However, they treated me remarkably well, considering the circumstances of why I was there. They honestly treated me as if I were one of their own. I must admit, however, that based on the racial stereotypes about how Black people are often treated in Rancho Cucamonga, by some White people, not all I was very surprised that I was not treated horribly bad in jail by any White, sworn personnel. I was simply treated as a person who was in jail.

Based on the nature of my job back in 2004, I did not really have a choice as to what housing unit I would be placed in at the jail. Since I had such a long-standing, intricate history of arresting people and sending well-deserved candidates to jail over an 12-year intermittent period of working in private security, the detention center classification staff felt that it was in the best interest of my personal safety that I be placed in protective custody (P.C.). There was a multitude of pros and cons that came along with being placed in protective custody. I was glad that I did not have to share a cell with any other inmates for the duration of my incarceration but, at the same time, I was looked at much more disrespectfully by inmates who were housed in general population housing units.

Never in my lifetime had I ever been accused of nor faced charges for something as terrible as murder but, with my extensive knowledge of the law, and my familiarity with criminal justice protocols, I knew that I could show no signs of weakness once I entered West Valley Detention Center! If need be, I had to be ready and willing, at any given moment, to do battle with whoever stepped to me and wanted to catch these hands!

The emotional and psychological torture of my incarceration first began to set in once I accepted the fact that I was officially cut off from all of my family members and friends!

BUT GOD

In a matter of a few short hours, I was forced to exist in a world where the rules of everyday society were no longer the norm. When the deputies had taken away my personal belongings, I was given a dark green uniform, an ugly pair of hard, plastic sandals, and undergarments that did not fit comfortably. As I moved through the jail facility from one place to another, I took notice that some inmates had different color jail outfits.

The one that I was most concerned about was the one I was wearing. For the most part, if an inmate was wearing an orange outfit, it meant that inmate was being housed in general population. If an inmate was wearing a red outfit, it meant that inmate was to be considered extremely dangerous or high-risk. A red outfit sometimes meant that the inmate was either a serial killer, or possibly a vicious gang member from a violent street gang or drug cartel. Once you enter the jail or prison system, you must live by a totally different set of politics and rules than what you're accustomed to as a free person on the streets. As for the dark green uniform that I had been assigned to wear during my stay, I later learned that the dark green uniform was designated for inmates who were considered to be classified as police officers, informants, rapists, or child molesters... and I was neither!

One of the hardest things I had to endure during my time of incarceration was being constantly handcuffed and shackled anytime I had to move from one place to another within the detention center. This meant that I was made to wear ankle cuffs, to prevent me from running, as well as long waist chains that were wrapped around my waist, restricting the movement of my hands. Once the long waist chains had been fully wrapped around my waist, as shown on page A3 of the March 12, 2004 publication of the Rancho Cucamonga Voice newspaper, I couldn't even raise my hands high enough to scratch the tip of my nose! The days that I had to be transported back and forth to court were the worst, because it meant that I had to be wrapped in chains and leg shackles for the better part of the day.

When it was my day to go to court, the deputies would wake me up very early in the morning to eat their horrific breakfast, and then prepare me to take the long walk down to where they staged inmates to prepare them to load the sheriff bus for transportation to court. This periodic process felt the same as cattle being rustled up to be pushed into a specific area where there was ultimately no escape. By the time I would finally make it back to my cell in the late afternoon, following a court proceeding, my wrists and ankles felt like the leg shackles and handcuff chains were still actually on me.

Once I finally got settled into the unit where I was going to be housed at, I quickly got a crash course in jail politics. For the first week of my incarceration, I pretty much kept to myself and did not interact with the other inmates in my unit. I was locked up for 23 hours per day, seven days per week, and I was allowed one hour of recreation time out of my cell daily. Any free time out of my cell was spent on making phone calls to my family, taking a shower, or outside in the caged exercise yard. As the weeks went by, random inmates began coming by my cell asking me if I wanted any reading materials.

BUT GOD

The first thing that I inquired about was how to get my hands on a Bible. Several inmates had given me tips on how to go about obtaining a Bible and, before I knew it, I finally had a Bible in my cell. In fact, I ultimately ended up with two Bibles. I had a blue, standard size Bible, and an orange, pocket-size Bible. Before too much more time had passed, a Black inmate had stopped by my cell to give me a lesson in jailhouse etiquette. He told me that everyone who comes out of their cell for their one hour of free time had to go around to each cell in the unit and ask if anyone in that cell needed anything. Sometimes an inmate would want me to take a few shots of instant coffee to another cell in the unit. Sometimes an inmate would want me to take a magazine to a certain cell, and bring back another magazine.

Sometimes an inmate would give me an empty plastic bag to fill it up with hot water from the sink in the pod dayroom. Once I took the hot water back to the inmate who requested it, I handed it to them by pinching the sides of the folded plastic bag and laying it flat on the floor so that the other inmate could pull it under their cell door and into their cell. Most inmates who requested hot water were either making instant coffee or using it to cook their Top Ramen noodles. Sometimes an inmate would want me to take certain food items to a specific cell, and bring back other food items in exchange. In jail, the barter system is a very efficient way for inmates to either maintain tangible items that they need for everyday survival, or acquire tangible items if they did not have enough money on their books to buy their own necessities. Sometimes, other inmates would come up to my cell and whisper to me that they wanted me to save the fruit from my food trays so that I can leave it in the shower for another inmate to intercept when they would come out for *their* free time.

Anytime inmates would come up to my cell and whisper that they wanted any fruit that I had coming, or hard candies that I purchased from the commissary, it meant that an inmate somewhere in our unit was making an illegal batch of jailhouse pruno. Jailhouse pruno is most commonly known as a homemade batch of prison wine, made with a variety of fermented fruits and hard candies that were used as sugars. I had enough problems to deal with when I had arrived at the detention center, so I didn't want to do anything contrary to the rules and regulations of the facility that would hinder me from going home sooner than later. The reason why the other inmates would *whisper* these requests to me is because having any left-over food or fruits in our cell was considered contraband, and we could face disciplinary action if the deputies were to ever find these items in our cell.

Every cell was equipped with a two-way Intercom system that the deputies in the pod tower would use to communicate with us. The intercom system in each cell was so sophisticated, the deputies could just push a button in the control tower and secretly monitor conversations between inmates in their cell. This gave the deputies the upper-hand on staying aware of any potential plans by inmates to either intentionally cause problems in the jail or possibly do harm to any jail staff or other inmates. There is absolutely no privacy in jail. Once I heard the heavy door slam behind me once I was placed in my cell, the reality of being unjustly incarcerated instantly sank in.

During my first three to four months of being incarcerated, I had nightmares and terrible dreams every single night without fail. More than twenty years later, I can still describe one particular nightmare as if it just happened yesterday! I had nightmares so frequently, sometimes I was simply afraid to go to sleep. Since I had such a hard time sleeping in jail, I made it a point to say up as long as I could to observe daily jail activities, so that I could learn how to survive in there, while also remaining alert and expecting the unexpected.

There was a really big television mounted on the wall of the dayroom inside of our unit, and there was a very strict policy on how the television privileges were to be shared. On a rotating basis, each race of inmates had control of the channels for the entire day. One day the Blacks had total control of the TV. On the next day, the Whites had total control of the programs we watched for the entire day. On the day after that, the Mexicans had control of the programs that we would all have to watch for *their* day, and so on. One of the most popular channels that most inmates wanted to watch for the day was the music video channel. This was the only way that I could stay up to date on new music or new artists that had released new albums. Truth be told, having control over which television programs I watched from day to day was the least of my worries, I spent the majority of my time there fighting to get back home where I belonged.

When the emotional and psychological exhaustion of being in jail became too much of a burden to bear, I oftentimes found myself laying down on the lower bunk bed with my blanket fully covering my entire body so that I could have a good, quiet cry! Jail is a very risky place to be caught crying because, to most other inmates, crying shows weakness, and other inmates prey on those who they feel are weak and vulnerable. Growing up in the church for most of my life, I have always been a firm believer that my faith in God would get me through most challenges that life could ever throw at me but, just being human, this experience felt much more difficult to overcome.

My faith and my overall level of spiritual health had gotten to the lowest point that I had ever experienced in my life. Even though I knew that the battle I was fighting was much bigger than me, I wasn't strong enough to even say my prayers at night or in the morning when I would rise. I started to rapidly succumb to the idea that, in those moments, I was only an inmate and nothing more. I wasn't even Dameon K. Wroe any longer—I was literally just a number that no one in jail cared about. The psychological torture of not knowing if I was ever going home again was a tremendous weight for me to carry, and it felt like I was carrying it all by myself.

Having a 50 years to life prison sentence hanging over my head every day was unlike anything I could ever realistically explain to anyone. Most people who truly, truly know me, know that I have always loved to sing. My spirit was so broken by being unjustly locked up, I was not spiritually strong enough to sing, to pray, or sometimes to even get up out of bed to find *anything* to be grateful for. Mentally, I really was *that* weak! Less than four months into my stay at the jail, I had to be placed on psyche meds just to be able to sleep. For the first two months of being locked up, I didn't even eat the food that the jail provided for me on a daily basis. The food was incredibly terrible, and quite disgusting. Once I learned how to start ordering food and writing supplies from the commissary store, I would primarily eat only the food items that I would buy with the money that I had on my books.

Prior to the shooting incident at the Sycamore Springs Apartments, I was a very outgoing, happy-go-lucky, fun-loving social butterfly who enjoyed being around people. After I arrived at the West Valley Detention Center, I was like a turtle who spent most of my time hiding my head inside of my shell, and I rarely wanted to come out. I kept other inmates away from me for as long as I possibly could. I didn't want to talk to them, I didn't want to listen to them, and I didn't even want to acknowledge their presence. For my own safety, and to protect the integrity of how I needed to defend myself against false charges, I purposely tried to stay out of sight and out of mind. The reason I made it such a point to keep to myself is because, as I was making my way through the booking process, another Black inmate explained to me the importance of keeping my mouth shut regarding why I was in jail.

He told me that every unit in the jail has what is called a jailhouse snitch. These are people who are in jail facing decades in prison, sometimes life, who would try to make me feel comfortable talking to them about my case, then go behind my back to tell the district attorney's office that I was in jail confessing details about the charges that had been brought against me. If the district attorney's office would have found the jailhouse snitch's allegations to sound credible, then the district attorney would have used that fabricated information as evidence against me at my trial.

Upon my arrival to the jail, it only took me a few days to learn that all of the inmates in my unit already knew about the details of my case, because many of them had a monthly subscription to all of the newspapers that were being circulated around San Bernadino County. Just like members of the general public, once the inmates got their personal mail distributed to them, all they saw plastered on the front pages of their newspapers was my face, and the one-sided stories they published that made me look guilty long before my trial even got started.

Of all the inmates in the first housing unit I was assigned to, I learned of four particular inmates that I would go on to remember for the rest of my life. I may very well have a life-long memory of these men, not because they made a positive impact on my life, but because their crimes were so violent, brutal, and utterly detestable. Two of these four men were in my unit fighting death penalty cases. Make no mistake about it, the people that I had to live among, for the better part of a full year, were not the type of people you want to honk your horn at because they're sitting at a green light taking too long to move forward. These were the types of individuals who would probably kill you for practice, as many of them had nothing left in life to lose.

Another big part of being surrounded by other inmates was to know and understand the dynamics of what each of those inmates were in jail for. When you move into a new house, in a new neighborhood, it's important to get to know who your neighbors are. In that process, you get to know which neighbors are friendly and which neighbors are most likely not going to like you being the new person on the block. Jail pretty much works the same way. The longer I stayed in the protective custody unit, the more and more other inmates began to educate me as to who was who.

The first inmate I was told about went by the nickname "Bear." Bear was a fairly tall, bald, White man with a noticeably less-than-athletic build. From what I was told, he was in jail because he molested a toddler and then choked her to death. Now, I'm not in any way a violent person but, after the other inmates in the unit had confirmed why Bear was in jail, I prayed for an opportunity to do physical harm to him, even if it meant that I myself would receive some sort of physical harm by the deputies for attacking him. No matter how hard I tried, I just couldn't stop imagining in my mind what that child's final moments on this earth must have been like because of a sadistic animal like Bear!

Anyone who knows me knows that I have an unwavering love for children, and all I could think about when I saw Bear's face was that little angel that he tortured. Because of his crime, Bear was never allowed to have a cellmate because his cellmate would have likely tried to kill him, due to what he did to that precious little girl. Violent crimes against children are not tolerated in the prison system by other inmates whatsoever—that's just the code. If enough people in the detention facility find out that an inmate is in there for a violent act upon a child, there will be a long line of other inmates plotting to kill an individual with those types of charges. Whenever it was time for Bear to come out of his cell and see if other inmates needed anything, I always laid on my bed with my blanket covering my face, to give him the impression that I was sleeping if he came up to my door. I didn't want anything to do with him at all. Even if I needed a magazine, some hot water for my coffee, or if I needed something passed on to another cell, I didn't want to use Bear as my errand boy… I just stayed away from him altogether.

My next neighbor that I had the displeasure of meeting was a man by the name of "John." To be honest, none of the other inmates ever told me a story as to why John was incarcerated at West Valley. Ironically, John is the one who ultimately told me about the details of his own case. For whatever reason, I guess he just needed someone to hear the angle of his potential defense strategy in deciding how he was going to fight his case. Well, subsequently, I was the wrong person for John to be talking to about his case.

John was a quiet, soft-spoken, nerdy-looking White man who looked to be in his late 30s to early 40s at the time. On this particular day, after being locked up in my cell for nearly the entire day, the deputies popped my door open and gave me an opportunity to go outside on the rec yard. Once on the yard, the deputy escorted me to the smaller enclosed cage within the bigger portion of that same rec yard. Just when I thought I was going to be enjoying some peace and quiet on the yard, the deputies brought out another inmate from my unit and placed him on the much bigger side of the enclosed yard... it was John.

For about the first 30 minutes or so, there was no conversation between John and I out on the yard—he stayed in his world and I stayed in mine. At some point during our awkward silence, John voluntarily broke his silence. "I know it's not cool to ask other people about their case, but I gotta say, of all the people in this jail, you seem to have the best chance of going home," he said. I was truly at a loss for words when he made that statement. Since I had never actually spoken to John before, I was curious as to why he made such a matter-of-fact statement like that.

"What do you mean by that," I asked him. He went on to tell me that he had been following my case in the local newspapers. He went on to explain, "From what I read in the newspaper, a guy tried to run you over with his pickup truck and you did what you had to do to defend yourself. I mean, you were licensed to carry a gun and you were working as a security guard. Right?" Without saying anything more than he had already said, I stood in agreement with John's statements. He went on to tell me that he knew exactly how I must have been feeling to be locked up in jail, because he was also being falsely accused of a crime he alleged he did not commit. Shocked to be hearing another inmate willingly tell me full details about his charges, John apparently felt comfortable enough to keep talking to me.

He went on to tell me that he was being charged with inappropriately touching a little boy who supposedly went to his church. He said that there was an event that his church was having and, allegedly, he did something to the little boy that was inappropriate. So, in my own mind, I put two and two together and easily concluded that John was being accused of molesting a little boy who allegedly attended his church. I feel like, having kept up with the details of my case in the newspaper, John must have felt that I had some reasonable knowledge of the law, because he started asking me for advice. In all honesty, I didn't have any legal advice to offer him, all I told him to do is pray about it.

John continued to share with me that the district attorney offered him a deal in order for him to get out of jail. He told me that the DA was going to give him credit for time served, if he agreed to plead no contest to a felony and register as a sex offender for the rest of his life. John became noticeably depressed about his situation the more he explained his circumstances to me. He was adamant that he did not do anything to the little boy, but then made the mistake of telling me that he had previously been accused of the same crime several years prior. Once he told me that, I just felt in my spirit that John was not going to win his case if he took it to trial and tried to fight it, because those are some extremely serious allegations that put other children at risk, based on John's propensity to touch children inappropriately if he was released back into the community.

As our yard time was coming to an end, I offered John the best possible advice that I could have given him. I told him that only he and God knew if he was *truly* guilty of what he was being charged with and, if it was going to mean no more jail time for him, to take the deal and not risk going to trial. I didn't tell John this at the time, but I gave him that suggestion because I knew in my spirit that he likely did something to that little boy, based on his admission of the prior allegation of the same offense. After our time on the rec yard was over, John was escorted back to his cell and I was escorted back to my cell—I never saw him again. Several weeks later, I started asking some of the inmates in my unit if they had seen John. It was at that time that one of the inmates had informed me that John took his case to trial and lost. He was ultimately sentenced to 44 years in prison as a result of his conviction. After hearing about what happened to John, I became even more passionate about fighting my case with every fiber of my being. Come hell or high water, I was determined to get back home by any means necessary! In order to increase my chances of beating my trial and getting back home where I belonged, I knew I had to get to work!

For the majority of the time I was in my cell, I was writing notes relentlessly about my case and my defense, that my attorney and I were planning to present to the jury. It might seem like an easy task to do but, in actuality, writing down notes about my case to pass along to my attorney was not as easy as it sounds. From what I had been told by several inmates, the deputies in the facility were known for randomly going through an inmate's personal mail, and sometimes legal mail, during cell raids or controlled inmate cell searches for contraband. As it pertained to legal mail, deputies were not supposed to be reading any documentation belonging to an inmate that was between that inmate and their attorney.

So, based on that knowledge, I started getting really good at writing pages and pages of legal notes for my attorney, and then hiding them in places where I felt the deputies would not think to look. This was very critical to winning my case because, if the Krause family or the DA had any friends or colleagues working in the jail, that friend or that colleague of theirs could have easily been a part of the team of deputies searching my cell and looking to find my legal notes… thus potentially compromising my entire defense.

When I was finally able to get a legal visit from my attorney, Donald J. Calabria, I knew for a fact that Deputy District Attorney Jeremy Carrasco's case against me was in deep trouble! Donald J. Calabria has always been an outstanding defense attorney, and an absolute force to be reckoned with. From what I can readily remember, when Donald Calabria came to the jail to visit me for the first time, our meeting did not even last a whole hour. Knowing what I knew about Donald Calabria back then, that short meeting was a very positive sign that we were going to win our case at trial. Jeremy Carrasco was no match for a defense attorney of Donald Calabria's caliber. Calabria was visibly concerned and upset that I was unjustly sitting in jail, but he appeared very confident that I had nothing to worry about.

During our initial meeting at the jail, I handed him all of the notes that I had been writing down each day in my cell, every time a new thought or new information came to my mind. Once he saw the organization and the factual detail of my notes, Donald Calabria was elated to see all that I had written. By looking at the detail of all of my notes that I saved for his review, he knew that I was making his job as my attorney ten times easier. Before my legal visit with my attorney was over, I could no longer hide the emotions that I had been holding inside.

In telling him how afraid I was about wrongfully being sent to prison, I began to break down and cry for a few moments. I specifically recall telling Calabria, "I don't want to go to prison for something I didn't do!" Almost immediately, he responded to me by saying, "I didn't come all the way down here just to leave you. You're not going to prison... you're going home! In the meantime, keep writing notes every day, just like these. Your notes that you give to me are so powerful, and the jury needs to hear this. I'm going to put you on the stand, because you are my star witness. You were there... you saw EVERYTHING!" As soon as our visit was over, and the deputies escorted me back to my cell, I continued to write down more notes for my attorney, in anticipation of his next legal visit with me.

When Donald Calabria had initially come to visit me, his visit with me made me feel like God was saying to me, "You see? I told you I'd never leave you nor forsake you. You can dry your tears now... everything's going to be okay!" The reason it was such an epic blessing to have gotten a visit from my attorney is because many of the inmates in my unit never got a legal visit from their attorneys at all! So many of the inmates in my unit had already been at the jail long before I got there, and they often voiced their anger and resentment at the fact that their attorneys had never made any effort to visit them in jail to go over the details of their case.

As I eluded to earlier, you can't show signs of weakness in jail if you want to have a greater chance at surviving the experience. That way of thinking is exactly what prepared me for the next inmate that I also had the displeasure of meeting during my stay at Stress Valley Detention Center.

One day, when I was coming back from court and being escorted into my housing unit, I noticed that the entire facility was on lockdown and all of the windows in the unit next door to mine were all covered up with tarps or blankets of some sort. This was strange to me because I knew that the deputies working in the control room were supposed to have a 360-degree view into every pod in my unit, so it made no sense as to why the unit next door had their windows covered up. By the time I entered my unit and walked upstairs to my cell, the inmates in my unit were still talking about what happened in the unit next door while I was away at court. It was explained to me that one of the inmates in the unit next door to mine had gone upstairs to the second tier in his unit, stood up on top of the second floor railing and did a swan dive onto the ground level concrete floor.

The man was allegedly depressed because of the amount of time he was facing in prison as a result of the charges that were pending against him by the San Bernadino County District Attorney's Office. About a week after the incident, the news of the man jumping to his death was all over the local newspaper. Sadly, the newspaper article mentioned the man by name, and further stated that the district attorney was about to announce that there was not enough evidence to charge the man for what he had initially got arrested for. So, in essence, the man killed himself for no reason—he was about to be set free in a matter of days had he not jumped off of that second floor railing. Thank God those windows in the unit next door were covered by the time I returned from court. It would have been an awful sight to see.

When I was finally let out of my cell later on that day for my free time, a White inmate, who referred to himself as "Warlock," called me over to his cell and asked me a very unexpected question about God. Talking to me quietly through the crack of his cell door, Warlock literally asked me, "Do you think that God will forgive me for what I did to be in here?" At a total loss for words, I explained to Warlock that I could not answer his question because I did not know why he was in jail.

Warlock went on to explain to me that he set up a drug deal to purchase a very large quantity of methamphetamine. He further stated that, once he arrived to purchase the meth, there was a total of three people in the house where the drug deal took place. He said that after he showed the three people his cash to purchase the drugs, he took out his .357 Magnum and shot each of the three people in the head, execution-style, stealing the drugs and keeping the money. In a much more humble voice, Warlock then stated, "The only reason I asked you if God would forgive me is because I see you walking around here all the time with your Bible in your hand, so I just thought you would know."

In speaking with him further, Warlock explained to me that he had already accepted the fact that he would most likely get the death penalty for the crime he committed, I guess that's why he felt so content with telling me about the details of his case—he didn't appear to be trying to fight his case to get free, he was only at the jail waiting for the day that it was time for him to transition to prison. By the time I got back to my cell for the night, I couldn't believe what I had just heard! One thing was for sure… I had to get out of there! After reflecting on the deep conversation I had with Warlock, I started to question myself as to the real reason I was at that jail. It felt like my entire purpose for being in that jail was to learn how to start depending on God more.

More and more frequently, I started to wonder if I was also sent there to be a light in the lives of people who were tormented by the darkness of the poor choices they made to end up there. Once I started to see the magnitude of what so many other inmates were going through, compared to what I was going through, I started to feel more confident about eventually being set free. Without even realizing it at that time, I was finally able to sleep better, I was able to write letters to my family to let them know how I was doing, and I was finally able to walk around the jail with my head held a little bit higher than when I first got there. The one thing that made the biggest difference in my life during my incarceration, was the fact that I was finally able to get myself to a point where I was finally able to pray.

However, the one thing that challenged my Christianity the most, hands down, was the fact that, as a Christian, I still had to pray for the very family who was relentlessly seeking my downfall. I had to pray for the very people who were unjustly seeking my life by way of a one-way trip to prison for the rest of my life.

That was the hardest part of my prayer life during my incarceration. Considering all of the challenges that I had endured in my life up until 2004, being incarcerated and maliciously charged with murder was the lowest point in my life, and was unlike anything else I had ever been through. I can honestly say that I was at rock-bottom, not knowing if I was ever going back home to my family, as a result of cruel and obvious lies. When I was finally able to utter a prayer within the confines of my cell, all I could ask for was forgiveness, for strength, and for God to keep me protected for as long as I had to be in jail. My prayer was very simple, "Heavenly Father, if You are with me in this place like I know You are, please continue to show me signs that You haven't left me." Each and every time I said that prayer, blessings came to pass!

Not long after I would say that prayer, one of the deputies came to deliver some very encouraging mail to my cell. The mail I received was usually a combination of greeting cards and letters from my family and friends. Most of the cards were words of encouragement sent by members of my church family, and my immediate family. Before I knew it, that very prayer had set a pivotal precedent for the remainder of the time I spent at West Valley Detention Center. There were times when I was literally on my knees praying in my cell and then, during those prayers, I could hear the distinct sounds of more mail being slid underneath my door by one of the deputies passing out mail for the night.

By the time I got up off my knees in prayer, I turned around to find several pieces of new mail from people on the outside who were encouraging me to stay strong, and that everything was going to be okay. Not only was that mail a sign from God that He was there in that cell with me, God also showed me how many people cared about me by way of in-person visits.

As any adult child would be, I was always happy to see my mother and my sister. Always being so overwhelmed with despair from day to day, as well as dealing with my fears of the unknown, seeing my mother and my sister during a visit was always the highlight of my days! They would always keep me up to speed on everything that was happening on the outside with my friends and family, and they would also keep me updated on the progress that Donald Calabria was making with my case. Since the visitation phone lines inside the jail were always being recorded, my family and I developed some very subtle, non-verbal ways to communicate through the thick glass in the visitation holding cell. It was my way of discretely asking my family how things were looking with my case, and it became their discreet way of telling me that things were looking VERY GOOD!

Whenever my family gave me a smile and two thumbs up, I knew that Mr. Calabria was building a strong defense for me and staying in direct communication with my family. Their smiles and their positive energy meant the world to me during our visits. I was also very grateful to my sister that, from the moment I turned myself in to authorities, she rallied all of my friends and associates together and gave them the information that they would need to also be able to visit me in jail. Once I had been settled in the jail for a while, I noticed that I was soon getting visits from my friends as well. At first, it really broke my spirit to have my friends looking at me through a jailhouse visitation window and wearing prison attire but, at the end of the day, I was fortunate that they were able to come visit me whenever they could.

Seeing my friends, and being able to talk directly to them, also lifted up my spirits in ways that I cannot adequately describe. I was especially humbled by the fact that several of them had driven nearly two hours away from their homes to come see me. God is so good! As I'm sure anyone could imagine, the hardest part of our visits were when my time on the phone had run out and my family and I had to go our separate ways. I wanted so badly to go home with them when they walked away from that visitation window, but the only place I could go was back to my cell to continue fighting to win my case. However, there were also quite a few times when my talk time on the visitation phone would get repeatedly extended so that I could continue my visit with my friends and family. Whenever my phone time got extended, I knew that was GOD'S hand at work... another sign that He was in the midst of my storm right along with me.

Each and every in-person visit that I got while I was in jail was like medicine for my soul because, had it not been for those visits, there's just no telling what I might have developed the courage to do, knowing that I had no business living my life behind the walls of a jail or a prison. In those moments, I was starting to become afraid of what the outcome of my life would have looked like if I would have given in to the terrible thoughts that once loitered in the dark corners of my mind. Although there are certain details about the dark state of depression I was in while I was incarcerated, I don't think that I can ever bring myself to share with my friends or family what those dark thoughts were back in 2004.

I'm just so fortunate and so grateful, and so blessed that God gave me the strength to survive and conquer the many hardships that the devil and his helpers took me through. More importantly, I am eternally grateful that God allowed me this special chance to still be on the time-side of life to even tell my story, in hopes of being a living testimony to others that God can and will successfully bring us through any challenge or any hardship that life may throw at us. Overcoming challenges in our lives is nothing but a test of our faith.

I can honestly say that, though my emotions were all over the place on a daily basis, I never felt a spirit of guilt by being locked up in jail, because I knew that my being in jail was a result of malicious people who were fabricating a smear campaign against me to get me sent to prison for the rest of my life. In a weird, yet beneficial turn of events, I started having unexpected visitors stopping by my cell from time to time. Shockingly, these visitors were not my friends nor family members, these visitors were deputies of the San Bernadino County Sheriff's Department who worked in the jail. Every time there was a shift change in the jail, the new deputies that were starting their shift would ultimately go around to each cell with a checklist and take count to make sure that inmates were in their assigned cell.

BUT GOD

Under normal circumstances, it was not popular among other inmates to allow everyone to see that you were having frequent interactions with the deputies. When other inmates would always see another inmate talking to deputies, the other inmates would assume that an inmate was snitching to the cops about something that could be a potential detriment to the livelihood of others in the unit. However, I had no control over these unsolicited visits from the deputies. Many of the deputies who worked at the jail knew exactly who I was because most of them had colleagues who actually responded to the scene of my shooting the night Michael Krause, Jr. tried to run me over.

Before I go any further, I must warn you that what I am about to say next may possibly trigger you to have some uncomfortable emotions. However, I waited more than 20 years to be able to tell these truths to the public, so all I can continue being in this moment is transparent and honest, so that you can actually feel the emotions that I myself was experiencing when these things were said to me! One day, during shift change at the jail, I was leaning against my cell door watching the TV in our pod that was mounted on the dayroom wall. As I was looking out of my window, I saw a deputy come into the pod with his inmate list, preparing to do a headcount of the inmate(s) in each cell.

He was walking with a purpose, as if he was in a hurry to finish his task. By the time he got to my cell, he looked into my window and said, "What's up, man?" As soon as I returned the greeting to him, he walked away and went to the next cell. Before he got all the way to the door of the next cell, he turned around and came back to my cell. When he approached my door again, he looked at me and said, "Wroe? What the hell are you still doing here? I thought you would've been out by now." Slowly sinking my chin into my chest, I simply replied, "Your guess is as good as mine, man!" Out of nowhere, the deputy took his keys out and opened up my cell door—he had to have known that I was not a threat! We stood at the entrance of my cell and talked for several good minutes about the circumstances surrounding my incident at the Sycamore Springs Apartments.

We spoke about general details that were already published in the newspapers, I didn't go into any great detail about other aspects of my case. Before exiting my cell and continuing on with his count, the deputy said to me, "Dude, I know one thing… if he would've tried to run one of us over with that truck, his ass would've got shot way more than once!" Although what he said to me in that moment might sound overly cruel to some people, I knew within myself that he was just being painfully honest—he didn't bat an eye when he said it! The one thing that stood out to me when the deputy made that statement is the fact that it was the deputy's way of reassuring me that the deadly force I used against Krause, to defend myself, was justifiable and appropriate, considering the amount of force Krause had used to place *my life* in danger.

It was one thing that such a powerful statement came from an actual deputy, but it was another thing knowing that this statement had come from even a *White* deputy. Based on all of their training, and mine, the deputies knew that my shooting was unfortunate, but legit. In cases like mine, there should be no difference between a police officer's life and a security officer's life. Every life is important and valuable... every life matters. Regardless of how people feel towards security officers, self-defense is self-defense. Michael Krause, Jr. had a valuable life as well, it's just a shame that he didn't think much about his safety or his life in the moment he made a decision to try to run me over with his truck. His decision to do that changed so many lives forever.

A few weeks after the deputy made the above statement and continued with his duties to finish his count for shift change, a different deputy stopped by my cell. The next particular deputy that stopped by my cell to speak to me about my shooting incident didn't come in, but he stood at my cell and spoke to me discreetly through the door. The second deputy obviously knew about some of the details surrounding my case already, and just wanted to know how I was holding up. All I could tell him in that moment was, "I don't belong here. I literally don't belong here!" After voicing his approval of the fact that the prosecutor should not have filed charges against me, the deputy simply said, "Hang in there, man. Everything's gonna work out."

When the deputy walked away from my cell, all I could do is walk over to the long, slender window near my bunk and just stare out of the window. For months on end, each time I found myself staring out of that lonely window in my cell, it took me at least five to six months to notice one common theme that was recurring each time I looked out of the window. It dawned on me that each time I looked out of that window, I noticed that the wind was always blowing in a westbound direction without fail. I thought it was incredibly strange that, no matter which day I was gazing out of my cell window, the wind was always blowing from east to west. How was this possible? Even if the wind *was* being blown in multiple directions, during the entirety of my incarceration, why did I only witness the wind blowing to the west? From a spiritual standpoint, I felt that God was trying to tell me something but, in those moments, I wasn't able to decipher the message. There came a time when, whether it was the small bushes outside my window along the fence line, or the high grass off in the distance between my window and a nearby freeway, I began to look forward to staring out of my window in hopes of seeing the trees and the tall grass still showing signs that the wind was blowing to the west.

This next introduction that I am about to describe is regarding my next-door neighbor in the jail's Administrative Segregation Unit, most commonly known to inmates as AD/SEG. With no prior warning, I was suddenly told by the deputies to gather up my belongings and to get ready to be moved to a different cell. It was my assumption that I was being moved to another unit just like the one I was already in, were there were about 20 to 30 other inmates, but I was terribly wrong. By the time all was said and done, I had been moved into the AD/SEG unit. Just as AD/SEG was short for Administrative Segregation Unit, the Administrative Segregation Unit was also known as *the hole*. This move made absolutely no sense to me because the AD/SEG unit is where inmates were sent for disciplinary reasons when they were being punished. I had never done anything to be punished for any reason so, in my mind, sending me to the hole was pointless, a waste of a disciplinary cell, and just mentally cruel.

Being in the hole was a much more dehumanizing experience than being in a dorm-style cell among more inmates. The Administrative Segregation Unit only had about four or five individual cells. There was one over-sized door at the entrance of the hole that primarily opened by way of another deputy pushing a button in the control room, which also monitored the accessibility of the unit via surveillance cameras. Whenever the deputies wanted to come into the hole to creep up on us, hoping to catch one of us slipping, they would use their jail key to open up the door to the AD/SEG unit. In this new housing environment, I had the bone-chilling experience of meeting a serial killer by the name of Wayne. Quite a few inmates voiced to me that they had issues with Wayne because of the barbaric nature of his crimes. They also warned me that Wayne had some very odd behaviors that would make one think he had some sort of multiple personality disorder or something.

The cells in the hole (AD/SEG) were surrounded by brick walls and hard, smooth concrete floors. It was also where I witnessed inmates washing their jail clothes in their toilets. I know it sounds gross, but I was shocked to learn how they came up with the actual process to wash their own clothes inside of their cells, instead of waiting for the jail staff to come around to issue newly cleaned clothing. The inmates would have certain food service workers discretely hide cleaning brillo underneath the grooves of their food trays so that the inmate(s) could use the brillo to vigorously scrub out the toilet to get it clean and ready for washing their clothing. Just the thought of that process wrinkled up my face and made me gag slightly.

    After my arrival in AD/SEG, Wayne was one of the last inmates to be brought into the unit. The cells were very poorly lit and extremely quiet, compared to the ongoing noise that I heard inside of the main pod. I spent my last three to four months at West Valley Detention Center in the hole, for non-disciplinary reasons. I had seen Wayne come into our pod several weeks before I ever had the chance to physically speak to him. I eventually got my chance to actually have a lengthy conversation with Wayne out on the rec yard one day, as the deputies had chosen to bring us out for our one hour of free time. Once we were out on the yard, Wayne was the one who had initiated a conversation with me first. Like other inmates in the facility, he was curious to know how a person like me had ended up in jail for simply defending myself. Wayne expressed to me that, unlike most of the other inmates, I struck him to be a very educated, articulate, and well-trained security officer who was just doing my job when I had to use deadly force to defend myself. Feeling as though Wayne was setting the stage for me to begin volunteering additional information about my case, I kept my comments to myself at that point, and just let Wayne continue to talk at will. Once again, I must warn you that, from this point forward, what I'm about to share with you could possibly trigger an emotional response.

In a shocking move that most inmates would never risk, Wayne inadvertently began telling me about the dynamics of why he was incarcerated at West Valley Detention Center. "I'm sure by now you've heard about my case and why I'm here," he offered. "I have no idea what your case is about, to be honest," I explained to Wayne. That's all it took for him to begin voluntarily talking to me about the explicit details of his crimes. Considering the fact that I was locked up just as he was, I had nothing but time to listen to whatever he felt like telling me.

Wayne explained to me that, prior to him getting arrested, he was a long-haul truck driver who had killed a total of four women that he described as being whores. As if killing them wasn't enough, he further advised me that he dismembered their bodies. He went on to explain to me that, eventually, he walked into a police station and tried to turn himself in. The way he described it, he walked into the police station and told an officer at the front counter that he was there to turn himself in for killing several women. For whatever reason, he said that the officer he was speaking to did not believe him and ultimately asked him to leave—Wayne refused to leave. Wayne then told me that, when the officer asked him to leave the station, he then took a Ziploc bag out of his jacket pocket containing a woman's severed breast, placed the bag up on the counter and said, "Now do you believe me?"

Once the officer realized that the object inside of the Ziploc bag was in fact a severed breast, Wayne said a few officers drew their guns on him immediately, and placed him in handcuffs without any further delay! As I'm sure you can imagine, I simply could not believe what I was hearing. When Wayne told me what he did to those four women, he had absolutely no emotion behind it. In the way that he was speaking to me about the crimes, his tone of voice suggested that the four women deserved what he did to them. He was talking to me about the details of his gruesome crimes as if we were standing there discussing the weather. Since he had no problem confessing his crimes to me, I informed him that I didn't understand why he was still in county jail and not already in state prison.

Wayne explained to me that the reason he was still being held at the county jail level is because he was still preparing his defense to get ready to go to trial and fight his case. I explained to Wayne that I didn't understand why he was planning to fight his case after just admitting to *me* that he killed the four women. He shared with me that he was fighting his case so that he could potentially avoid getting the death penalty.

After Wayne had finished explaining to me all of the details of his case that he wanted me to know, he then asked me a baffling trivia question. "You know why I turned myself in, don't you? I feel like, out of everyone in here, you of all people know why I turned myself in," he humbly asked me. I looked him square in the face and said, "I'm guessing you turned yourself in because you realized that you needed help, and that enough was enough. You knew that the killings would have continued had you not turned yourself in."

After I said those words to him, he looked at me with a very frightening smirk on his face and said, "I knew you understood why I did it!" Talking to Wayne was the most frightening and chilling conversation I've ever had with anyone in my entire life. Back inside of the AD/SEG unit, I also got a chance to witness some very different sides to Wayne.

During our 23-hour daily lockdown period, Wayne appeared to have a fairly normal side to him. Whenever he needed something, for some reason, he always came to me first before he went to ask any of the other inmates in the hole. Whenever Wayne would appear at my cell door, looking at me with an awkward grin through my window, it usually meant that he wanted a few shots of instant coffee in exchange for a 2-pack of Grandma's Oatmeal/Raisin cookies. He would slide a 2-pack of Grandma's cookies under my door and, in return, I'd give him two servings of Maxwell House instant coffee. When you're in jail, you can never consider someone as a friend, but that coffee and cookies exchange that Wayne and I often shared was the closest that he and I ever got to being friendly. Even if other inmates didn't like me for whatever reason, I learned that respect for one another is what oftentimes kept the atmosphere in our unit from reaching a boiling point.

After being in the hole for approximately two months, my zeal to get back home was growing stronger and stronger. Being in the middle of a serial killer and a serial rapist of elderly women, my spirit was starting to get weak again, and depression was right around the corner. At some point, my level of patience with Wayne started to wear thin because his personality would go from one extreme to another without warning. Whenever I stopped showing interest in talking to Wayne, he turned to antagonizing the other inmates that were housed in AD/SEG with us. My other next-door neighbor was allegedly a drop-out, Nazi Low-Rider gang member. He was always cool with me, but he and Wayne got on each other's nerves because Wayne was always placing photo copies of his victims' dismembered bodies against my neighbor's cell window.

It was at that time that I overheard my neighbor threating to pop his cell door open and come out on the tier and attack Wayne if Wayne didn't get away from his door. These were the moments when I would decide to cut everyone off and read a few more chapters in my Bible. Reading multiple chapters in my Bible not only allowed me to temporarily escape my reality of being in jail, but it gave me hope that my nightmare of being incarcerated would soon be over. If it wasn't for me getting access to that Bible at the beginning of my unwanted stay at Stress Valley Detention Center, I would have lost my mind way before I ended up in the hole! Looking back on everything that I went through to prove that I was not guilty of murder, I didn't realize it back then, but being in jail seemed like I had been involuntarily enrolled in some kind of Bible Boot Camp! This idea of being enrolled in a theoretical Bible Boot Camp is the very foundation that leads me to my final, and greatest testimony!

My last commissary trade that I had done with Wayne consisted of me giving him two more shots of instant coffee, in exchange for him giving me another 2-pack of Grandma's Oatmeal/Raisin cookies. Still to date, Wayne got his two shots of coffee, but I didn't stay in the AD/SEG unit long enough for him to return the favor. Without notice, I was moved from one AD/SEG unit to another. The next AD/SEG unit they transferred me to was sure to be confirmation that God had been using everyone in my surroundings to speak directly to me, and I was about to receive the lesson of a lifetime.

Once I had arrived at the AD/SEG unit in the new pod that I was transferred to, I immediately noticed that it was much more quiet than the other unit I was in. Carrying myself with the same demeanor that I had always displayed, I simply went to the cell that the deputies had escorted me to, cleaned it up to make is as inhabitable as possible, started reading more of my Bible, and kept to myself like I had always done. There were times when keeping to myself, rather than interacting with others around me, made me feel as though I was right back in the quicksand of depression all over again.

Even though I didn't talk to them very much, the inmates in the new AD/SEG unit would come over to my cell door on their tier time and introduce themselves to me. In this new housing location, I was the only Black inmate—the other inmates were Mexican. These inmates now living to the left and right of me looked like the scariest human beings I had ever been in the midst of, besides Wayne. Every visible part of their bodies were covered with tattoos. My next door neighbor had so many tattoos on his face, there was literally no more room left on his face to put even one more tattoo! From what I can remember from 20 years ago, I recall him telling me that his name was Richard. He was supposedly a former member of the Mexican Mafia. He was the one inmate who seemed to always have an interest in talking to me, for some reason, but he never talked to me about what landed him in jail.

Whenever Richard was out on his tier time, he hardly ever came out of his cell for more than 30 minutes. There was literally nothing to do while we were out on our tier time, except for pace back and forth in a long, dark, concrete hallway. If we had someone to call, there was a telephone at the far end of the tier that we could use to make a few phone calls. Until it was my time to come out for my tier time, I stayed in my cell for 23 hours per day, just sitting up on my bunk reading my Bible. Since it was so hard for me to estimate how much longer it would be before I was able to go home, I challenged myself to read entire books of the Bible while I had the time to do so. When I tell you I read the Bible daily, I mean to tell you that I read entire books of the Bible. I read the entire book of Matthew, Mark, Luke, John, Acts, Romans, Job, Psalms, Genesis, Exodus, Judges, 1 Kings, 2 Kings, Proverbs, 1 Corinthians, 2 Corinthians, Galatians, Ephesians, Hebrews, and Revelation. These are just some of the books of the Bible that I specifically recall reading. Reading these scriptures and staying focused on the stories that each book told distracted me from most other things happening around me that probably would have gotten me in trouble if I made a decision to focus on jail life too heavily. Sometimes it was hard to stay focused on my reading if Richard was out on his tier time. Since I knew he didn't always come out of his cell when he could have, I gave it no extra thought that his cell door was wide open and he could come out as he pleased… until I would look up from reading and see him standing quietly at my window.

Often times when Richard was standing at my window, he wouldn't even alert me to the fact that he was standing there. I could tell that Richard was curious as to what a person like me was doing in jail, but he never asked me too many questions about my case. Most of the questions that Richard asked me about were based on what my life was like outside of the jail walls. Ever since he had eluded to the fact that he was a former Mexican Mafia gang member, I wasn't overly excited about telling Richard too much about my private life, because that's why it's called a *private* life. He didn't need to know anything other than what I felt like telling him.

Of all the books of the Bible that I listed above, the most difficult book for me to read in its entirety was the book of Job, by far! It took me the better half of about two or three days to read the book of Job. Once I had made it past the first several chapters, I could feel the despair and the depression starting to settle into my spirit again. I didn't really want to continue reading anymore, but I had made a commitment to finish what I started. By the time I had made it to Job 30:1, I was no longer depressed or in despair, I was extremely angry!

I was angry that I had been falsely accused of murder. I was angry that I was away from my friends and my family. I was angry that I was being railroaded by the San Bernadino County District Attorney's Office. I was angry that I wasn't able to sleep in my own bed. I was angry that I had to eat disgusting food every day of my incarceration. I was angry that I was being targeted for malicious prosecution because of the color of my skin. I was angry at the fact that Job's story talked about him losing one thing after another. I was angry because I had started to take notice that Job and I had so much in common. I was angry at the fact that certain people that I knew would come to visit me didn't ever come to visit me at all. I was especially angry at Michael Krause, Jr. for trying to run me over with his pickup truck a second time because, if it were not for his actions, I would have never been sitting in jail in the first place.

The more I kept reading further and further into the book of Job, I had finally got myself to a point where I just sat on the edge of my bunk and I cried. I tried to push through the tears and just keep on reading, but I was not able to continue reading any further. All I could do in that moment was hold my head down in despair, staring at an open Bible that was telling a story that felt exactly like what I myself was experiencing. At some point, I had to quickly bring myself back to the reality that I was still in jail, and I could not afford to let another inmate see me sitting on my bunk crying.

Have you ever had that chilling feeling that somewhere in the room, someone might be looking at you? Not long after I had decided to stop reading the book of Job, I began to notice that there was an awkward silence in AD/SEG, as I was sitting on the edge of my bunk with a now closed Bible. Something in my spirit told me to look up and, when I did, Richard was standing at my cell door and looking into my window with his hands cupped over the sides of his eyes. "You good, bro?" he asked curiously. Initially, I couldn't utter a word to respond to his question. I knew that if I would have said one word, I would have broken down. From that moment on, I had no other choice but to keep it real with Richard and share with him how I was feeling. I remember my conversation with Richard as if it were yesterday!

Me: No… I'm not good.

Richard: Why? What's wrong?

Me: What's wrong is, I don't belong here! I'm trying to read this Bible, but I just can't take it anymore.

Richard: What are you reading, bro?

Me: The book of Job, but I just can't read anymore of this story… it's too depressing.

Richard: What is so depressing about it?

Me: Because, the more I keep reading, the more I see that Job's story is my story… I'm Job right now. I feel like I have lost everything! I've lost my family, I've lost my friends, I've lost my freedom… I don't belong here!!

Richard: What chapter are you on?

Me: Chapter 32.

At this point, Richard looks at me with a confident grin on his face and says, "Bro., keep reading… it gets better!" As soon as he said that to me, the first thing on my mind was asking him, "How would you know?" The reason I was entertaining that thought in my mind was solely based on Richard's appearance. He was a former Mexican Mafia gang member who lived a lifestyle of a career criminal, and he had tattoos all over his face as if he hated himself. In my mind, there was no possible way he knew more about the Bible than me, so I had assumed. But God! The next day, when I decided to pick up my Bible and start reading again, God humbled my spirit and silenced the voices in my head, allowing me to witness that everything Richard had told me was factually correct—things got better for Job. Just as things started getting better for Job, things also started getting better for me.

Once I got strong enough to keep reading from my Bible, I noticed that I was also in a better place, spiritually, and was able to get into a much more consistent prayer routine. However, since this book is all about being honest, I have to be honest and talk about one of my greatest spiritual challenges. The absolute hardest thing for me to do while I was in jail was to pray for the Krause family... the very family that had been actively trying to get me sent to prison for the rest of my life! I told God straight out, "God, I know I'm not supposed to be telling You this, but I'm not about to pray for the very people that are lying on me and trying to unfairly get me sent to prison—I'm just not doing it!" Being a Christian for as long as I have been a believer, I was all too familiar with the scripture that commanded me to love my enemies and also to pray for those who persecuted me.

Based on these scriptural teachings, I knew that I had no other choice but to pray for the Krause family, and even the prosecutor that was leading the charge against me. The more I considered the spiritual meanings of these scriptures, I became fearful of the possibility of not going home unless I showed God that I was willing to be obedient and just pray for them. I may have only been able to muster the strength to pray for them only once or twice, but at least I did it.

In my back and forth exchange with Richard, God humbled me and pricked my heart to understand that I was not the only one who understood the scriptures. God also showed me that the anger I had bottled up inside of me, as a result of certain people not coming to visit me, should have been a feeling of joy. You see, God knew that being in jail facing such a serious charge as murder was my absolute rock-bottom moment in life. God knew that I was spiritually, emotionally, and psychologically weak. Because I was weak in so many different areas of my life, God knew that I *only* needed people around me who were much stronger than me. Since God already knew that He was going to deliver me from the grasp of my enemies who sought my downfall, He knew that allowing other weak people in my circle to get close to me would have done more harm than good.

Once Richard had restored my hope, and my overall positive outlook of being freed, I picked up my Bible again and began to finish reading the entire story of Job. As I got almost to the end of my reading, I came across a scripture that hit me like a ton of bricks, and that very scripture convicted me of not putting my full faith in God. Every great accomplishment I've made over the course of many years of my life, I stepped out on faith to achieve them all but, in that cold, dark, lonely cell, I allowed my faith to reach an all-time low. The scripture that forced me to reflect on my situation was found in Job 38:4-41. By the time I had reached verse 18, the tears began to fall down my face again because, in my spirit, I knew that these verses were God's way of letting me know that He was about to break my chains and deliver me back home to my family and friends where I belonged.

Paraphrasing Job 38:4-41 in my own words, I felt like God was saying to me, "Where were you when I created heavens and earth? Where were you when I gave the sea its measurements? Where were you when I commanded the rain to fall upon the earth? Where were you when I separated the light from the darkness?"

In other words, God was saying to me, "Son, I don't need your help to deliver you from the hands of your enemies… I got this! I got this. I have already promised you that I would never leave you nor forsake you, so stop doubting Me and let Me do for you what I promised you I would do."

God definitely made good on His promises because, in less than three months later, God broke my chains for good and made it possible for me to finally post bail and get released back into the loving arms of all my friends and loved ones! I was so glad and overjoyed when I found out that I would soon be going home! As I started to reflect a little bit deeper into the unfortunate set of circumstances I found myself in, as a result of our broken judicial system and what appeared to be a racially motivated, malicious prosecution, I began to see that, what my enemies tried to inflict upon me for my downfall, God turned it all around for my good so that I could be a living testimony to others as to just how good and how faithful God is to His children who live their lives for Him! One of the things I had been looking forward to for the longest time, before I got out, was an IN-N-OUT Double-Double, fresh fries and a Sprite. I couldn't wait to eat real food again! Before I could get my eager hands on that combo meal, the devil tried to throw a few more darts at me before I was released.

When it was time for me to get released from jail, the deputies came to my cell to escort me on a very long walk down to the area where my personal property and civilian clothing would be returned to me. After changing out of my inmate rags and into my own clothes, I walked over to the counter where another deputy was preparing copies of my release papers and other items that belonged to me. As the Hispanic deputy was taking his sweet time to process me out of jail, a White sergeant walked over towards the counter area and just stared me down as if he had witnessed me run over his dog or something—he appeared to be extremely angry! The sergeant stood a few feet behind the deputy who was processing my release papers, and just continued to stare me down and give me dirty look after dirty look.

He never said one word to me but, if looks could kill, he would have taken me out with his devilish looks alone. After I had finally got released, it took me a few days to realize that it wasn't really that White sergeant who was giving me those dirty looks... it was Satan! Satan was extremely angry that God had broken my chains. Since God had surrounded me with a hedge of protection, Satan's darts did not hit their mark—Satan and his angels had been defeated! One thing that I want people to learn from my experience is that spiritual warfare is a real thing… it's not a game! When you start to build a more intimate relationship with God, and you begin to witness for yourself how God will dispatch His angels to surround you with His unwavering love and protection, God will allow you to see things in the spirit that the enemy doesn't ever want you to see or find out.

When I was finally back home and getting settled back into society, it took me a long time to readjust to being independent again. Within just a few short days of getting released, a longtime friend of mine hosted a Welcome Home party for me at his home. When I arrived at the party, it was the greatest feeling in the world to see all of my friends, family, and supporters welcoming me back home with open arms, and demonstrating how much they missed me, as I had also missed them! Although many of those same people and I have grown apart, I still owe them an eternal debt of gratitude and acknowledgement for the fact that they stood in my corner and supported me through the darkest ever moments of my life. I am extremely grateful for their visits, for their kindness to my family while I was incarcerated, and I am also very honored that several of them put their jobs and their careers on the line to publicly and selflessly risk their livelihood to support me no matter what. I was extremely happy and blessed to be back among my friends and family, but I was not the same person I was prior to the shooting incident at the Sycamore Springs Apartments. All I wanted to do was stay indoors every day and hide from the world. I didn't want to come out of the house and do the things I was usually accustomed to doing.

The first few years following my release consisted of successfully completing a 3-year probation period, extensive visits with a psychologist, and trying to unlearn all of the bad habits that I had picked up in jail. It took me a long time to learn how to trust people again because, at that time, I was just coming out of a situation where so many people had turned against me. My shooting incident back in June of 2000, coupled with my shooting incident at the Sycamore Springs Apartments in 2004, left me with a variety of mental health triggers that reminded me of each shooting incident. It took me several years to get myself to a place where the trauma related to those situations no longer bothered me as much as they did in the past. When I first came home from jail, I still had to take prescription medication to help me sleep peacefully at night, because every few weeks I would mentally re-live every single detail associated with the imminent danger I

was able to escape in both incidents. I am very happy to report that I no longer have to take any kind of medication to sleep or carry on with my day-to-day responsibilities.

God is good! As of the date of this publication, I haven't had to take prescription medication for more than 15 years. After every trial and tribulation that God has allowed me to overcome, I must admit that I never could have come this far if it wasn't for the power of prayer and my determination not to allow the turmoil of my past to dictate the trajectory of my future. Throughout my entire professional writing career, my goal has always been to show society how to turn negatives into positives.

Based on all of the negative publicity that I have unfortunately been exposed to for more than 20 years, I feel like many people in the public have unfairly judged me as a result of misleading Google searches by those who simply sought to learn more about me as an author. The title *Road to Redemption* is more than just a book title, it is a movement that seeks justice and full restoration of my rights as a law abiding citizen. It is a powerful statement that describes how passionate I am about reclaiming my name, restoring my integrity with the public, and rebuilding the broken pieces of my professional writing career that have been damaged by a race of people who may never admit to themselves how factually wrong they were to try to send me to prison for life!

I obviously don't know who this book is supposed to help, but I sincerely hope and pray that this book helps to shine a bright, positive light into the life of that one person in the world who has, for years, allowed the failures, disappointments, and hardships of their past to prevent them from living a better quality of life *today*. I hope that something I've said in this chapter gives others in our world the empowerment and the heart-felt desire to forgive themselves, *today*, for mistakes that they have made in times past. I hope that my testimonies and my stories about life's uneven journey, will give others a renewed sense of accountability for the decisions that they make, understanding that, good or bad, every decision we make in our life has a consequence of some kind.

Furthermore, I hope and pray that my testimonies shared in this book will cause more parents to play a more active part in molding their children to be positive, productive members of society... getting all of us one step closer to world peace and unity. It's extremely important that we teach our children at a very young age why it is so important for them to respect authority and obey laws. When we teach our children how to grow up to be hateful and disrespectful towards others, especially people in authority, based on what they may see us doing as parents, we are setting our children up for failure later in life.

To every person in society who made a decision to unfairly and prematurely judge me, based on the slanderous lies spoken against me in Google search results, I want to make it clear that what happened to *me* could have easily happened to YOU, or YOUR Black son... or YOUR Black nephew... or YOUR Black father... or YOUR Black brother... or YOUR Black boyfriend... or YOUR Black fiancé... or YOUR Black husband... or YOUR Black uncle... or YOUR Black grandfather... or even to YOUR Black friend.

After my release from jail, I had already been expecting the attorney for the Krause family, Jeffrey Weaver of the Winet, Patrick & Weaver Law Firm, to come after me immediately and make me a part of their thirsty civil lawsuit. By the time all was said and done, I was ultimately responsible for making payments of $125.00 per month to Jeffrey Weaver, that would later be handed over to the Krause family. Based on the fact that Michael Krause, Jr. put *my life* in jeopardy when he ended up being fatally shot, I should not have had to give his angry family one red cent! I am not the one who caused their grief, Michael Krause, Jr. and the actions of Scott Martinez are the cause of the Krause family's grief, whether they will ever choose to admit that or not.

Just as the monthly lawsuit payments to the Krause family were starting to become a financial burden on me, God intervened and sent me a guardian angel… a very well-respected, highly esteemed attorney by the name of Rupert A. Byrdsong of the Ivie, McNeill & Wyatt Law Firm. After consulting with attorney Byrdsong, and telling him my situation, he agreed to represent me and mediate between myself and Jeffrey Weaver, the attorney for the Krause family. Before I could even mentally process the information that attorney Byrdsong had relayed to me, after his meeting with the attorney for the Krause family, I was told that any further obligations of me to continue making monthly payments to attorney Jeff Weaver were completely dissolved and no longer a burden for me to carry or worry about! I cannot begin to describe the feeling of joy and overwhelming gratitude that came over me when attorney Byrdsong had given me such amazing news. Because of my strong belief in God, I had no doubt that God was going to bless attorney Byrdsong for the way he delivered me from the grasp of my enemies and freed me from a level of financial ruin that I would not have been able to recover from.

It was almost like God had waved a magic wand over my entire financial situation and just took it away from me as if it were never put in place. I later learned that, in June of 2014, the brilliant and highly esteemed Rupert A. Byrdsong was appointed to the bench, and is now Los Angeles County Superior Court Judge Rupert A. Byrdsong. After what God pricked his heart to do for me many years ago, I can honestly say that, if anyone should end up in Judge Rupert A. Byrdsong's courtroom, he will definitely demonstrate fairness, professionalism, integrity in how he rules on a case, and, most importantly, he will treat everyone that comes before him with respect. I cannot possibly thank this man enough for what he did for me.

Just as my former employer, Southwest District Patrol, was negligent in not having adequate insurance coverage to include me as one of the armed guards permitted to patrol the Sycamore Springs Apartments on the night of January 1, 2004, Southwest District Patrol was also negligent for NOT informing me that their insurance policy would not have covered me as being an armed guard on that particular property when they hired me and asked me to work at the Sycamore Springs Apartments. Had I known this information back in January of 2004, I would have NEVER accepted that assignment. Because of his incorrigible behavior back then, it doesn't mean that Michael Krause, Jr. would not have been fatally injured by a different security officer, but he surely would not have been fatally injured by me, because I would not have agreed to work there if I knew there was no insurance in place that would cover me and protect me from liability in the event that I had to fire my weapon for any reason.

All of the traps that my enemies laid out for me, to get my foot caught in, they caught their own foot in the very traps that they laid out for me. In His written promises, God promised me in His word that He would never leave me nor forsake me, and He kept His promise to me. In His written promises, God promised me that He would make my enemies my footstool, and He kept His promise to me. In His written promises, God promised me that no weapon formed against me would prosper, and it didn't, because I was found *not guilty* when my enemies thought that they had killed my spirit. In His written promises, God promised me that the effectual, fervent prayer of a righteous man would availeth much and, because of prayer, God kept His promise by breaking my chains and setting me free from the bondage of my enemies. In His written promises, God promised me that every evildoer who would rise up against me would be defeated right before my eyes, and He kept His promise. In His written promises, God promised me that He would restore the years of my life that the locusts have eaten, and He's already in the process of doing that, and more.

For the time that I was unjustly incarcerated, fighting for my life all over again to get back home, I constantly dwelled on the scripture John 14:1-3 which states, "Let not your heart be troubled. You believe in God, believe also in Me. In my Father's house are many mansions, and if it were not so I would have told you. I go to prepare a place for you, and if I got to prepare a place for you, I will come again and receive you unto Myself that, were I am, there ye may be also." The more and more this scripture kept coming into focus in my mind, the more confident I felt that I would soon be released from jail and back home with my friends and family where I had always belonged, and it finally came to pass!

8
★ ★ ★ ★ ★

WHAT GOOGLE NEVER TOLD YOU!

In order for you to fully grasp all of the information you have read in this book up until this point, I encourage you to go to the Google search engine and enter a search under **Dameon Wroe shooting** so that you at least have something to compare against the truths that I have shared in this book, and the additional information that I will be providing in this final chapter. Before I go any further, I want to direct your attention to the next organization that I am about to publicly call out for publishing a blatant and total lie to the public about me, all for the sake of selling a story by any means necessary. It gives me great pleasure to embarrass the Los Angeles Times newspaper for trying to discredit the San Bernadino County Sheriff's Department Detective Bureau.

In an online article published by the Los Angeles Times on February 19, 2004 under the heading

> Guard Faces Murder Count in Shooting, Staff Writer Lance Pugmire wrote, "However, investigators determined the guard's life was never in danger, said Joe Gaetano, the

supervising deputy district attorney handling the case,"

Joe Gaetano and his so-called investigators should have exercised their right to keep their mouths shut because, if they were not there to witness what happened to me from start to finish, their opinions have never had any value! If the Sycamore Springs Apartments would have had some type of surveillance camera that was set up to monitor the incoming and outgoing traffic at their main entrance gate, a murder case against *me* would have **never** been filed, because the video would have clearly shown Michael Krause's pickup truck accelerating into me and knocking me backwards before I fired my weapon to defend myself! *People* may lie, but videos don't.

Since they blatantly lied to the public in their publication, I would love to see the Los Angeles Times newspaper publish a current (2024) article to explain to the public why they lied and contradicted the Inland Valley Daily Bulletin, per the very first article citation shown on the reference page of this book. The headline of the article published by the Inland Valley Daily Bulletin on January 3, 2004 completely destroys the manufactured version of events that were unethically published by the Los Angeles Times newspaper. The shameful article that was published by the LA Times is further evidence of White America's continuous and systemic belittling of the Black man in this country.

To many White Americans, Black men are oftentimes viewed as uneducated, illiterate, and just plain-old stupid.

WHAT GOOGLE NEVER TOLD YOU!

Historically speaking, the Black man in America has been the biggest target of racial profiling, false arrests by police, and also unfair convictions, convictions that afford agenda-driven prosecutors to elevate their careers by securing as many convictions against Black men as they possibly can, even if it means fabricating a bogus case against us. For anyone who doesn't believe the statement that I just made, go back and watch the movie *The Hurricane* starring one of the greatest actors of our time, Denzel Washington. For anyone who doesn't believe the statement that I just made, get on the internet and research how many Black men are still being let out of prison today, after being locked up for decades for crimes that they never should've been arrested for, thanks to advancements in DNA evidence.

Since my acquittal back in 2004, some very positive things have happened to me and *for* me, but I'm sure the reason why the public has not heard about it yet is because it's positive news. By now, you have had plenty of time to witness a variety of untruthful, inaccurate things about me, thanks to Google. Now let me share some things about me and about my past that Google will never tell you. The following attributes that I am about to share with you are personal achievements and accomplishments that I am very proud of, and anyone who truly knows me can validate that these things did in fact happen. Twice in my lifetime, prior to 2004, I saved two people from drowning at Lake Meade during two separate houseboat trips I went on with a group of friends. Of all the people who were on the houseboat, I was the one who was willing to partially disrobe and dive into the cold, choppy current and swim out to the person about to drown. I was able to wrap a long tow rope around the both of us so that we could both be pulled back to safety of the houseboat. During one of these same houseboat trips, I was awakened early one morning to the terrifying screams of two or three women who were sharing a tent about 100ft. away from where my tent was set up. By the time I had ran over to their tent to find out what the problem was, the women came running out in obvious fear. I learned that the women were terrified because they heard the rattle of a rattlesnake that had found its way into their tent while they were just beginning to wake up. I eventually captured the rattlesnake, trapping it into a large bath towel and removed it from their tent to make them feel safe.

What Google is never going to tell you about me is that, once upon a time in the year 2000, I helped a CHP officer on a traffic stop who asked me to stand by with him until his backup arrived. I was on my way to work at the Edward's movie theater in West Covina, when I observed a CHP officer detaining four to five male Hispanic men at the intersection of Valley Boulevard and Lemon Avenue. I was the first car sitting at a red light at the intersection, facing westbound on Valley, and the CHP officer was directly across from me at the adjacent corner of the intersection, facing eastbound on Valley just before Lemon Avenue.

There were three Hispanic males with their hands on the hood of the officer's patrol car, while the officer was standing at the rear passenger side of the patrol car struggling to take the fourth male into custody. Seeing that the officer was by himself and struggling, I went through the intersection in the number one lane of travel and asked the officer if he needed me to standby with him until an additional CHP unit arrived to help him. The officer indicated that he wanted me to stand by with him. I drove a short distance further and made a U-turn in the middle of the street and pulled up behind the CHP patrol vehicle—the CHP officer was aware that I was armed at the time. I exited my vehicle and detained the other three males at the front of the officer's patrol car. Seeing that the officer was physically struggling to get the handcuffs on his subject, I un-holstered my weapon and held it in front of me in a *sul position* to discourage the remaining subjects from trying to help their friend overpower the CHP officer who was arresting the other individual.

Once the officer got the man handcuffed and secured in the back of his patrol car, I holstered my weapon as he appeared back at the front of the patrol car. He then thanked me for stopping to assist him, shook my hand, and I went on my way. I never saw that officer again, but I could tell by the tone of his voice that he was grateful that I observed what was going on and came to help him before the situation turned worse.

Sometime in 2013 or 2014, while on my way home after picking up my kids from daycare, I pulled over on the side of the road to help two other men pull a woman out of the window of her SUV that had flipped over multiple times as a result of a terrible car accident. After we pulled the frightened woman out, and escorted her a safe distance away from her vehicle, I got back into my car and drove home. That was a very prideful moment for me because, as my children were in the back seat looking on, I was able to demonstrate to them the importance and the value of showing kindness to a total stranger when the need presented itself.

I also pride myself in being an excellent father to my children, primarily due to the fact that my own father has never been an active part of my life the way that I am involved in the lives of my own children.

After filing for divorce more than ten years ago, the court awarded me primary physical custody of my children. For the first year of my legal separation, the court also awarded me child support for my *step-son*! Yes, you read that correctly—my step-son. Ultimately, my primary physical custody of my children was later amended by the court to reflect sole custody. Being awarded sole custody of my children has been one of the greatest accomplishments of my life, because it proves to the world around me what type of father I am. Many people have told me how lucky I am to have been awarded sole custody of my children, especially due to the fact that I am a Black man living in California. Historically speaking, sole custody being awarded to a single, Black father in California is unheard of. As for me, I never considered myself as being lucky that I had sole custody of my kids… I have always considered myself as blessed to have my kids 100% of the time. Furthermore, I want to make it abundantly clear that the court did not just *give me* that opportunity, I was the parent who worked hard to *earn* it!

From 2011 to 2020, I finally had the mental and emotional strength to write and publish three more books; *No Longer Silent—By Way of Poetry*, *Modern Day Mentor*, and *Their Voice Matters: Child Custody Solutions for Effective Co-Parenting*. Each of these titles have their own special significance in my life but, of these three books, the one that moved me the most was Modern Day Mentor. After my encounter with Michael Krause, Jr. back in 2004, my goal has always been to use *Modern Day Mentor* as a tool to allow me to personally mentor young adults between the ages of 18 to 25. As young adults transition further into adulthood between these ages, they need a realistic sense of guidance from responsible, older adults who understand where they're trying to go in life and who can teach them what it's going to take to get them there successfully. Since Michael Krause, Jr. was only 19-years-old when he passed, I have decided to dedicate the rest of my life mentoring young adults his age, so that what he got himself into with me never happens again to any other unsuspecting families. None of us can reverse the aftermath of what has already happened but, moving forward, what I can do is use my gifts and talents of mentoring to help other people his age make better life-decisions that will ensure their safety in troubling situations.

After the release of my book *Modern Day Mentor* in 2019, I was offered an opportunity to be an Ambassador for a local STEM club within the San Gabriel Valley that works with elementary, middle school, and high school students. From 2019 to current, I have been teaching Financial Literacy to primarily elementary and middle school students.

Trying to get back on my feet, professionally pursuing my writing and public speaking endeavors, has been quite the challenge. However, interacting with my Financial Literacy students has been such a huge blessing to me and has just simply kept me focused and grounded. My students know first-hand how much I love them and care about their future success in life, and that makes everything I'm still fighting for even more worthwhile.

Based on my ongoing involvement in their lives, my students know that I will never give up on them. My students have proven to be a healthy distraction for me. The more I work with them on events and activities that help to push them towards their educational goals, the less time I have to dwell on past life events that trigger past trauma.

Another thing that Google is never going to tell you about me is that I am an advocate for children who are bullied at school. On three separate occasions, a parent or guardian of a child has contacted me to inform me that their child was being bullied by another student. After I stepped in and acted on their child's behalf, it was reported back to me that the bullying had stopped almost immediately in two of the three cases. With the remaining case, the bullying stopped completely after about 30 days. With my zero tolerance attitude towards bullying, I also have a zero tolerance for people in our society who feel like they can go around terrorizing our communities whenever they feel like it, and think that they should not have to face any consequences for their actions.

Now that this book, and my truths, are available to the general public for consideration, I find myself fighting for my life all over again but, this time, I am fighting to regain all of the esteemed opportunities that have been stolen from me as a result of so many lies posted on the internet about me. When people or organizations find out that I am an author, mentor, life coach, and former recording artist, one of the first things they do to find out more information about my other accomplishments is look me up in the Google search engine. For at least 15 years after my murder acquittal, all people have been drawn to is headline after headline that made me seem like a murderer, even though a jury found me not guilty. That negative publicity from Google search results like the ones featured on the front cover of this book killed so many paid opportunities for me to reach higher heights in my pursuit of success in the public eye.

When my book *Modern Day Mentor* was released back in 2019, a long-time acquaintance of mine contacted me and asked me, "Would you consider offering me a multi-purchase discount if I buy some of your books to give away to my employees?" Flattered beyond belief that she believed in me enough to want to share my work with her subordinates, I calmly asked her, "How many employees are we talking about?" After mumbling some quick, approximate numbers under her breath, she said, "About five hundred!" By the time I had checked my own pulse and discovered that I had not yet fainted, I immediately said, "Yes, of course!!" At the time of her inquiry, she worked for a huge organization which had offices in several different states around the U.S., and she was put in charge of a huge project that her company had tasked her with facilitating.

On top of purchasing five hundred books from me, she expressed to me that she was also interested in hiring me to come down to Nebraska to be a keynote speaker, and speak directly to her staff about how important mentoring is in an organizational setting to promote company growth. She made it clear to me that not only was she going to fly me out to speak to her people, she also offered to put me up in a hotel and pay to fly my children out to be with me if I was unable to find a babysitter. I was beyond blown away! She then informed me that she would be getting back to me in several days to confirm the purchase of the books, because she had to run it by the head of her company's purchasing department first. The moment she told me that, I felt in my spirit that the deal would ultimately not get approved, based on all of the negative information about my malicious murder trial that her colleagues were sure to research on the internet before approving the purchase of my book. To date, the sale of those five hundred books never happened. People who were too afraid to take a chance to get to know me for themselves apparently believed the internet's version of lies that slandered my character, my integrity, and my credibility.

Through it all, I still continued to trust God, and I made up in my mind that I was never going to give up on myself. For every rejection that I endured, my skin just kept on getting thicker and thicker. It is now my desire to use this book as a platform to publicly thank everyone who came together to make my freedom from jail possible. I am forever grateful to my friends, my family, my church family, and my extended family for all coming together to help me get back home.

I'm also thankful for people like Mr. Tavis Smiley for having the vision and the foresight to create the KBLA Talk 1580 radio station back in 2021. For many years after being released from jail, I felt that no one in society wanted to hear my voice. During intermittent times of great depression, I was made to feel like my voice no longer mattered. Based on that thinking, I stopped pursuing new opportunities for a while because of the backlash I felt I was getting from the public for defending my life against a person who tried to take it away from me. There came a time when a very dear friend of mine informed me that she was going to be appearing on the KBLA Talk 1580 radio station as a special guest of radio hosts Robin Ayers and Danny Morrison to promote her amazing new business.

As any good friend would do, I made sure there was nothing on my calendar on the date and time her interview was scheduled to air. As I sat listening to the talk radio interview in its entirety, I started to think to myself, "Wow! Robin Ayers and Danny Morrison seem like some extremely down-to-earth people." I consider myself a fairly good judge of character, and I had concluded that Robin and Danny were two people that I definitely wanted to listen to again, so I started following them on social media so that I could learn more about the topics they would often discuss on their show. I stepped out on faith and started engaging them in their content more and more, letting them know that I was really enjoying listening to their show. Before long, I fell in love with their show and their overall vibe so much that I started recommending people in my own network to like, share, and follow them and KBLA Talk 1580 on social media.

Soon thereafter, I started calling into the show's hotline to offer my perspectives on subject-matter which matched the level of experience and expertise that I have in many areas. Robin and Danny enjoyed my feedback so much, it didn't take long for them to start looking forward to me calling in to the show to add my own down-to-earth flavor to the various topics of discussion. To date, I have been extremely blessed to have appeared on the Danny Morrison Show with Robin Ayers many times, and we have since established a very solid, respectable connection with one another. In all honesty, the way that Danny Morrison and Robin Ayers accepted me with open arms for the person they saw me to be, they are two of the most influential people in my circle that lit a fire under me and kept on encouraging me to finish this book! Watching each of them constantly winning and constantly working in unison to keep the Black community united and vigilant with letting their voices be heard, regarding issues that favorably or adversely affect our culture, had an incredibly powerful impact on me, and I love and appreciate them both for taking a chance to believe in me when others just flat-out shunned me and seemingly turned their backs on me.

Danny Morrison ultimately got another broadcasting opportunity to shine on a different network but, no matter where he goes, he is someone that I truly respect and admire, and I will always follow and support him because of how genuine and how supportive he has been of me and my endeavors. I echo the same sentiments about Robin Ayers. She is a won-

WHAT GOOGLE NEVER TOLD YOU!

derful person with an amazing personality, and she has such a passion for the work that she does out in the community via the KBLA Talk 1580 AM platform. Robin has a daily talk radio show that she does on the air from 6:00 PM to 7:00 PM Monday through Friday, streamed live on YouTube and Instagram called The RA Report. Equally, I thank her beyond measure for taking a chance on me and letting me prove myself to be the stand-up person that I have worked hard to become over the course of my 24-year professional writing career. I love her like a big sister and I just enjoy being in the midst of her positive energy. Another group of people that I have grown to love and appreciate as well is the RA Squad. Over the course of the past few years, I have really gotten a chance to communicate and engage with various RA Squad contributors in the YouTube comments on the show, and I very much appreciate them as well.

Before I close the final chapter of this book, which took an unspeakable amount of courage and determination to finish, I want to leave you, the reader, with knowing that I am now a huge advocate for mental health wellness for individuals and families who have experienced personal or family trauma. If you are someone who has experienced a life-changing, traumatic event, I want to encourage you to seek professional help in speaking with a psychologist or other mental health therapist who can help you make sense of your emotions and help you navigate through other feelings of sorrow or depression. It's not a bad thing to need help. It's not a bad thing to need someone to talk to on a professional level.

For me, the *Road to Redemption* means using this book to begin my new journey of reintroducing myself to the public and making it clear that I am trustworthy and passionate about using my God-given gifts and talents to empower my community. This journey will also include working hard to prove to business and educational organizations that, despite the negative things that have been said about me over the years, I am deserving of a fair chance to be a mentor to youth in our communities who need to be surrounded by a positive role model who has first-hand knowledge and experience with helping then get from where they are in life to where they are trying to go. I am a pillar of my community and an asset to the people that I serve in those communities. I know that this journey is not always going to be easy, but what I do know is that it's definitely worth the effort to continue seeking complete justice to reclaim my name, after bouncing back from the hellish way that I have been treated by a broken judicial system that I had always worked hard to respect.

Because of the hard work that I have put into accomplishing all of my professional goals, I deserve to be redeemed and sit at tables with leaders of communities and heads of organizations. Because of the hard work that I have put into mentoring youth and young adults, I deserve to be redeemed and have more opportunities to speak at high schools and colleges to continue empowering future generations. Because of the hard work that I have put into learning about the criminal justice system, I deserve to be redeemed enough to have future opportunities to train and educate the youth in our communities on how to stay out of trouble with law enforcement and obey the laws of the land. Because of the hard work that I have put into everything that I do, I deserved to be redeemed and looked upon as a person in the world who is capable of bringing people together for the greater good of the public, as well as for the greater good of all humanity.

I want a fair chance at having my name restored to be in good standing with the public. I want a fair chance at being considered for big opportunities again. I want the public to judge me based on who I am today, not by who I was portrayed by others to be 20 years ago. I want to be given a fair chance at demonstrating how much worth I bring to the table when it comes to my ability to empower others and coach members of our society on how to be better versions of themselves. I want to be trusted again with building better, more meaningful business and personal relationships. In a nutshell, I want my life back.

Now that this book has finally been published, and my truths have finally been revealed to the public, I feel so much more at peace within myself. From this point forward, I refuse to sit silently on the sidelines of life and let an internet search engine control the narrative to my story. For the first time in more than 20 years… I can officially say… I'm finally free!

★ ★ ★ ★ ★

REFERENCES

Johnson, Jannise. "Teen Killed by Security Guard: Officials Believe it was Self-Defense." *Inland Valley Daily Bulletin*, January 3, 2004. Front-page article.

Pinion-Whitt, Melissa. "Guard surrenders to authorities." *Inland Valley Daily Bulletin*, February 19, 2004. Front-page article, continued on page A6.

Litz, Paige. "Wroe to face murder charges: Security Guard Charged in Shooting Death of Teen Will be Arraigned Monday, Judge Rules." *Rancho Cucamonga Voice*, March 12, 2004. Pg. A3.

Leveque, Rod. "Security Guard Trial Headed to Jurors: Paramedic Refutes Defendant's Story." *Inland Valley Daily Bulletin*, 2004.

Leveque, Rod. Newell, Jason. "Guard Acquitted of Murder: Jurors Deadlock on Lesser Count." *Inland Valley Daily Bulletin*, September 24, 2004. Front-page article, continued on page A6

Leveque, Rod. "DA Files to Retry Guard on Manslaughter Charge." *Inland Valley Daily Bulletin*, October 6, 2004.

Casetext.com. August 2, 2010. *Krause v. Western Heritage Ins. Co.* Retrieved on March 1, 2024, from https://casetext.com/case/krause-v-western-heritage-ins-co

Leveque, Rod. "Guard Wroe Weighs Plea Agreement: Judge Tells Him it's an Outstanding Deal." *Inland Valley Daily Bulletin*, March 5, 2005. Front-page article, continued on page A6.

Leveque, Rod. "Slain Man's Family Sues Guard, Others: Wrongful Death Alleged in 19-year-old's Shooting." *Inland Valley Daily Bulletin*, March 5, 2005. Front-page article, continued on page A6.

Bible Gateway. *Yea, though I walk through the valley of the shadow of death, I will fear no evil: for thou art with me; thy rod and thy staff they comfort me.* Psalm 23:4. [KJV]. Retrieved on May 24, 2024, from https://www.biblegateway.com/passage/?search=Psalm%2023&version=KJV

Bible Gateway. *Let not your heart be troubled. You believe in God, believe also in Me. In my Father's house are many mansions, and if it were not so I would have told you. I go to prepare a place for you, and if I got to prepare a place for you, I will come again and receive you unto Myself that, were I am, there yo may be also.* John 14:1-3. [KJV]. Retrieved on May 24, 2024, from https://www.biblegateway.com/passage/?search=John%2014&version=KJV

Pugmire, Lance. February 19, 2004. *Guard Faces Murder Count in Shooting.* Retrieved on May 24, 2024, from https://www.latimes.com/archives/la-xpm-2004-feb-19-me-guard19-story.html

www.ingramcontent.com/pod-product-compliance
Lightning Source LLC
Chambersburg PA
CBHW071855290426
44110CB00013B/1157